The Gutter's Priest

And The Violent Taketh By Force

Victor Holtz

PAGE PUBLISHING
Conneaut Lake, PA

First originally published by Page Publishing 2021

ISBN 978-1-6624-5470-7 (pbk)
ISBN 978-1-6624-5471-4 (digital)

Printed in the United States of America

I would like to dedicate this book to so many of the people that influenced my life: my Lord Jesus, my mom, Faye Pope, my dad, Tommy Holtz Jr., my grandfather and grandmother Annie and Tommy Holtz Sr., Marion Boyd, William Jackson, Mildred Jackson, Ethel and Curley Taylor, Margret and Sandy Murry, Buddy Pope, Christine and Joseph Bryson, Donald Tylor, Eric Jerome Williams, Alexander Ware, Cynthia and Jerome Humphry, LJ and Mae Boyd, Robert and Pamela Hackney, Tom and Carrol from Pazzalley's, and Joe Rodriguez. I've learned because they gave of themselves that I might take. I have rounded some very dangerous curves, and for that I am forever in your debt.

Preface

In the distance a mist of clouds, coming closer, as they seem to overlap each other forming a portal through time as buildings , and landscapes evolve into something new within the center of the mist a figure emerges walking slowly as his attire also changes suitable with the times. Now wearing a full length coat and a floppy hat covering his eyes. Everything around him is affected by change and yet his garments seem to remain humble and even tattered with each transformation as he approaches the portal's exit. His presence is of one given to teach with authority and yet his voice is tempered as he opens his mouth and speaks. "If you can believe... All things are possible to those who believe." And the man said with tears in his eyes, "Lord, I believe... Please pray for my unbelief."

I think that said it best. Once again failure was defeated by faith, and yes... I was there, as I have witnessed thousands of such victories, fewer now than there were in the beginning.

I have also witnessed the wisdom of man giving into his own understanding and what that has brought forth, particularly the weakness of his faith.

Oh, forgive me... I have not properly introduced myself.

I am Melchizedek, The first high priest of God.

I am said to be without beginning. I am said to be without end.

It has been given to me over the centuries to be one of those chosen to care for and bear witness to incredible adventures.

I would like to take you on one such a modern-day adventure that begins upon the streets of Saint Augustine in the state of Florida.

How a young man's belief inspired a city.

And I suppose to say this story sounds unbelievable would be an understatement, yet these things happen all around you more than you know.

This is an amazing story of intrigue, suspense, love, and misfortune.

There are many twists and turns in life that make up the becoming of a man…or woman. There really is a way that seems righteous to a man, and you'd be surprised what a man will consider to be righteous given the circumstances of his existence.

You're about to go down some pretty intense streets.

Some of them you will recognize. Some of them will make you cringe. And I am hoping that most of you will take something away from these adventures, something that perhaps you'll keep within your hearts for life as we adventure this story of Aaron Daniels and the lives of those around him.

And so behold what can happen as the violent…taketh by force…

Introduction

The place is Fort Walton prison work camp, Fort Walton, Florida.

There is the rumble of thunder in the distance as an inmate at the Florida state prison stares at the window in anticipation of his release as the prison has been shut down for bed time. The flashes of lighting illuminating the darkness.

Clouds that seem to roll hurriedly across the sky are merely glimpsed through a window in the distance as they race to remove the subtle shades of bright blue from every area of the sky.

His name is Aaron Daniels, prison number 314933.

"What is your understanding?" someone had spoken to him earlier the night.

These words now echo throughout his consciousness, his desire to sleep is amplified by anxieties. What troubles him now for the first time in his life is what can only be described as his manhood or rather the lack there of. He fights to remain amid the storm hours before his release.

He lays there on his bunk, oddly enough as he begins to finally drift off to sleep it is as if he can hear the woods more than 200 yards from the prison. The brush of the wind against the leaves , the crackling of the rain against the old wildered leaves.

The greys and dark blue and the faded of crimson within the clouds.

He is made curious as for a moment he hears the sound of leaves cracking under the weight of footsteps.

He turns in his imagination toward the tree line of the forest beyond the walls but sees nothing.

Still, there is something out there…and it's getting closer.

Finally, mental exhaustion of the anticipation of his release weighs on him and the thoughts of reconnecting with loved ones has claimed his mind into a place of serenity. Softly he drifts away and find himself in memories of happier times; times of innocence's long gone, but indeed not forgotten.

He is on his grandfather's farm. The retired pastor Mason.

There two boys enjoy a game of basketball in the dusty-brown hard dirt yard of the country farm home. An old bicycle rim is nailed near the top of a slim, seven-foot pine tree with a plywood backboard attached to it.

There is also a barn just across the yard on the other side of the makeshift basketball court, and through the open door of the barn, his grandfather has just finished with his work. He rolls out a bicycle and places it alongside another bike.

The boys both notice the repaired bike and come running.

"Grandpa, Grandpa!" they yell as they run into the waiting arms of the pastor.

The younger of the two boys—Jonny—looks up at his grandpa with a large smile.

"Thank you, Grandpa."

The pastor's smile is equally as large as he replies, "Why, you are very welcome."

He continues his deep, burly voice that has a comfort to it like the distant rumble of thunder itself.

"Now, how about the next time you two have a flat tire, you both come in with me, and I'll show you my tools and how to fix it yourselves. You're both coming of age now…"

The two boys seem anxious, and both nod.

Then the pastor asks, "Okay, so who wants one to grow on?"

"I do, I do!" the two boys yell as they race across the farmyard through the porch and into the front door.

Soon they both return, holding the pastor's Bible as he eases himself into a worn leather recliner on the screened in porch. The two young boys slide two beanbag chairs and rest on them at their grandfather's feet.

They lay across the beanbags comfortably and listen as the pastor begins to read.

"Today's lesson is from the book of Jeremiah. It is the first chapter, the first verse."

He clears his throat and begins to read:

> Then the word of the Lord came to me, saying:
> "Before I formed you in the womb, I knew you;
>
> Before you were born I sanctified you; I ordained you a prophet to the nations."
>
> Then Jeremiah replied, "Ah, Lord God! Behold, I cannot speak, for… I am a youth."
>
> But the Lord said, "Do not say I am a youth, for you shall go to all to whom I send you, and whatever I command you, you shall speak. Do not be afraid of their faces, for I am with you to deliver you," says the Lord.

The pastor closes the Bible and asks, "So…why don't you tell me what you heard, starting with you, Aaron, since you're the oldest."

The young boy's eyes begin to wander, then a sheepish grin lights his face as he submits his answer, "I don't know, Grandpa."

Jonny does the same, "Me neither, Grandpa."

The pastor pauses for a moment and then explains, "What God is saying, I believe is this. We are all…kind of like a light bulb. See, as he has given us, we each have a wattage… Some of us can only light a small room. Some are born with great wattage and can even light giant stadiums such as the Gator Bowl. But you see what is important…is that you are willing to activate that light, to become… turned on.

"It's there inside you, so don't ever be afraid to speak, especially if you're right, and especially if it's the truth. Always remember…you were created…not replicated… There is something special about just you. Do you understand?"

The boys nod, and there is a shining sense of enlightenment upon their faces.

The pastor smiles and says, "Okay, you two go and play."

The two boys move quickly and are out the door and back to their basketball game in moments. The pastor sits and watches them from the porch.

The pastor suddenly turns. Startled, he sees a familiar face staring at him through the screen.

"Algeon, you scared me half to death!" he shouts.

The old man with his gray whiskers and floppy begins to laugh but then manages to say, "Well, Pastor, I 'spec that was gonna be yo reaction, but ya need to know, wasn't planned out that way."

Now the pastor is laughing and asks, "So what brings you by, old friend?"

"Nothing, just goin' to my sister's house, thought I'd say hello on account of me seeing ya car from the road. I thought you'd be home. You sho' are good with them boys of yours. 'Spec furlong they grow up to be fine young men."

The pastor seems distant for a moment as he takes a deep breath.

"God only knows, Algeon. The Lord once said, 'Out of the mouth of babes God has perfected praise.' And you know, when I look at them I think…they're born. They are born crying, maybe because they sense they're leaving the very essence of God…and they instinctively seek love.

"Finding it, they stop… They are thankful, and so they stop, they smile…but then we begin to teach them the things that we have…learned, often wanting them to do what's right, but they follow our examples more than our words, and they grow up, and soon with our own teaching, we have perverted the love they once knew, replacing it with all types of emotional baggage, and so soon they are gone… Those things inside of them…they feel so…natural…so real. So gone is that great want for true love, the love of God. Suddenly there is only the want of what we see. The need to possess it. Because of the status it brings. I tell you, Algeon, the day will come when all things doing with God will be found archaic…and even fabled. The Bible tells of it."

Algeon looks at the pastor with a puzzled look on his face.

"Pastor, I 'spec you know more about them things ta come more than the likes of me, but ain't that the kinda thinkin' that got us here? See, I'm just a simple man, Pastor, but the minute I start to believe that God's no longer got control. Well, I 'spec that's about the time I just assume it ain't worth gettin' out of bed no more."

The pastor's eyes wander, staring deep into the eyes of his good friend, and he finds warmth.

"You're right, Algeon. Through faith God formed the worlds and flung stars into space. Blessed is the first-born son, the Bible says. Maybe I should trust in that with regards to my grandboys. I'm afraid I worry too much in my declining years."

Algeon looks upon the boys shooting hoops.

Then he looks up into the sky as the dark clouds begin to angrily roll in. There is a cool breeze, and even the boys take note. Algeon looks back through the screen at Pastor Mason.

"Ya know... I guess we just gotta believe, Pastor, in God's mercy not leaving us to ourselves and letting this world get outta hand."

The pastor looks upon his grandsons with a smile of relief. He then turns back to Algeon.

Algeon looks his pastor in the eyes and smiles.

"But don't get me wrong, Pastor Mason...there's a storm a coming and more than one in life. If you live long enough, I 'spec it's natural from time to time to get ya self a little wet. Gotta ask ya self, can ya stand the rain? Them boys of yours look good and ready for that to me."

He waves goodbye to all.

There is a loud, sudden clap of thunder, and Aaron suddenly turns as there is the sound of the rain and wind blowing against the windows as though the winds were trying to find its own direction whirling in a frantic rage against the dorm. But this is a night Aaron Daniels cannot seem to rest, and this rain takes him again back into the night this all started.

Now he hears the rain beat against the window of his Dodge Charger.

He escapes through the windows of his memories yet again.

Chapter 1

Watcha Back Drive

Two years earlier.

It was two years earlier, in downtown St. Augustine, Florida—America's oldest city.

The cathedral bells rang twice in the morning as the wind and rain are coming across the St. Johns River from the northeast with great force.

The waves crash into the embankment along the scenic city bay front splashing into the street.

A '74 Dodge Charger makes its way downtown and parks just in front of the Trade Winds Tavern nightclub. The streets are empty as Aaron Daniels—better known as AD—sits first for a moment and thinks, *You're really gonna do this. This is what we've wanted for so long.* He sits and stares at the windshield as the rain beats against it, the wipers swishing back and forth. He takes a deep breath and makes his way from his car while fighting a wind that so easily blows his umbrella inside out.

As he makes the adjustments, he begins to make his way across Cathedral Place and down Charlotte Street.

As he reaches the cobblestone road just along the side of Galleria del Mar Art Gallery, he stops to consider whether or not he should've parked closer. He then remembers the plan and realizes the distinct sound of his Charger would only add to the risk at hand.

He crosses Bravo Lane, and soon he reaches Bridge Street, concealing himself from the rain under the trees. There he stops to think about what he is about to do.

He looks back just over his shoulder and smiles, as if to say goodbye to the world he's known.

Then there is a pause and a gaze at the ground before him shaking his head, as he realizes it is the only world he's ever known. But then he looks ahead and smiles as there is the world that is before him. He looks toward the sky, and as the rain beads upon his face, he begins to wonder what else could have him out in such miserable weather yet feeling so…good—his Tracy.

A sharp left and a quick right finds him at the chain link fence that separates his girlfriend and her neighbor's yard.

After jumping it soon, he is at her window.

He taps on her window, but there's no response. Impatiently he taps a second time and is immediately startled by her face appearing through the window, with a finger pressed to her lips.

She slowly opens the window and directs an intense "Shh!" at AD, then climbing through the window, she almost falls into his arms in the dark night.

They walk carefully huddled together across the yard, their steps illuminated slightly by the mostly smothered moon and the wave of lights and shadow that seem to strike against the earth as the wind blows the limbs and the leaves.

AD heads toward the fence, but Tracy laughs quietly.

"Oh baby, you jumped the fence, and for me," she whispers as she heads for the front gate.

Aaron grabs her and fiercely whispers, "What about the plan? Someone will see us!"

She shakes her head and says, "Baby, it's two in the morning, and storming, and uh, dark. We didn't plan on the weather two weeks ago. Right now, I can't see us. Let's go."

AD shrugs his shoulder as they head through the front gate down the street and to the Charger.

Aaron throws her overnight bag into the trunk. Once inside, their lips meet, and there is a grin upon their faces as they look into each other's eyes.

"Are we really going to do this?" she asks.

Aaron jokes, "Tell me you've changed your mind, and you're walking back by ya self."

As he cranks the engine, he begins heading opposite the direction of Jacksonville.

Tracy asks, "Where are we going?"

Aaron's face displays the difficulty of the explanation to come then says, "I just have to take care of a little something first."

There is a look of anticipation on her face, and she asks, "What kind of little something?"

Aaron mumbles, "A small little…pick-up."

Tracy is heated! "Uh-uh, so your good cousin who you've been working for doing God knows what, he can't just pay you what's due to you for services rendered? No, he's a pimp, AD, and he's pimpin' you!"

Aaron laughs.

"And what's so funny?" she asks.

"You, already sounding like a wife. You took that and went there, with *all* that."

"I'm just keepin' it real," she replies.

"Well, for your information, I've already got the grand on me, and I'm picking up another five grand for doing this as a wedding present." Tracy's mouth drops as AD continues, "Oh, now ya got teeth showing and things. Like now I can see you got your daddy's tonsils?

He points toward her mouth.

Her month snaps shut as she quickly slaps his hand away.

"Five thousand dollars?"

"Yep." He smiles.

Staring out of the windshield, she looks almost dazed, then she says, "I don't like it."

"Say what? You say that now, but with what you got, that gives us seventy-six hundred dollars to start our new lives on Straight Street, off Watcha Back Drive."

But Tracy is visibly despondent, saying, "But, baby, nobody's gonna give you that kinda money for something like this unless there are risks."

"Don't sweat it, Tracy. I told Jonny you'd be with me. He assured me it would be all right. He's getting out the game himself in the fall. He decided to go to University of Florida and play basketball. They've been sweatin' him so hard to come play for them. So his hustling days are almost over too."

But Trancy is still shaking her head, saying, "Yeah, well, you can't get wet unless you get in the water." She smirks.

Now Aaron is shaking his head then says, "What's that, like some ancient Chinese cookie saying?"

"Yeah, Aaron, it means, let's take what we got and run. Baby, what you telling me make sense for Jonny, but he ain't here now, is he?"

But then Aaron pulls into a gas station and says, "Too late, we're here."

Tracy looks around and asks, "Where? A gas station? Oh, you need ta pull up. You ain't doing this at no gas station. Boy, they got cameras all up in here!"

Aaron pulls into the BP gas station off of US 1, near the 312 bridge.

He then pulls along the side of the building in the rear near the restrooms.

"Here's the game plan: You stay here. I'm going just over into the parking lot over in the shopping plaza. From the corner of the building, you'll be able to see me at all times."

He hands Tracy an envelope with the money in it for their future.

"Why can't he do it? If it's nothing, Aaron?"

Aaron smiles and replies, "'Cause there's always risks, Trace."

"But you said..."

"Trace! Come on, hell, baby, let me do what I do, okay?"

She takes a deep breath and exits the car.

AD drives into the parking lot and parks. He looks around and waits as the rain picks up. Through the rain, he sees a man staggering in the parking lot. The guy is obviously drunk.

AD's eyes wander the area, looking for his contact. Again, he notices the man who is now on the ground, facedown.

Jesus, Aaron thinks to himself as he checks his watch. *I'm either very early or he's running late.*

He looks around the parking lot, and still no sign of the car he's expecting. He looks again at the man still lying in the rain.

Aaron takes a deep breath as he begins to notice that the rain is calming, and this man appears to be lying facedown with his head in a puddle.

Jesus! Aaron thinks to himself as he quickly gets out of the car and starts toward the man.

As he gets closer, he notices air bubbles, and the man is struggling

Oh my god! He rushes toward the homeless man. *Please God, whatever you do, don't let this man need mouth to mouth. Stacy is probably watching, and this is gonna be a thing, Lord.*

He rolls the man over, and the man's mouth is covered with foam, and then in a violent cough he coughs the foam all over Aaron's jacket.

Aaron cringes.

Wow...really... I mean, yeah, I should have been more prayer specific, but ya know what? It's cool, I can wash this before I give it away.

The man looks around as Aaron begins to help the man to his feet, his left arm draped over Aaron's shoulder.

Observing Aaron's jacket, the drunk man says to Aaron, "Jeez, buddy, that looks both really nasty and yet oddly familiar."

Aaron smiles and thinks, *Least wasn't no mouth to mouth. I'm just wondering why this smells like it could stain to the white meat?*

The man lifts his head and asks, "Where am I?"

Aaron nods and says, "Actually, I'm pretty sure you haven't seen that place for hours."

"Ya think so?" The man looks at Aaron with a seriousness on his face.

Aaron smiles and says, "Let me get you out of this rain, man."

"Ya do that for me?" Now the man seems solemn.

"Yeah, dude, you somebody folk too. Come on."

Aaron helps the man to a bench in front of a store and sits him down.

"You gonna be all right?" he asks, propping the man up.

17

"Yeah, yeah… Thank you. Wait!" The man grabs Aaron's arm and goes into his own pocket, pulling out about four dollars and some change. "Here, take this."

Aaron laughs and says, "My first instinct was to roll you, but naw, man, it's okay."

"Wait!" The man reaches into his jacket pocket and pulls out a damp Fantasy Five ticket, holding it out toward Aaron. "Ya never know."

Aaron just smiles as he wipes off his jacket with an old newspaper and rainwater.

"Naw, man, we straight. You just have a nice life, go out, and win ya self something."

Aaron turns to see the car he's been expecting coming into the lot.

"Hey, I gotta go." He runs back into the rain, cleaning his jacket with an old piece of newspaper. He walks to the now-parked car and taps on the window.

The man in the car looks and hollers, "Yeah?" with an intimidating look in his eyes.

"Im Jonny's friend!" Aaron yells back.

The electronic lock sounds, and Aaron gets in.

The man looks toward the drunk on the bench and says, "You brought back-up. Should I be worried?" nodding his head toward the man on the bench.

Aaron smirks and says, "You got jokes. Jonny didn't tell me you were a funny man, guess he never saw ya shoes. Tell me, ya grandchildren made you wear them."

The man smiles and asks, "Where's your car?" Aaron points to the Charger. "Yeah, that's the one I'm looking for."

He pulls over next to it. Aaron grabs a grocery bag. The man takes the bag, a quick peek, and he hands Aaron a small package for Jonny. The man quickly inspects the product.

"Are we straight?" Aaron asks.

They bump fists, and Aaron heads for the Charger.

The man's car doesn't move. Aaron thinks he's probably on his cell phone with Jonny. Aaron moves out toward the BP but is caught by the stoplight. While AD is held up at the red light, he checks his rearview mirror to find a blue Crown Victoria coming off 312 and moving fast toward the car he'd just left.

Suddenly lights start flashing. Two detectives—Rodgers and Billips—quickly get out of their car, guns in hand, and pull Aaron's contact out of the car just as the light changes.

Aaron pulls around the back of the BP where Tracy's waiting. He hands her the package.

"Get this to Jonny, Use ya cell phone to get a cab. Now get in the bathroom while I lead the cops away. Don't call me, I'll call you!"

"Aaron?" she cries out.

"Now, Tracy, damn it!"

Aaron then speeds off but is unable to get out onto US1.

One of the detectives places handcuffs on the man in the parking lot; the other is visibly scanning the parking lot.

The man looks up at the Charger across the street and says, "You're kidding. You mean the kid's a cop?"

They both follow his eyes, and Detective Rodgers spots the Charger and Aaron looking back.

"Billips, take him. I'm going after the car!" Rodgers yells.

Aaron gets out onto US 1, heading north, but then quickly crosses over to the South Dixie extension to South Dixie highway.

The Crown Vic is suddenly with him, lights flashing.

Aaron finally goes around into the Winn-Dixie parking lot just short of state road 207 and stops.

Rodgers stops, getting out quickly, and screams, "Put your hands where I can see them!"

He trains his gun on the back of Aaron's head. He snatches the door open and pulls Aaron out. He slams Aaron against the trunk of the Charger and cuffs him and then looks into Aaron's face.

There is an obvious look of disappointment on Detective Rodgers's face, and at first, he says nothing. Then he takes another look at the interior of the car. No one. He then notices the gas needle says full. Then Rodgers remembers the gas station.

"Damn! He couldn't have had time to buy gas."

By now, Tracy is passing Aaron's parked car in the Winn-Dixie parking lot and sees her man handcuffed with his face toward the highway, pinned against the trunk of his own car.

He sees the taxi and can only hope that Tracy is among the passengers.

But there are another pair of eyes on Aaron as well. A green four-door box Chevy pulls slowly into the Chevron station just the other side of the highway. A man sits and watches.

Damn, AD, you almost made it, man. Fucking round with Jonny, now the whole thing done blew up.

The man puts the car in drive and slowly drives away.

Too bad, kid. I really liked you.

Chapter 2

Missed

The other officer "Billips" arrives with the other suspect in a patrol car. He gets out and looks confused as he walks over to Rodgers, who is having a cigarette.

"You called a patrol car? What were you thinking?" Billups asks.

Rodgers motions his head toward the Crown Vic. Billips walks over and looks inside.

He then goes back to Rodgers and asks, "Who's that?"

Rodgers answers, "His ID says Aaron Daniels."

Billips shakes his head, saying, "This is bad, partner. This is so not good...so now what?"

Rodgers throws his smoke to the ground and says, "Look, as far as I can see, we may still be able to make this work."

Billips is puzzled and asks, "Okay, how? How do we make this work?"

Rodgers smiles and replies, "By making this not about us. We got bad intel. It's not our fault."

Rodgers steps away and takes out his cell phone and makes a call.

"Yeah?" a deep yet clammy voice answers with a hint of contempt.

A reluctant Rodgers answers, "We missed him."

"Why am I not surprised?"

"It's not our fault!"

"Again, why am I not surprised?"

"The kid wasn't there."

"What ta ya mean the kid wasn't there?"

"Look, we picked up his mule. Now, I have a plan…"

The voice on the phone becomes angered and shouts, "You have a plan!" Then the clammy voice replies with a slight chuckle. "Tell ya what. You can get cute and start planning shit, but ya shit go wrong, and I'll shove it up ya ass sideways, holding a great big pig. So tell me something… Ya still got a plan?"

The man with the clammy, deep voice hangs up the phone and turns to a man sitting behind a mahogany desk in a large study, looking out of a large picture window overlooking a manmade lake.

The man from the phone walks over to the desk. His name is Cole.

In the reflection of the glass, their eyes meet, the man behind the desk closes a green folder and places it into a safe secured behind his desk.

"Mr. Mickelson, that was Rodgers. They missed. They say Blain didn't show. Everything went according to plan except he sent in a mule."

The man behind the desk then stares again into the darkness as the wind and rain begin to pick up.

"So, Mr. Cole…we simply have a minor setback. Still, it doesn't change the facts, and one of them is that his network is quite conducive to our projective quarterly income for that area."

Mr. Cole's lips snarl and says, "With all due respect, Mr. Mickelson, I can remember when hostile takeovers were, ya know, hostile. By now, Blain knows something is wrong…"

Mickelson raises his hand, and Cole stops.

"Perhaps, but he would have sent a trusted agent for such a large transaction, don't you agree? No, they won't panic, and he'll simply cut his losses and go off to school." Mickelson turns back to Cole and continues, "We'll have to convince him that his interests would be better served in St. Augustine and not at the University of Florida."

Cole smiles and says, "That's what I'm saying. I'm just the man to convince him."

Mickelson smiles and slowly shakes his head, saying, "No, no, Mr. Cole. A truly good employee is one who has incentives to consider. If he feels he's working for himself, he'll do a better job and will be less likely to make mistakes. He built this whole thing up from scratch. He'll need to feel his child has taken on a life of its own. It will be what comforts him at night when he thinks of how…we took it away."

"So how do we get him to stay?" Cole asks.

Mickelson turns back to the picture glass window and stares again into the rain before answering, "He's a gamer. I believe I've got a little game of my own."

Chapter 3

The Preparation

Jacksonville, Florida. At 4139 Moncrief Avenue, Bobby Cox and his wife, Nurse Penny "Cricket" Cox, are at long last celebrating the transfer and start of her husband Bobby into his new job after moving to Florida from Bloomington, Kentucky.

They lived with Penny's mother, sister, and brother for months to hold off expenses as Penny and Bobby searched for a house. Siblings such as Charles and sister Peanut engage in light but loud banter in the living room just outside Penny's room.

Their mother enters the room to intercede.

"Children, children Lord ha mercy, ya daddy—God rest his soul—wasn't a loud man, and yet I done had three of the loudest children the city has even known. But I did the DNA test on both of y'all, three or four on you, Charles, and y'all are mine, so tell me, what y'all arguing 'bout now?"

Charles's eyes widen, and his mouth drops.

"Momma, that's cold, okay, that's just wrong, but you need ta know your daughter is dating a boy so dumb that he thinks Jell-O is a verb 'cause it moves."

Now Peanut snaps her fingers.

"No, you didn't. How 'bout that old lady you call yo self dating. Momma, she's so old she can remember when the dust was still two for a penny. How 'bout she can remember when shoestrings was a style. Momma, I think I saw her twice in your high school yearbook."

Her mother's mouth drops and asks, "Well, wait just a minute. How old do you think I am?"

Peanut covers her mouth in silence.

Their mother just nods her head and laughs.

"Anyway, you two need to keep it down. Bobby has to start his new job in the morning, and he's gonna need his rest. Now y'all outside his room, making all this noise, so get."

The two head into another room toward the other end of the house.

Charles continues, "Shoestrings? I got ya shoestring. You know I was there when the boy spelled snow s-n-o."

Bobby sits on the end of the bed, staring at Penny as they both begin to snicker at her family's antics.

Bobby shakes his head in disbelief and asks, "You're not going to miss that?"

Penny holds one of Bobby's suit and shirts in her hands. Bobby stands up.

Then she replies, "Yes…and no. You haven't seen them really go at each other."

Bobby laughs and says, "Come on. How bad can it be?"

Penny gives Bobby a look and says, "Peanut was upset with Charles because she thought he told Mama that she snuck out one night, so the next morning she woke him up by putting a lit match up his nose."

Now Bobby's mouth drops, and he asks, "A lit match up his nose? While he sleeps? Who does that? That's not a real thing?"

Penny nods, saying, "Exactly, sometimes I imagine real crime scene tape in their future."

Now she begins to use Bobby as a mannequin as she decides which suit he should wear on his first day of work.

Pat is so excited. Bobby is just amused with his wife he affectionately calls "The Cricket."

"Bobby, be still. What about the blue suit with the light-blue shirt, and the red tie?"

But before Bobby can even speak, Penny continues, "No, wait, the light-brown suit with the paisley tie and the dark-brown shirt."

"Are you gonna walk me to school too, Mom?" Bobby jokes.

"Ha, ha, you know you'll never get another chance to make a first impression."

"So what did you wear your first day at the hospital?"

Penny stops and rolls her eyes.

"Cute, Bobby. The dress is too small, and your toenails would run my hose still. That would be an impression." She pauses for thought. "No, maybe you should wear the traditional black suit with the white shirt and black tie."

Bobby laughs. But then there is her expression, and Bobby takes note.

"I'm… I'm sorry, you were serious?" Putting his arms around her waist, she shakes her head yes as their lips gently touch. He asks, "What would I do without you?"

She kisses him back and says, "Exactly! So the brown suit, the pink tie, and the maroon shirt."

"Oh Pat, I hate that pink tie. I think your mom brought it for me to see if I'd leave you, but I stayed, we got married. We should drop the pretense. Besides I'm a conservative."

"No, we're poor. There's a difference. You need to be expressive, to be successful, Bobby."

Bobby grimaces and asks, "So what does pink say?"

She presses the tie under his chin and replies, "Pink says confidence. Pink says, 'Yes, I am a confident man. You all should fear me.' Who else would dare wear a pink tie on the first day but a confident man?"

Bobby chuckles. Pat rolls her eyes

"You…you were doing that serious thing again."

"Pink is brazen, Bobby. It says, 'Soon you shall all work for me, my peers." She raises one of her fingers in the air. "Or, I'll be okay once the LSD wears off."

Then pulling him in front of the mirror, she matches the brown jacket against his chest with a maroon shirt and the dark-pink tie. There is a look of approval.

"Okay, maybe you got something."

Penny's eyes raise as she smiles and says, "A woman knows these things."

Their eyes meet.

"God, you're beautiful when you're right," he whispers as he gently pulls her to him and kisses her.

She quickly jumps and pulls away and says, "Bobby, you'll be wrinkling ya suit."

"Oh," he catches himself.

She takes the garments and lays them across a chair and then rushes quickly back into his arms

"Now, what were you saying?" she asks as she presses her body against his.

*****

Back at the Mickelson estate, Mr. Cole goes into the library to be alone. He sits at a desk where he has one of his many metronomes adorning the desk.

Taking the metal ball on the end he pulls it back and lets it go. *Tick, tick, tick, tick.*

His mind now wonders of the events of last week. He was sitting in the back of the limo when the phone rang.

The voice on the other end sounds troubled.

"Cole, somebody broke into the house."

Cole pauses and then, "The house? What da ya mean somebody broke into the house? What, like a thief?"

"No, Mr. Cole. We tag him. He's one of yours."

"Mine?"

"Yeah. We traced him back to one of your affiliates, a Mr. Big Boy Morris out of Palatka."

"Big Boy! That doesn't make any sense. Give me the information!"

"His name is Arnold Jackson. He handles distribution…"

Now Cole remembers the man coming home with a beer in his hand. As he closes his back door, he is startled to see Cole standing there with a gun in hand, fitted with a silencer.

Cole asks the man, "You know who I am?"

The man answers coolly, "You're the strange man standing in my house with a gun."

Cole smiles and says, "Yeah, that's right. But I'm also ya boss… or at least one of them. I'm here tonight, Arnold, 'cause I'm afraid I'ma need to know who else you working for."

The man's eyebrows raise, and he says, "Hey, look, I just took the merchandise where Big Boy tells me. If something feels light, I don't package, and I don't weigh the stuff."

The two men stare each other in the eyes.

Cole nods in approval, then he asks, "So tell me about the house you broke into in the Ville last night."

Suddenly the man tosses the beer can and lunges at Cole. But Cole is too fast, and the shot hits the man in the forehead.

Cole begins to search the body when he finds an ankle holster with a police-issued 9mm handgun

A cop? No wonder he was so cute. But still, how did he make the house? That thought rests upon Mr. Cole's mind.

Tick, tick, tick, tick.

Chapter 4

Owed to Jonny Blain

Later that morning in St. Augustine, Billips comes out of the interrogation room with the man Aaron made contact with.

He meets Rogers coming down the hallway and says, "He's not talking. He's an old con."

"Yeah, I read his jacket." Rodgers smiles and continues, "I had the kid in a holding cell last night and kept him away from those jailhouse lawyers."

"We don't have anything on him," Billips replies in frustration.

"He doesn't know that. It's his first rodeo. We'll have to go to Plan B."

"Which is?" Billips asks.

"We lie. We get paid to lie. Jesus, Billips, Sometimes I swear the best part of your deducting skills ran right down ya mama's leg. Just relax, listen, and back my play."

The detectives go to the booking and instruct the officers to bring Daniels into an interrogation room.

Shortly after, Aaron is seated, and the detectives come in, and Rodgers starts in right away.

"Okay, kid, this is your first arrest, and look at you. You jumped right into the big league. We have the drugs, and your codefendant is taking a plea, so you're looking at ten years."

"At least," Billips adds.

"Ten years…" Aaron's face goes white with anxiety and fear.

Billips starts in, "Yeah, hotshot, we've got you on video and audio making a hand-to-hand transaction. Not to mention fleeing, eluding, and reckless endangerment. But you're not who we're after, kid."

Rodgers's hand presses against Billip's chest as to say, "Calm down."

"We want Jonny Blain," Rodgers says calmly.

"Jonny Blain?" repeats Aaron, more out of surprise than curiosity.

"Please don't even try it. Better than you have tried to lie to us, son. Again, you're out of your league."

"Yeah, kid," adds Billips.

"Unless ya just got nothin' better to do for the next ten years, you'll spare us the bullshit, sign a statement, and take ya little ass home."

"Yeah, kid, go home, get the clap, or something, 'cause you don't get rid of whatcha catch in the chain gang, and you look to me to be a real hot date," Billips adds with a slight smile.

Aaron's mind goes adrift. He can still hear the detectives, but he can also see Jonny's face.

He sees him as they'd shoot hoops in that old bike rim on their grandpa's farm.

He sees him the first time they stole candy from Buckam's grocery and ran down the tracks to eat it.

He sees him again on prom night when they double dated because Jonny was too young to drive.

He can see him at the championship game and all those victories in between.

Now Jonny is on his way. Aaron could not be the one to come between Jonny and his dreams of playing basketball. Besides, Aaron was no snitch.

"I'm sorry, Detectives. I don't know what you're talking about."

Rodgers smiles and says, "You know what? I told my partner here you'd say that. Oh well, we'll get Jonny Blain, and as far as you're concerned, kid..." Rodgers hands Aaron a business card and continues, "Seriously, you really don't want the drop the soap. I've heard sometimes if they like you...they'll knock it out ya hand, ha ha ha."

The detectives leave the interrogation room, and Rodgers pulls the waiting officer to the side and says, "Listen, that kid goes into protective custody, you got it? Sick cellblock. I don't want him mixing with the population, at least not yet. Also, make sure that if he wants me, day or night, that I'm called, paged, whatever! You understand?"

The officer grins and says, "I gotcha, Detective. You think you got a bed wetter?"

Chapter 5

Welcome to the Jungle

In Jacksonville, Bobby arrives to work at the federal building, downtown. He passes through security and reads the listings posted near the elevator. Once upstairs, he is directed to Mr. Morganstein's office.

Mr. Morganstein is the assistant to the public defender's office, and chaperone. After the tour, Bobby is shown his office, but his assistant is nowhere to be found.

Bobby settles in by unloading the small box of things Penny insisted he'd need to give the office some identity.

He sits comfortably behind his desk in his leather chair. He smiles as he gazes out of his window and then at a picture of his cricket as he places the picture on his desk.

He then takes notice of his phone.

The call box is particularly interesting. Sliding the box toward him as he leans back with his feet propped up on the desk, he pretends to push a button.

"Katie, hold all of my calls this morning."

He is suddenly startled by a voice from behind him.

"You know what? I'm just gonna take for granted you didn't mean to say that out loud, and your getting a handle on those voices you insist you...hear calling back at you?"

Bobby jumps, flustered and embarrassed, and explains, "I thought the door was closed."

The lady smiles and says, "I'm sure hoping so. Believe it or not, I'm Katie."

"You're kidding?"

"Nope, I'm your secretary."

Bobby looks closer to find "Katie" on her name tag.

"You're kidding," he thinks aloud.

"Yeah." She smiles. "I guess mother really does know best."

"Uh... I'm Bobby."

"Yeah, I know, and I'm so glad to meet you. You have imagination or...really good pills, whatever works. You may need them around here." She smiles. "Anyway, I'm here for you. So you're not one of those guys that get here and become a clog in the machine punching a clock. I've been here seven years now, and I usually break in the new bees."

Just then there's a light tap on the open door. To Bobby's surprise, there stands a tall, slender but shapely blond, her long hair full of body and quite attractive. The only signs of age are the wisdom in her eyes and the reservation in her smile.

"Ms. Daniels," Katie says with a smile and then starts for the door. On her way out, she turns to Bobby and gestures to him that the phone thing will be their little secret.

Ms. Daniels looks at Katie as she leaves, then back at Bobby. She seems pleasantly amused.

"Well, I see you've already made a friend. That's good. Your assistants—especially Katie—can be your first line of defense when it comes to making your life bearable. I'm your second. Hi"—she reaches out her hand—"I'm Sellenia Daniels, your boss."

Bobby is surprised—and pleased.

"You're the head public defender?"

"That's right, Mr. Cox, and I also want to welcome you to the DCA branch of our office. Now allow me to tell you a little about what I expect out of this office, Mr. Cox—good work and results. We get appeals here every day, some without any statutory merit, but others with legitimate arguments who simply need us to examine the facts and subject them to plausible laws and status.

"Now, you may find that some of these people may have indeed committed the crime for which they are incarcerated, and their desire for freedom may hinge only on a loophole in the law. Let your passion be for the loyalty of your oath. Loopholes are supposed to be explored. How else will we know they are there to fix them? We are not here to write law but to interpret it to the level in which our clients' rights are upheld. Many—and do mean many—of them never had that opportunity."

She walks over to Bobby's window and continues as she gazes across the St. Johns River.

"You've walked into a storm, Mr. Cox. A storm that was created by the State's Attorney's office and all over Florida. Their political agendas are in play, you see, in Florida. There is no grand jury system in this state, so the DA determines who should be arrested. It's a numbers game to them. They flood the jails with the poor and offer them deals in lieu of justice. So they sit there and they sit there until many of them see the deal as their only way out. A closure, if you will. The DA's conviction rate goes up, and those who, for whatever reason, are unfortunate enough to find themselves taking deal after deal, generally find themselves writing to us eventually."

Sillenia looks at Bobby, and she smiles and says, "It's not supposed to work this way, Mr. Cox, but because it does, I'm asking you to take it to heart also. Be diligent about these people, would you?"

Bobby sits back on his desk and says, "Ms. Daniels—"

"Please, call me Sillenia."

"Okay," Bobby continues. "Sillenia, I love a good fight. When can I get in?"

"Sooner than you might think. We also work some pro bono cases to get you some courtroom exposure and so I can see what I got, and yes…that was meant to apply pressure, so I hope you're not gun-shy."

She smiles.

Bobby grins and says, "Gun-shy? You're really not feeling the tie, huh?"

Chapter 6

Best-Laid Plans

Back in St. Augustine, Aaron lies in his cell in the medical block of the St. Johns County Jail. He can only think of Tracy and what she must be going through.

They've been together for some six years, the last three behind their parents' backs.

Now he thinks of his parents. How will he explain this? He's on camera doing a drug buy! Complete with audio. Aaron is almost glad there's no bond. They're gonna hit the roof.

Aaron goes to his first appearance to hear the charges against him. He is visited by the medic. The nurse asks the guard why he is being held in medical isolation. The guard doesn't know, so he tells Aaron to pack up and get ready to be placed in the population.

His cell door is popped shortly afterward, and he gathers his bedroll and hygiene items and places them on a table in the middle of the dorm. Now he can see the whole cellblock. Most of these people are asleep, but one catches his attention.

A man awakes to use his toilet. The man washes his hands and turns to find Aaron standing at his cell door.

"You remember me?" Aaron asks, but the man looks at Aaron in confusion. Aaron laughs, "I pulled you out of the puddle last night."

"Yeah? Yeah! That was you?"

"Yep." Aaron smiles.

"So what they get you for?" the old man asks.

"It's a long story. What about you, what are you in here for?"

The man giggles and answers, "Evidently, I was having a little too good of a time."

"No!" Aaron snaps.

"Player haters," the old man responds as he burps.

Aaron laughs and asks, "So how long do you think you're looking at?"

"Oh, I'll get out today. Yeah, we do this every so often. So what about you? When you jump, or don't 'cha know?"

"No clue." Aaron sighs.

"Well, what's your name anyway?"

"I'm Aaron Daniels."

Reaching his hand through the cell, the older man says, "I'm Derrick Philmore, and I do remember what you did for me."

While shaking Aaron's hand, there's a sincerity that is evident in the man's cracked, wrinkled, hairy face.

"I don't have anything of material, young man, but such as I have to give, I pray you will receive God's blessing be upon you."

A voice comes from the intercom, instructing Aaron to get away from the prisoner's door, and Derrick releases his hand. Aaron picks up his bags and goes through the dorm door.

A guard meets him and commands Aaron to follow him.

*****

Days go by at the county jail. Rodgers comes over from the jail to his office within the sheriff's office and, grabbing Billips, heads out to their cruiser.

"What's up?" Billips asks.

"I had a request from the jail. One of my snitches is trying to get some time off his ass, dropped me some info that—if it checks out—could put us back inside with Mickelson."

"Mickelson? The kid's got something on Jonny Blain?"

"No, and those idiots stuck Daniels in population."

They reach the car and soon are heading down US 1 South.

"I still don't understand. What are we doing?" Billips asks.

"We're gonna catch another fish for the fry."

"How's that work?"

Rodgers hits the steering wheel with his palm and says, "I swear we're the same age, but while I was watching *Police Story*, you must've been watching *Police Academy*. The only thing you have to have is knowledge of the terrain. It's as simple as that. I've been a cop in this city for eleven years, seven of them before I ever heard of Cole. I'm a director of operations in my town. Cole my ass... He the muscle... Mickelson is the only one we have to impress."

"You got plane?" Billips asks with obvious concern.

"It's simple. I got a tip on a player called City Boy Style. He's a big-time runner out of the Westside, but he's extended his reach to the Overtown area. He doesn't see turf, and that's who we're gonna reel in to take over Jonny Blain's action."

"But Jonny is a player. This guy City Boy is a runner."

"So how'd you think Blain got started? Look, somewhere along the way, he met with the right contact. That's what we're gonna do for City Boy—make an introduction."

"So where are we going?"

"Eddie's trapped."

Soon they park just down the street from Oneida.

After a few minutes, a silver BMW pulls up just before Eddie's place.

Billups is impressed and says, "Wow, maybe the City Boy is ready for the bigs. Nice ride."

Rodgers shakes his head and says, "It ain't his. He's renting it from a baser. Actually, the very baser we're gonna convince to give him up if he wants to continue driving that car."

A man runs inside the gate and up the outside stairs. Two knocks and he's in.

"At least he was smart enough not to park in front of Eddie's place. You see a BMW in front of that dump, you almost gotta call SWAT," Billips jokes.

Shortly, the man comes back downstairs and back into the BMW and drives off.

"Right on cue." Rodgers smiles.

"We're not gonna pull him?" Billips asks.

"What for? If what my snitch tells me is true, he ain't got no dope on him, only brings what he needs. Besides, a truly good bust is made in a controlled situation. One that I control. Besides, we don't want him thinking he's being watched. We'll keep sitting on him, watching the traps. Sooner or later, he'll take us back to his supplier. They always do. Then we'll knock the supplier down, and City Boy will be looking for a new supplier. Enter Mr. Mickelson." Rodgers smiles.

Chapter 7

Consciousness

Back at the jail, Aaron lays on his top bunk. His parents have informed him of their plans to visit, and he can't help but play that over and over in his mind.

The speaker system informs the cellblock of Bible study. Aaron is restless and welcomes the opportunity to get out of the cellblock.

Some twenty of the cellblock detainees make their way into a classroom where they are met by an elderly white gentleman with smiles and greetings. After they've been seated, he asks that they would join hands in prayer. They open the Bible up to the book of Mark, chapter 12, verse 41. The pastor begins to read.

> Now Jesus, sat opposite the treasury, saw how the people put money into the treasury, and many who were rich put in much. Then one poor widow came, and threw in two mites, which makes a quad ran. So he called all his disciples to himself and said to them,
>
> "Assuredly, I say unto you that this poor woman has put in more than all those who had given to the treasury; for they all put in out of their abundance, but she out of poverty, put in all she had, her whole livelihood."

Then the teacher reminded the class that they were seeking the mysteries of Christ Jesus.

One man stood and suggested that people often give less than they're capable of.

The teacher expounds on that point on various levels.

"Being that God has no need for your money, let's talk about what's really important: Us. I mean, he gave his son a sacrifice to satisfy the issue of sin. Everything has a spectrum, and each spectrum has its points. In creating everything, he had to allow for these spectrums. But he created a remedy for our sin condition because free will meant we would sin against what is good in accordance with God's word. Moses gave us a time and a place to make sacrifices for the sins of man once a year. He even gave us what should be sacrificed, the blood that should be used. He gave us the law, or the ten commandments, to show us why we needed to be saved from ourselves and our sins. But then God took it to the next level. He gave us a man, his son, to be that sacrifice and used his blood to take away the sins of man once and for all so that we could have life with him.

"Now, of course, there is still sin and the evil one. And he still wants his pound of flesh. While he didn't see that coming, he didn't give up. See, God made this gift available unto whosoever could believe it. So the enemy, or the Devil's, job is to make you think there is no God, and so there is no sacrifice, no heaven, no hell...but your spirit? See, he can't keep quite what you're hearing in your spirit. People may say there was a big bang, and here we are, but within your spirit...ask yourself... There are roughly 6,500 different identifiable dialects of language in the world. The big bang theory would ask you to believe that these forms of communications that tie us all together were formed from men grunting at each other. Let that sink in for a minute. Scripture tells us in the beginning was the word, and the word was with God, and the word was God. Now, who grunted enough Hebrew language that brought about that?"

The pastor laughs, as does the classroom.

"How are your study habits toward Jesus? We say we believe in God and Jesus and heaven and hell, and yet what of our purpose? Are you without reason? So complex a creature as yourselves given thoughts and dreams hopes...but all for nothing? One of the things Jesus promised was this life and its abundance. But he also gave us a mission. Even his very own. Seek out to share this message of salvation. Don't let it all end here. Who would you see lost for eternity in utter darkness to a being that can't allow anyone to survive him? You see, just as God is good and inclusive, the other end of that spectrum…is not."

All are quiet, and then the pastor asks, "Do you feel who you are? Have you examined your dreams as impossible as they may seem? They were given you for a reason. Dare to believe you are exactly who God says that you are…or do you really give two mites?"

That evening Aaron spends hours in the Bible, reading it but then studying it also, taking notes. He is fascinated by the life and words of Jesus, his understanding of who man is.

Now, there was the question. What could he do? He knew he was no pastor. But there was this sense that people were dying, people that he loved, but then there were just people that he knew too. He is just AD, but he thought to himself, *Okay, but what if God is saying, "I can use you"?*

Chapter 8

What Meets the Eye

At the federal building the next day, Bobby is early and eager to get a jump on the business at hand. Sillenia had promised him a case to work—pro bono—that would bring him actual courtroom exposure.

She told him to remember that this is not a test and that people actually had something to lose. Exactly what it would become would depend on his work ethic.

He is pleasantly surprised to find Sillenia's door open, and voices coming from inside her office. He is also surprised to find Katie at her desk, arranging files.

"Good morning," he says, catching her by surprise as she pores over a file.

"Oh, hi! You're in early."

"So are you, aren't you?"

Katie nods and says, "Well, I know Ms. Daniels, and she's going to expect you to be on point, so I also have to be on point in assisting you to the best of my ability, right?"

"Your help is greatly appreciated, Katie. So what do we have?"

"God, I love the way you say that! We got Mike Moore. He was said to be seen by the arresting officer exiting a car that was found in his possession."

"He was driving the car?" Bobby asks.

"The officer says yes, but Moore denies it. Now, his prints were found in the car, but not on the driver's side."

"So whose name is on the registration?"

"A known crackhead who suddenly claims the car was stolen, but at the time of impound, no police report was filed on the car as being stolen."

Bobby nods and says, "I wonder why. So are they charging Moore with grand theft auto?"

"No, the deal is, he takes three years, and they drop the grand theft if he takes the possession."

"Wait a minute. You said Moore claims he wasn't driving, so where did he get arrested?"

"Inside the residence at 20 Scott, St. Augustine, Florida."

Bobby takes the file, and Katie hands him a cup of coffee as he goes into the office.

Twenty minutes later, he comes back out and looks at Katie, who returns his gaze with a smile.

"Katie, did you read this entire file?" The look in her eye answers the question. *Of course, you did.*

"Counselor, I believe you have an argument," Katie says, smiling.

"You're damn right, I do."

Just then Sillenia appears from around the corner down the hall, with a tall, neatly dressed man in his mid-forties. Their body language suggests an intimacy between the two.

Bobby looks at Katie, who is also watching the two, smiling at each other.

"So who is that?" asks Bobby.

"That's Rollie Wade. He heads the Justice Department upstairs."

"The Justice Department is upstairs?"

"Well, this is the federal building," Katie replies.

"So he's like the FBI or something?"

"I'm not sure. All I know is their boss, the Attorney General, is the same as the FBI, and he's the man. And he is quite taken with Ms. Daniels." She laughs.

Rollie Wade and his team of special agents also play a very pivotal part in what is to unfold.

Rollie goes back upstairs where he finds agent Danny King waiting for him outside his office. Danny is his long-time trusted assistant and righthand man. He greets Rollie with a report in his hand.

"Peggy told me you were downstairs, so I figured I'd wait. How's Sillenia?"

"She's great. I take it this is about Mickelson?"

"As you requested. Our surveillance team has picked up some interesting information."

"What ya got?"

"First transformers," Danny says with a smile.

"Excuse me?"

"Mickelson has a surplus of power going through his mansion that our technician says doesn't quite jive with our blueprints or schematics."

Rollie looks up from the report and asks, "Best guess?"

"I've thought about it, and frankly, Rollie, I'm stumped. We know he has a high-tech security system, a state-of-the-art titanium alloy vault, and all of the creature comforts that come with being a master criminal living in a ten-million-dollar estate. Still, we can't account for where the extra power is being channeled."

"What about an emergency generator?"

"He has two, and that's the problem. While one is idle, there seems to be another one fully operational going twenty-four seven, but what for?"

Rollie turns and looks out of his window into the city nick-named Bold as Danny awaits instructions.

"Okay, Danny, let's make this priority one: get with the counterterrorism unit and get us some satellite surveillance of the inside grounds. Tell them we picked up some unusual power surges that we believe could be consistent with a threat to national security, something being built. Also, get some people out there to test the density of the surrounding properties. I wanna know if there any caves or caverns that run through are close to his estate."

"I'm on it, but weapons of mass destruction? Isn't that stretching it a bit? They may contact Homeland Security?"

"Well, it's stretching it a lot, but it'll have to be checked out, then it's just a matter of existing data being made available through inner department channels. Homeland won't be a problem until counterterrorism show cause."

Danny smiles and says, "And so having an old friend heading up counterterrorism has its advantages. Hey, Willie is a head of that department, isn't he?"

Rollie looks back at Danny and says, "You're learning, Danny."

"I'm learning, Rollie."

"Also, get me an in-depth work up on Mickelson's staff. Go beyond the whitewash cover of legitimacy. Let's see what their particular talents are. I'm willing to bet the power is tied to a particular training."

"We're on it."

Danny leaves as Rollie picks up *The Florida Times-Union* newspaper. He's an avid sports fan, a competitor by nature—an asset that has contributed greatly to his success.

He notes the signing of an intent letter by Jonny Blain and its expected impact on the Florida Gators basketball team. He remembers the team that made it to the final four and reads how the youngster could be the missing link to return the Gators to NCAA basketball respectability.

He finishes the sports, and then an article catches his attention, a police officer killed while off duty in Putnam County. No motives are given, and the authorities suspect the murder to be the act of one man. No details have been given on the crimes.

Chapter 9

Exit Strategy

Back at Deerwood Estates, Cole walks into Mickelson's office, where he also maintains a desk.

Mickelson is on the phone then says, "Ah, Mr. Cole has just walked in. Please explain your idea to him."

Cole looks to Mickelson who indicates Rodgers on the phone with a smile. Cole snarls and takes the phone. He listens for a minute, but then cuts Rodgers off.

"Wait, I know about City Boy Style. He doesn't have the natural or intelligence to run the type of operation we need to control a crew, or have you noticed he doesn't have one? I got his role mapped out! Who gave you guys permission to think anyway? You think I'm just yelling to feel myself vibrate? Just take the money and wait for instructions, you'll live longer!" Cole hangs up the phone. "One of these days…"

"You'll give them their fifteen minutes of fame?"

Mickelson turns the paper toward Cole and then holds it up so he can admire his handiwork.

Cole smiles and says, "Too bad they don't release details. This guy was one for the books. He made me consider recording the whole damn thing!"

With a proud swagger, Cole makes his way over to the bar.

"So I take it everything went well. Nobody saw you leave?" Mickelson asks.

"Those bozos outside make for perfect alibis. They never knew I was gone. Hell, I could have done one of them on the way back in for as relaxed as they were. But that cop…something just felt wrong about him."

"Oh my." Mickelson laughs. "Well, dear boy, he was smack in the middle of our drug transaction, and he wasn't invited."

Cole nods and says, "Ain't it funny, though, how fast the cops outed him as being a cop? I mean, he was inside. Why not use that vehicle again to get another one back in? I mean, he wasn't on location. At any rate, we're good on exit strategies."

"Outstanding, Mr. Cole. One never knows."

Chapter 10

And Then We Said Goodbye

Aaron has a visit that morning from his parents, one long expected; and every point imaginable is covered. Disgrace, embarrassment, shame, and that little issue of "When you comin' home, son?" do make it in at the two-minute warning.

Aaron smiles and walks back to his cellblock, wondering if his parents—whom he knew loved him—were aware that all they'd focused on was what his arrest had done to them.

He's barely made it back to his cellblock when he is called again for another visitation. Surprised, he thinks of Jonny. He really doesn't need to be tied him in any way; the cops could put it together.

He'd been lucky so far, as that neither Rodgers nor Billips seem to be local prep high school fans. He doesn't know much about law, except what he'd seen on *Law and Order*, but he doesn't feel good about his chances.

He sits in the booth, and moments later, what couldn't be worse. Tracy comes around the corner and sits across from him. His eyebrows rise as his eyes widen.

Before she can pick up the phone, he indicates that people are listening. She nods as their eyes meet, and his anxiety instantly melts.

"What are you doing here?" he asks.

"Where else would I be?"

She places her hand against the glass. He does the same, placing his hand over hers. For a moment, comfort finds them.

"Did you get that?" he asks.

"Uh…oh, yeah. I've got it with me. What do you want me to do? I mean, I tried to get you out, but you have no bail."

"Yeah, I know. Listen, I need you to go to the place and wait. You may have to get a car and work for a while. We'll have to wait this thing out. They got nothing on me, okay?"

Tracy smiles, and his face quickly mirrors hers.

"But I don't want you coming back here. Don't even write to me unless I write to you!"

The look in his eyes suggests that she might be in trouble, and she looks around.

Her head drops, and when she looks up again, there is a single tear rolling down her cheek.

Forgetting that the phone in her hand lies on the desktop, she speaks, and Aaron is forced to read her lips as she asks, "How long?"

"I don't know, Trace…but you can't ever come back here! Ever!" he stresses.

The emotion fills the room as they stare into each other's eyes and seemingly struggle to catch their breath, watching their words.

"You should go," he whispers into the receiver.

The look on her face tells all she wants to say. Not being by his side doesn't seem right, yet she knows she has to leave.

She struggles for words, but they all seem so intimate and not to be shared by strangers. She nods and hangs up the phone and says, "I love you," while staring through the glass. He nods as well, and then she is gone.

He starts the long walk back down the corridor to his cellblock. With each step, his mind drifts to the night of his arrest. He can hear the sound of his sixteen-inch firestone tires peeling across the highway as he mashed the accelerator of his 342 engine in his candy apple-red charger that barely broke stride, darting through traffic across the two-lane highway of US 1 on to the South Dixie Highway about three seconds ahead of the police Crown Victoria in hot pursuit.

He remembers luck was with him when he reached South Dixie Highway and the fishtail that almost led to catastrophe.

He remembered adrenaline pumping coursing through his veins, yet there was a greater fear. And all just to take the heat as far away from her as possible.

He remembered seeing the 207 intersection and the red light, having to dart into the Winn-Dixie parking lot and finding all other exit options blocked.

He can still see the rearview mirror and the officer's gun trained on the back of his head.

He remembers her voice saying, "Ya don't get in the water, ya can't get wet."

He sat there, drenched in water, in the back seat of the police cruiser. Now he was in the deep end, wondering if he had it in him to just swim.

Back in his cellblock, he sits alone inside his cell, the cost running through his mind of what was at stake. Would he get ten years? Would Tracy wait? How could he ask her to? This could all go away if he would turn state on his first cousin, but deep down inside, he knew these were not real places; he couldn't get there, not like that.

What he was left with was a mindset to prepare for the worst. He knew others that had been down the road, and they'd survived. So would he.

Chapter 11

The Hurry Up

The day is sunny and bright as Bobby finally has a court date to defend his client, Mike Moore, against the possession charges. They reach the courtroom and find a small group of Moore's supporters already there. Bobby—eager to prove himself as a trial lawyer—mentally prepares himself. This is an important hurdle to clear. He gets his papers in order, checking his watch as the first case starts to unfold. Now his client is brought in, and Bobby introduces himself.

"Mr. Moore, I'm Bobby Cox. Sir, I understand that you don't have much faith in the legal system. You've been wronged. Now, often we see an opportunity as attorneys, and we want to take advantage of it. Kind of like the hurry-up offense of a football game, keeping the run defense on the field in a passing situation, you understand?"

Mr. Moore nods with skepticism and asks, "Aren't we here to pick the jury?"

"Yeah, we can do that, but I was thinking, after going over your case, and looking at what's expected to take place right here right now, I see a run defense on the field on a third and eight. You've been in jail now, like, eight months, right?"

Mr. Moore nods, though he is still visibly confused.

"I think it would be in your best interests if we waived a jury hearing and be heard by the judge right now today. I made sure we were the last case on his docket."

Sillenia comes in and takes Mr. Moore by the arm as she sits beside him.

"Mr. Moore, I am Sillenia Daniels, and I'm Mr. Cox's boss. I'm here because I believe in what Mr. Cox wants to do here today. Sometimes there are considerations that juries don't quite take into consideration that a judge must, or answer on appeal. Remember the state's witness is a police officer. Sometimes that's all a jury needs to see to convict. The judge, on the other hand, would really have to consider the evidence in its entirety. We believe the judge would be in your best interest."

Mr. Moore looks back at Bobby and then at Sillenia and asks, "Are you guys telling me I could go home today?"

Bobby nods, saying, "That's a very real possibility, yeah."

Mr. Moore looks at Sillenia and asks, "And this guy here is new? He ain't all buddy-buddy with the state attorney?"

Now Sillenia smiles and replies, "That's right, Mr. Moore, he's fresh off the pressors, and he's trying to impress his boss."

There is great look of enthusiasm on Mr. Moore's face as he looks back at Bobby and says, "Yo, man, kick yo game, dude. Show this lady you like pimp Willie slap a silly...state attorney silly! Do what you do. I don't know why, but I'm really feeling you right now, feel me?"

Sillenia smiles and says, "So, Counselor, you heard the man, kick ya game."

Soon after, the bailiff calls the court to order. The state calls Mike Moore's case to select a jury. The judge addresses the state attorney.

A small-framed man with thick glasses and wavy hair stands and says, "The state is ready, Your Honor."

Then the judge turns to the defense.

Bobby stands and says, "Your Honor, my client has elected to waive his right to jury trial, and we would request that the judge hear our case. The state has indicated that they are ready, and as this man has been incarcerated for almost a year, we are certain we can resolve this issue this evening."

The judge looks over at the state and says, "If the state is prepared, I'd be more than happy to resolve this case today."

The state attorney stands and says, "We are prepared, Your Honor, with one exception. We don't have the arresting officer here, and he's our key witness. We could have him brought over, but he was not aware that the defense would waive their client's right to a jury trial."

Bobby stands and addresses the court.

"Your Honor, we took it upon ourselves to have Officer Gabriel brought over, and he is—even as we speak—waiting to be called to the stand."

The judge looks over at the prosecution.

"Well then, what ya say we get on with it? That being said, you may call your first witness."

The wavy-haired man is momentarily found speechless, but he has already declared his readiness.

"The prosecution calls Officer Gabriel to the stand."

The officer walks with a confident swagger to the stand. Officer Gabriel, who is reading from his notes of the arrest, describes the events of that night.

Then Bobby begins the cross-examination.

"Officer Gabriel, you've testified that you came around the corner of N. Whitney and Scott Street to notice the defendant come to an abrupt stop and then throw his car into drive after seeing you. He then went back into the front yard he was leaving, and exiting the vehicle, he ran through the front door of the residential address 20 Scott Street. That is your testimony?"

"Yes, sir, it is," the officer answers.

"And because of the angle that you first saw the car, that was how you could tell there was only one person in the car, correct?"

"Correct."

"How do you know the defendant wasn't already in the apartment and the person really driving hadn't just dropped him off?"

"He couldn't have been. He was driving. You see, as I approached the vehicle, I saw one person emerge, and he opened the front door of the apartment as I testified. As I reached the car, I noticed the driver's door was still open. No one followed him."

Bobby nods as in agreement and says, "So the testimony of Mr. Moore's cousin that he entered the house first had to be a fabrication to protect her kin?"

"Had to be," the officer answers.

Mr. Moore leans over toward Sillenia, who is sitting beside him, and asks, "Ain't he supposed to be establishing my alibi?"

"He just did," she whispers back and smiles in a sinister fashion.

Bobby continues, "So you're certain beyond a reasonable doubt that Michael Moore was the person you saw going into the door at 20 Scott Street?"

"Yes, sir, I am."

"How tall are you, Officer Gabriel?"

"Excuse me?"

The prosecutor stands, saying, "Objection: relevancy."

Bobby turns to the judge and says, "Your Honor, I assure you that my line of questioning goes to the heart of my client's line of defense."

The judge pauses for a moment, but then says, "Overruled, the witness will answer the question."

The officer then looks to Bobby and says, "I'm six foot two."

"Six foot two, and let's just say for the sake of argument that you're at least three inches taller than my client?"

"I guess so."

"Tell me, Officer Gabriel, why was the car fingerprinted?"

The officer smirks and says, "Because I noticed the perp wearing gloves as he approached the front door. I was already sure that he'd say he wasn't in the car. I was betting he didn't have them on the whole time."

"Yet no gloves were recovered…"

"No, he must've had his cousin ditch them."

"You think?"

"That's my guess."

"Because you're sure he was wearing gloves."

"Yes, I know he was wearing gloves."

"Do you know Mr. Moore from the streets, Officer Gabriel?"

The officer adjusts himself in the seat and says, "Sure, our paths have crossed before. He's a dope dealer. He's working my beat."

Bobby's eyes turn to the judge and says, "So he's been…how shall we say…targeted?"

"No! But he has been observed. They all are. If you sell dope on my turf—my beat—I'm watching."

"Ever catch him? Selling drugs?"

The officer looks sternly at the defendant and says, "No."

"So he's on your wish list?"

The officer gets a little flustered, saying, "I didn't target him."

Bobby walks over to the table where the state's exhibits lay. He picks up a picture of the Chevy Lumina that was found to contain the drugs and then walks over to the officer.

"This picture was taken less than an hour after the arrest. What does it show?"

The officer looks and says, "It shows the dope in the middle console, in plain view."

Bobby looks at the photograph and says, "Yes, but what's that on the floor of the passenger side?"

The officer looks as if for the first time, answering, "Looks like paper to me."

Bobby nods and says, "It is paper, Officer Gabriel. It's a Sonny's Barbeque wrapper, to be exact. Now, did you notice something very interesting on the passenger's door?"

The officer looks and says, "It's a cup in a cupholder."

"Yeah, that's what I see too. But I also notice that in this photo, all the ice has not yet melted. How do you explain that, Officer Gabriel, if no one else was in the car? A man, five feet, eleven inches, just driving along… Two car doors, but he keeps his drink in the passenger-side car door? I mean, I heard of leaning, but you ever see somebody lean like that?"

"So someone else may have been in the car earlier, before this incident occurred. What's your point?"

"See, now, I don't understand that. Why would he panic? He was at his cousin's house already, his license was good. Why not just pull up into the driveway and toss the drugs under the seat?"

The officer smiles and says, "'Cause he's a criminal, and they always slip up."

Bobby then walks over to the defense and takes out six pictures from an envelope. He gives two to the DA and two to the judge. They are labeled exhibits 3 and 4. He shows a copy of exhibit 3 to the officer and calls it to the attention of the court.

"Officer Gabriel, what do you see here?"

The officer looks and answers, "It's a picture of a guy with the car the drugs were found in."

"Yes, it is. Now do you see any similarities in the way this guy is dressed and the defendant?"

"Yes?" The officer shrugs his shoulders. "They both have similar jerseys"

"Would you believe this photo is from the bank just down the street from the BBQ stand and taken less than thirty minutes from the time of the initial encounter with the defendant?"

The officer sighs.

Bobby smiles and tells him, "It's also clear that there is indeed a passenger in the car, Officer Gabriel."

Bobby then shows him the photograph that is exhibit 4.

"This is my client's fingerprint card, and this is the thumbprint enhanced. Stained with barbeque sauce from the cup of ice from the passenger's door, it shows up surprisingly well, doesn't it?"

The officer's gaze shifts from the photo to Bobby's eyes.

"Okay, so that's his print," admits Officer Gabriel as he compares it to Mr. Moore's fingerprint card. "So he could have put that there earlier!"

Bobby then walks over to the defense table and takes out a photocopy of the Sonny's receipt.

"Officer Gabriel, this receipt has a date and time of April 11, 2003, at eight forty p.m. You stopped the defendant's car at nine p.m. that evening, according to dispatch."

The officer smiles and says, "They place him in the car!"

"They place him at the counter!"

"So there you go!" Officer Gabriel gulps.

"Then who ate the ribs?"

"What?"

"It takes every bit of fifteen minutes to drive to 20 Scott Street. You're saying that he ate the ribs, reaches over and uses the passenger-side cupholder, and then as he pulls into the driveway, he gets a call or something and begins to pull out, sees you, and in a moment of panic, leaves the drugs, puts on his gloves (because nobody eats ribs with their gloves on) and exits the vehicle? You're six foot two, maybe you could make that lean while driving, but my client—why would he? He could just move the cupholder, and he'd still have a bag of ribs if he were driving the car, wouldn't he? This is beginning to look like maybe he was the passenger being dropped off as he stated, or there's at least enough here to suggest a reasonable doubt especially when you consider the speed in which this all went down and give the street lighting."

The state's attorney jumps up and says, "Objection! Is there a question?"

"Sustained." There is a pause and an awkward silence.

Then Bobby asks, "What if he was a passenger being dropped off at his cousin's house. In which case, he would have been the first one inside the door, just like his cousin said? There were two guys wearing football jerseys and are about the same weight and height. It was nine o'clock at night with only a street light and a brief chance to catch a glimpse of a profile of a fleeing suspect. My question is can you swear beyond a reasonable doubt that you know you saw Mike Moore enter that house?"

The officer looked over at Michael Moore and sighs.

"No. I guess, I can't."

"Thank you, Officer Gabriel, no more questions." Bobby turns toward the defendant and smiles.

There are mumbles of approval throughout the courtroom.

The officer leaves the witness stand and stops at the defense table.

He looks down at Mike, and with half a grin on his face, he says, "Catch you later."

Soon the charges are dismissed, and Mike Moore and his family are reunited, as Bobby and Sillenia stand in the corridor after the hearing.

Bobby is amused and says, "Nobody told me you would be here."

Sillenia nods and says, "Nobody had better. There's very little you can learn about an attorney on paper. Maybe even less by word of mouth, but when you're their boss, and you just show up as second chair, that's when you know what you got."

Bobby nods with a smile on his face.

Amid the passersby, Bobby reaches out and grabs one by the arm—much to Sillenia's surprise.

"Sillenia, this is Cricket, my wife."

The long-haired woman peeks from beneath a Boston College baseball cap.

She slowly extends a hand and says, "How do you do?"

Sillenia is pleasantly shocked as she shakes Cricket's hand.

Bobby hugs Cricket and tells his boss, "I'll see you back at the office."

He takes Penny by the arm and pleasantly leads her toward the stairs.

"Crick, what are you doing here?"

"I just came down to lend some support."

"In disguise?"

"Well, I didn't want to make you nervous."

"So this is an incognito type of support thing. You may have well had stayed home and used the force?"

"You could feel it, huh? Anyway, what's important is that it worked. You won. What's next?"

"Next?"

"Yeah. Bobby, I got the whole day off. Got any more good ones we can win? I'm really feeling myself. We got this," she says as she puts up her dukes and begins to shadowbox.

Bobby laughs and says, "I'm afraid that's all for today, babe."

She stops as if in shock and says, "What, that's it? I hope you don't get paid by the case. I mean, don't get me wrong, free time's great. You should give your mind down time to recoup and relax even take in a game, but as expecting parents, we'll have to step it up a bit. Of course, I know that also means that I'll have to do more—I mean, technically, you've done enough—but maybe you can do, like, two, even three, a day and really up your worth?"

"I do work more than just one a day, and I certainly work on more than just one case a day even when I'm not in court. See, there's a docket…"

Suddenly Bobby is stopped in his tracks as he watches his wife walk along in front of him down the end of the stair. He can no longer hear the words coming from her mouth as his mind is gathering information.

"Did you say parent? As in a baby?"

Penny turns to him with a smile on her face and a light in her eyes.

"Very good, young counselor. You're going to be a daddy."

Chapter 12

Partners

Back in St. Augustine, just across the 312 Bridge in an apartment complex known as Coquina Lakes, Detective Rodgers is relaxing, stretched out on his living-room sofa.

He watches television with his hand draped over the head of his Blue Nose Pitbull as his rings.

"Hello?" It's Billips. "What're you doing?"

"Watching the tube, why?"

"I'm right off 312. I'll be there in Coquina Lakes in about three minutes. I've got something you should see."

"Work? Can't this wait 'til morning??"

"Just put Rex in a room and open the door." Click. The phone hangs up.

Shortly after, Billips arrives. Rodgers lets him in, and they walk over to the kitchen table.

"So what do you got that's so important?"

Billips drops a copy of the property sheet from Aaron's car.

"We were looking for evidence of Jonny and cocaine residue we didn't even notice what we were really looking at."

Rodgers reaches into the icebox and takes out two beers.

"Yeah, I saw that stuff. The overnight bag? He's seeing some girl. I doubt seriously if he's going to turn on Jonny just because he can't see a girl. She probably left it in the back seat. He threw it in the trunk. Where are you going with this?"

"Well, I thought the same thing, but then I checked his wallet, looking for something—anything. Look what I got."

He hands Rodgers a copy of a marriage license.

Rodgers reads the name, "Tracy Austin. You don't think…"

"Yeah, I do. You were right about the gas station being a drop-off, but we asked the attendant and the cab driver about a man. We never thought to ask about a girl. We were expecting Jonny Blain, not this kid, and certainly not his girlfriend."

Chapter 13

Choices We Make

That night Aaron is called from his cellblock. He's told to go to the booking office. From the sound of the men in the cellblock, this can't be good.

One man yells, "New charge!" and the others seem to agree.

Aaron has done some things, and he racks his brain to think of what it could be. He's taken into an interrogation room. Soon Rodgers and Billips enter. Aaron is sitting down as the men stand over him.

Rodgers leans right down in Aaron's face and gets straight to the point.

"Where's Tracy Austin?"

Aaron thought they overlooked his property. Though surprised, he is still relieved that there is no new charge.

"What does my girlfriend have to do with this?"

"We can put her at the BP gas station that night, sport."

Billips yells, "Now she ain't home, and no one's seen her, so where's she at?"

"You're trippin'! There was just me. She put that stuff in my car days ago, little by little. We were sneaking off."

"Maybe..." says Rodgers as he walks around the table. "Maybe she was, and maybe she wasn't. You see, it really doesn't matter at this point in the game. You need to know a couple of things about us, Aaron. One: we don't play fair. Two: we just...don't give a fuck.

"You see, we know you're trying to protect your friend, Jonny Blain, and we're really tired of fucking around with you. Now you have a decision to make, Aaron: your girlfriend or the boyfriend. Now, frankly, I don't see you coming off like fuckin Batman, okay, so just tell us what we want to know, and we'll give you both a walk. We don't want you, Aaron. But if you don't play ball, we'll do you and your little girlfriend too. We'll just end up getting Blain sooner or later… Whatta you say?"

Aaron's eyes close. With all that he wants to say, he finds that he can't even utter a word. His only ace is that Tracy's in hiding, and her address on her license is her old one.

He needs time to think then says, "Look, you're asking me to snitch on a friend. I'm gonna need time to think about it."

"Think about it!" yells Billips, but Rodgers interjects.

"Okay, Aaron. The clock is running, and if we find her first, all bets off. You try and mess with us, and I got a feeling Tracy's not gonna want to be as loyal as you. Don't let this blow up in your face with both you and Jonny catching time. Remember, we're not the DA, but we can recommend."

Aaron nods and is soon taken back to his cell.

Once back, he's confronted by cellmates that want to know if he's caught another case. They don't see a booking sheet, so they assume he's been asked to snitch. Some even wonder if their names came up.

To most, now, he might as well be a grenade. Now something about his presence quickly scatters people.

He's heard about a jailhouse lawyer in his cellblock, a guy who has figured out some key points of law for some of the inmates in return for canteen items.

Aaron goes upstairs and employs the young man to take his case for ten dollars' worth of canteen.

The young man stops all his work and listens to Aaron's situation.

"Wow, talk about a rock and hard place. Okay, first of all, only the state can make deals. A lot of times guys sign papers for cops and get jilted. Look, it's your first offense. And they say you got caught selling drugs. Just make a deal with the DA yourself. You'll probably get off easy. You tell 'em she was with you, but you dropped her because you didn't want her to know what you were doing. They just want a conviction, man. They'll YO you anyway."

"YO?" Aaron is confused.

"Oh, youthful offender. You'll probably get off with a year and a day."

Chapter 14

Dropped Wire

Back at the federal building in Jacksonville, Rollie is at his desk when Danny comes in with a look of excitement.

"Rollie, you were right about counterterrorism—the photographs came back."

Danny places the photos across Rollie's desk.

"What's key here, Rollie, is what we don't have."

"Elaborate, please," says Rollie as he observes the photos.

"We got lucky, Rollie. Our local surveillance has taps on the phone. They have been so careful not to give us anything to make a case. Now we know why. Look here."

Danny points to the middle photo showing Mickelson's office.

"Key note." Rollie looks surprised as he checks the log against the time of the pictures.

Images show someone is on the phone, yet there is no tape.

"You didn't get a trace?"

Danny shakes his head.

"We got no trace, no dial tone, no ring. But most importantly is the no dial tone."

Rollie's puzzled but then asks, "Dropped wire?"

Danny nods and says, "He's set up his own electronic bypass phone service, a dropped wire of sort, that's my guess." An impulse signal directed toward a relay that transports a signal into a super conductor. The signal is so faint its barely detected among the social domains that are being transmitted but that only means the connector and its conductor is fairly close.

Rollie stands and gazes out into the city.

"So the trace won't be easy. Finding the line—that'll be problematic in this electronic age. It could be anywhere. However, the relay is limited. He may have modern technology on his side, but he'll think and plan old school. Nothing in his profile suggests anything different." Rollie ponders and continues.

"What we're looking for is his source. The base of that technology, it won't be on the property. There are legal ramifications. A good attorney's going to argue that such measures were taken to ensure privacy. The sensitive nature of the information that comes into his home. He has a law degree and the expectation of privacy."

Danny agrees as he reviews another document and says, "We tried to trace the signal we got scrambled. The main bounced us from zip codes like 41093 in Ashland, Kentucky, to 03867 in Rochester, New Hampshire, to 16335 in Meadville, Pennsylvania, to75007 in McKinney, Texas. That should get us a court order in itself."

Rollie ponders, "They know we're right outside. The court order would stall as we'd be forced to explain why, to show our hand to his lawyers. I don't want to cross that bridge yet. There's something else to consider. What's the best way to protect a dropped wire?"

Danny thinks and says, "Old days, military issue, I don't know. Keeping it encased and covered underground?"

"Good answer, but an even better one with today's technology is out of line of sight from your own ground, points, and measures under your own control. Totally protected…unless someone knows it's there. Check the surrounding properties. Find me all of Mickelson's holdings, personal property, and properties posted as real estate for sale contracted to his company. About the relays. Gentlemen, it won't be in a high-traffic area, and the final point, the point of origin, will be miles away. Let's go to work. I'm suddenly feeling that there's more to Mickelson than maybe even we know."

Chapter 15

The Deal

That night at the St. Johns County Jail, Aaron reads through the Bible, the Gospel of Christ according to Matthew. He becomes perplexed at Matthew: "The Kingdom of Heaven suffers violence, and the violent take it by force." He sits up and gazes into an active dorm. He thinks for a moment, *Who can I ask?* as he notices things going on all around him.

Four men sit at one of the three dining tables, playing spades; two more sit at a table, frantically trying to hear the TV over the card game. Four others engage in a game of dominoes as one of the men stop and yells at a guy sitting on the toilet in his cell.

"Hey, put some water on it! The water free! Think we wanna smell yo shit?"

Aaron asks himself, *Who would even care what this means?*

*****

A few days pass, and early one morning Aaron is surprised when he is instructed to get ready for court. Apparently, the state has accepted his plea.

He is escorted in shackles into the courtroom and is then approached by a very attractive public defender, Mrs. Pezzic.

She calls him aside, "Mr. Daniels, to be honest, I haven't had any time to go over your case. The state attorney said you contacted them with a plea?"

"Yes, ma'am."

"Am I to understand that you're willing to plea out to three years, with the stipulation that no charges be filed against Tracy Austin? Is she your girlfriend?"

"Yes, ma'am."

"And she was with you that night?"

"Mrs. Pezzic, can I not even talk about it? Would that be cool with you?"

She smiles and says, "Okay, Mr. Daniels, but the state wants to get this done today. I see the date you were arrested, and it's your first offense. Perhaps given a little time, I could work this sentence down a bit, if I had just a day or two..."

"No!" demands Aaron, cutting her off. "Please, Mrs. Pezzic, it's important that the deal go down today and that this all ends today. And Tracy's out of this. Please!"

Mrs. Pezzic nods and says, "Okay, Mr. Daniels."

Her eyes can see his concern, and there are no implications that his girlfriend is even under investigation.

"I'll go talk to the state, and we'll get this done."

"Thank you, ma'am."

As Mrs. Pezzic walks away, Aaron is both relieved and scared.

He looks over his shoulder constantly, worried that Rodgers and Billips may walk in any moment and screw up the works. He looks over to see Mrs. Pezzic talking to the state. He can only hope that she's hammering out his condition and that his plea is not in vain. He gazes at the judge reading over another case. But then Aaron notices the Florida State emblem just behind the judge on the wall.

It's a Native American girl standing on the shore of a beach, watching the sunset. He remembers that the writing underneath the emblem said, "In God We Trust."

Suddenly instead there are simply two words: "Trust God." Aaron closes his eyes tightly then looks at the writing again. Still, it says, "Trust God."

He looks at the man shackled next to him and says, "Hey, man, that thing on the wall behind the judge's head...what's it say?"

The man looks at it and turns to Aaron.

"It says 'In God We Trust,' but trust me, get a good attorney if you can afford one."

Aaron stares again at the emblem, and suddenly the fear is gone.

Chapter 16

Options

Hours later, Rodgers storms into the sheriff's office and walks hurriedly to Billips's office. Billips is just hanging up the phone when Rodgers comes in and closes the door as gently as he can, considering his outrage, then angrily turns to his partner.

"The kid fucked us!"

"What? What kid?"

"The Daniels kid. I just went over to pull him. It seems he's already in court. In fact, on my way over there, I saw the bus coming back. He pleaded!"

"He pleaded out?" Billups looks with confusion in his eyes.

"Yeah, and get this: the state gives the Austin chick a free walk. Says they didn't have enough to convict him, let alone her."

Billips mouth drops and says, "So they couldn't give us a little time?"

"Yeah, well, they've never heard of Blain, or Mickelson, or that son of a witch's bitch, Cole. All they care about is quota. Come on, let's go."

"Where?"

"Maybe we can find the girl. She can't know what's gone down yet."

"On a four-year-old school photo? How?"

Rodgers turns to his partner and whispers angrily, "Damn it, Detective, we detect."

Chapter 17

The Dream

Aaron goes to sleep that night with a sense of uncertainty about today's events.

His knowledge of the law is limited; his thoughts are only that he'd done the right thing. Tracy had begged him not to go through with it. He couldn't let this touch her. He drifts into the night and begins to dream.

Suddenly he's in a dark vehicle moving down the highway.

There are only small, diamond-shaped slivers to see through in the back of what appears to be a prison van.

He sits at the end of the van, staring into the darkness of the wooded highway. Suddenly there is a man walking through the tree line. In an instant he's gone, but Aaron is sure he saw this man in a place uncommon for a man to be. Suddenly across from him…people. How many, he is unsure.

One of the men across from him. He is bald, with a beard and mustache. There's someone beside the bald man who is humming a piano chord, the same tune over and over.

Dig, dig, dig, dig, dig, dig-dig dig-dig-dig-dig dig, dig-dig, dig-dig, dig, dig, dig…

Then the bald man begins to sing in a deep, sorrowful voice:

> *Searching my memory*
> *Racking my mind*
> *As I ponder how I came across all this time*
> *And ew wee…*

(Chord)
Don't even know when or how it all went bad
Now I'm riding to the pound
And I show feel sad
And ew wee…
(Chord)
As I leave these walls inside my mind
As I stop…
To retrace place and crime
And I know that looking back won't set me free…
(Run)
To my wife I have betrayed this ring
As I got
I got my whole life changed
And I had to kiss my child goodbye in chains
And ew wee…

The bald man finishes his emotional and heartfelt ballet, and at least most people could feel his grief.

Then there came a voice out of the darkness in the back, a voice of contempt.

"Damn, man, you come to prison to get soft? That's fucked up. You ain't got no pride about ya?"

The voice continues mockingly the bald man, "Oh, I miss my baby! You should've thought about that before you snatched that old lady's purse!" There are a few snickers of laughter. The voice is visible now. A young man with tattoos in his face. "But don't worry. I've got some homeboys who'll take real good care of you in your time of solace."

Now there are even more voices in the darkness that snicker.

He continues to taunt the bald man for the remainder of the ride.

"Got damn, minstrel singing nigga!"

The bald man simply holds onto a wooden cross that hangs from his neck and stares into Aaron's eyes through the darkness. The bald man's eyes are just two dull orbs, filled with sadness and loneliness floating in a sea of emptiness with only the occasional reflections of cars and street lights through the diamond shaped slivers.

They reach the reception center, and everyone is brought out of the van and unshackled.

The bald man stands next to Aaron, but looks over his head at the young man who taunted him at the end of the line.

The young man is tall too, and staring back at the bald man.

Soon a sergeant steps in and turns toward the bald man.

"Truck Turner! I thought that was you on my ledger. I had to come and see for sure."

"Yeah, it's me, Cappy. How ya been?" the bald man replies.

The sergeant walks over and shakes the bald man's hand.

"Doing okay?" the sergeant asks.

"You know…the same old shit, different day."

Then the bald man smiles and leans over and whispers something in the sergeant's ear. The sergeant then informs everyone to strip to their T-shirt and shorts. Then the sergeant tells the only other guard to take a break while the sergeant prepares the newbies.

After the guard is well out of sight, the sergeant calls the git over and leads him behind the van, instructing everyone else to stay in line and face forward.

A few moments pass, and the sergeant comes from behind the van and goes into the restroom. Once the door closes, the bald man takes off his shirt and boxers and walks behind the van. From behind the van, the bald man's voice can be heard.

"Who's your daddy, bitch boy?"

The git weakly replies, "Oh man…"

There is a crack, followed by a gurgling sound.

Crack!

Crack!

The bald man's voice is heard again, "Who's your daddy, nigger!" *Crack!* "Say it!"

The git's voice is barely audible, "Please, man… Okay, okay… You my daddy… You my daddy, man, please, I'm sorry, man…"

There is a ripping sound, and the bald man reappears from behind the van, wiping what looks like red raindrops from his naked body with a torn shirt.

He throws the shirt behind the van and then clothes himself in his boxers and T-shirt.

The sergeant immediately returns from the bathroom and heads behind the van.

"Damn! I guess you must've slipped and fell, huh?" He laughs and continues. "Those gold teeth over there? Don't even worry about 'em. They're just contraband now!"

He gets the battered young man to his feet, and though he looks like he's been hit by a car, the sergeant walks him back to his place in line then shouts, "You boys coming in here... Newbies, you're gonna wanna watch your steps 'round here. There are a lot of slippery places on the compound."

He steps back in front of the beaten git and looks him square in the eye, saying, "Know what I mean?"

The bald man looks down at Aaron, who is now looking up at him.

The bald man is expressionless and says, "I wasn't always a godly man. I guess I can still be...a little sensitive."

Aaron looks down the line at the git and thinks to himself, *Yeah...yeah, I get that about you.*

The jailhouse doors slide open loudly for breakfast, and Aaron awakens.

Chapter 18

Being Bobby

Days have gone by, and Bobby Cox is still walking on air at the expectation of being a first-time dad.

He enters the federal building with pep in his step that has people around him noticing his mood.

"Hello, Fred," he said, speaking to the security guard as he walks through the metal detector.

"Good morning, Mr. Cox."

Bobby rushes and makes his way into the crowded elevator. His eyes are glazed. His mind is years away, enjoying his son's first catch in the front yard of his new home.

"Your floor?" the young lady behind him asks as the doors open and are about to close.

"Uh, yeah!" Bobby stops the doors and is soon down the hall to his office. He finds Katie already at her desk. "Morning, Katie."

"Papi."

"Huh?"

Katie smiles and says, "That's what we call our dads in Puerto Rico."

Grinning, Bobby asks, "You're Puerto Rican? Who knew?" as he walks into his office, still beaming.

"I did, though I think my mom is on to me," Katie jokes to herself as she grabs some files and starts in behind him. "Bobby, I've got your caseload, and you have been made honored—though I don't think I'm not supposed to tell you."

"Honored? How so? And who are you not supposed to tell me from?" he asks as they both stop to wrap their minds around the statement.

Katie pulls the largest folder from the stack and puts it in front of him.

"This one, it's one of Ms. Daniels's. She's been trying to work this kid's case for over a year. I guess she thinks a fresh perspective would be in this kid's best interest."

Bobby looks confused and asks, "If she hasn't been able to work the case, what makes her so sure he's innocent?"

Katie shrugs her shoulders as Bobby examines the brief.

"Looks pretty open and shut to me. The police officers say he was found trespassing in a posted area. Officer started to detain them for questioning when one of the officers observed the defendant drop a brown paper bag, his right hand…bag containing narcotics. The kid only got five years, and at that he lost the case in a jury trial."

Katie shrugs her shoulders again and says, "Maybe that's the problem. If it's really that simple, and the guy's caught dead to rights, why take it to trial?"

Bobby looks at Katie and then again at the brief and says, "Says here there was a witness for the defense that testified he was there and that he dropped the bag the officers confiscated."

Katie smiles and says, "So that's a start."

Bobby raises his eyebrows and nods his head, saying, "Not really. The jury has the right to decide which argument they want to believe. They just didn't believe the witness. The state attorney discredits him."

"Why? Why not just drop the charges against one kid and press charges against the other one?"

"Doesn't work like that. I mean, where's your case? The defense would then have testimony from the cop on the scene IDing the other guy as the bagman. He would have been subpoenaed for the other kid's defense."

"You're telling me that even if the cop made a mistake…"

"That's right, Katie. Once he files a charging affidavit, he doesn't get a do-over after he's written a statement into evidence." Bobby reads on. "That's odd," he says to himself.

Katie is right over his shoulder.

"What, what?"

Bobby looks up and finds himself inches from Katie's face.

"Katie, why don't you brew me some of that French vanilla coffee that you make so well and let me look into this. If I find something incredible, you'll be the first to know."

She realizes she is in Bobby's personal space.

"Oh, okay!" she says, hurrying out of the room.

Bobby sees something already. Now he begins to read the dispatch report. He is puzzled and understands why this case feels not right.

Chapter 19

When Tracy Met Lisa

Meanwhile back in St. Augustine, Tracy is sitting around her new apartment, and almost everything she does reminds her of what Aaron's first take would be once he got home.

She is sure she knows what he would say, how he'd react. She decides to take his advice and not let days go unproductively.

She takes a couple of thousand dollars and goes car-shopping. She finds a Honda Accord in nice condition. She then spends much of the afternoon finding an insurance agency that is practical.

Afterward she decides to drive by the gas station where she last spoke to AD as a free man, the BP. She pulls into the Taco Bell next door to it and plays that night again in her mind.

Time passes, and the smell of the food is enticing, so she goes inside for something to eat.

There is a man ahead of her in line, wearing a pair of baggy shorts, a tank top, and sneakers without socks. His hair is long and blond. The cashier is a redhead with a very nice figure. Her hair is cut short and close, and she's chewing gum like there is no tomorrow.

"Next!" she almost yells at the blond-haired man. As he makes his way up to the counter, he looks straight into the cashier's very nice cleavage; she's left the top buttons undone on a uniform that might be called a little tight.

The man smiles and comments, "So much for thinking outside the buns." He laughs and continues, "Hey, Red, you know what I'm really thinking?"

She looks off and then rolls her eyes back at the guy.

"Let me guess, how you gonna talk the redhead upon the handlebars of that cheesy beach cruiser you rode up on. Let's not go there. Tell you what: I have a friend who works at Krystal's, just got his operation, you can hardly even tell us apart now. He's looking for a stud, and he has a car."

The man steps back and says, "That's just rude. I think I want to see your manager!"

She turns and yells over her shoulder, "Mom!"

"Yeah, honey?" answers a voice from the back.

The man turns to look at Tracy and says, "Do you believe this? The manager's her mother. I'm taking my business elsewhere."

As he's leaving, the cashier yells, "That's Krystal's across 312, straight down US 1, south on the left, can't miss it. Ask for Rochell. It'll be our secret."

Tracy can no longer contain herself and bursts into laughter.

The cashier joins her, but then she asks, "Hey, ain't you Tracy Austin?" Tracy is stunned and looks hard at the cashier as she continues. "How quickly you guys forget the shy and quiet ones."

But then Tracy's eyebrows rise in recognition.

"Oh my god, Lisa Monroe?"

"Yeah, it's me, Lis. So that was you I saw sitting out there, staring at the BP. I thought you were trying to decide whether you should get gas or go hungry. You ain't gotta walk. I can spot you a taco or two."

Tracy laughs and says, "No, no, it's nothing like that."

"So what're you doing?" Lisa asks.

The question catches Tracy by surprise, and she responds, "I'm job-hunting, as a matter of fact."

Lisa smiles with excitement and says, "Really? We just had to fire a girl today. *Mom, I still need you!*"

"Yes, yes, I'm coming!" Lisa's mom makes her way to the front.

Lisa seems to be just what the doctor ordered: someone who could make light of any given situation, witty and quick, and at a time when Tracy could use a friend. This seems to be a nice clean place where Tracy could feel comfortable, so she accepts the job.

Chapter 20

All Day, School

Days go by at the jail. Shortly after the shift changes, an officer comes by with a log sheet and stops at Aaron's cell.

"Daniels, you'll be transporting to DOC in the morning. Go ahead and get all your stuff together. You'll be leaving the cellblock before breakfast. Check your inmate handbook for the things you can take with you…and good luck, kid."

Aaron looks up into the officer's eyes as the officer stands there.

He says, "Aaron, three years ago, I was at that state championship game when you hurt your knee. People talk about Jonny Blain, and he's a great player, but you're the guy that made it all come together. I remember you had thirteen assists that night, and only six went to Jonny Blain in a game decided by two points. You were my MVP… So good luck, kid. I'll be praying for you."

Aaron lays back in his bunk and remembers that game. Jonny had thirty-six points, and yet the thought that someone had noticed his accomplishment, much less thought of him as the MVP, was a small token of comfort for a night that would pass quickly. Aaron is taken away under the cover of darkness along with six others.

They stop at Lake Butler, and then he is transported to Jackson CI within two weeks.

A week after that, he is transported to a camp called Graceville—or so the sign says as he happens to catch it through the little catacomb slits in the window.

He's made one friend over the last two weeks: an inmate Eddie Boyd, better known as School. They've been traveling together since

Lake Butler West Unit, and it seems that they would be on this journey together. They get off the bus and are searched again then given their bedding and instructions about what is and isn't allowed and then turned loose into the dorm and yard.

After securing their things and making their beds, the two take off for the recreation yard. School is a slender, blond-haired, green-eyed boy from up north who grew up in the hood of Lansing, Michigan, and Brooklyn, New York.

A white boy who both talked and related the black experience was something Aaron had not seen much of in St. Augustine. This guy was real, and he had already proven he could be a good friend.

School is hyped as they make their way toward the ball court and begins to sell out.

"Okay, son, this is where the rubber meets the road dig, and I peep yo game, yo just looking through ya photo album, so I got you."

Aaron smiles and says, "So you can just look at my stats and know my game?"

School smirks and says, "Stats? What stats? I looked at those pictures of your girl, Gee. Miss got the body, angel face, those eyes. You got moves, boy. You're not to be played close. A little better than a midrange jumper, quick first step, can take off the dribble."

"You learned all that by looking at my old lady's pictures?"

School laughs and says, "Naw, man. I learned that from your stats. The girl told me you got the kinda heart to play the game to win."

Aaron smiles and notices across the yard from them is a young man wearing gray sweat shorts. The young man has his boxers rolled up on the ends, and the impression is that he's wearing bikini panties.

Aaron points and says, "Check it out!"

School quickly knocks his hand back to his side and says, "Damn! I forgot you fresh fish folk. Ya never point in the chain gang, feel me. What's freaky to you is like Beyoncé up in here to some of these brothers, ya dig."

School pulls Aaron aside and continues, "Look, man, you don't want punk problems behind the gate. You piss 'em off an' they tell their war daddies you hittin' or frontin' on 'em. You go down like good gas."

Aaron is amused and asks, "You serious?"

In a most sarcastic voice, School replies, "No, I think you're being too critical, and the boy's got potential! Ya damn right, I'm serious. And another thing, watch out for brothers with a free Coke and a smile. Trust me, you don't ever wanna get that thirsty."

The two boys reach the ball court. There is a game going on, but soon the attention is turned from the competition on the court to the two muscle-bound men at the other end of the yard at the end of the ball court. They square off, and they look at each other with expressions of discontent.

They are Buddy Row and Bam, two of the most feared inmates on the compound. From a distance, the guards also notice, but this is the kind of trouble where somebody's bound to get hurt. They are unseen and agree they'd both be easier to subdue minus some fight.

It looks close. The question is, how far has it gone already?

Bam tells Buddy, "Look, man, I notice since yo boy got transferred to our dorm, and since he made house, man, a lotta shit been walkin' from my house, and I'm thinking it's making its way to yours. Now he may not have known better, but that shit in Dorsey's locker and a few more is mine, and I know he gave it to your house 'cause it damn sho ain't in mine, and I want mine back!"

Buddy is just as intense as the two size each other up.

"Yo, man, if you got a problem with my boy, you right to bring that shit to me, but what you doing? You tellin' me all loud? Uh, you frontin' on me, nigger? You need to know, people not knowing how to talk to people—that's how the graveyard got started!"

Meanwhile, a man sits on the bench not ten feet away, reading a newspaper. He has yet to acknowledge what seems to be happening all around him as the crowd gathers.

One of the bystanders taps the old man on the shoulder.

"Aren't you gonna do something? Stop this?"

The man stops reading and looks over his paper at the two men. He is an elderly black man with salt-and-pepper hair and has the air of an inmate who is respected by all. His presence, even as an elder, has a calming effect, and even Buddy and Bam take notice of what he will say.

He answers in a voice that is heard by both Bam and Buddy Row, "And what does this have to do with me?"

Surprised, the two inmates turn their attention away from each other and focus on the old man.

The old man turns his attention back to his paper as he continues, "Is it not written that a house divided cannot stand? Are they not of the house of misery and deceit? Why do you marvel? That it has come to this? Even now and assuredly whosoever should survive will be carried off near dead...and who among you shall weep for them? Indeed, their spoils will be plundered among you, for surely you will not see either of them again and life will go on."

The old man turns a few pages and begins to read the paper, holding it up to his face.

Buddy Row and Bam look at each other and then at the crowd around them. They begin to turn almost back-to-back, yelling at the crowd, "So what y'all looking at?"

"Yeah, y'all looking for a show, ain't no show here, motherfuckers. Step off!!"

"Think you gonna split up my shit? Ain't nothing!"

"Yeah, my shit best not be touched either. We got some smartass head start, motherfucks, in here too, thinking a nigga already gone ta jail!"

The crowd scatters quickly and soon disperse.

The two young men go their separate ways.

Aaron and School look at each other and then at the old man behind the paper.

"Damn!" Aaron says, grinning.

School is also in disbelief, saying, "Yeah, Pops got some big old hairy cahoonas on him. That's like OG status for real."

Aaron looks at School with confusion and asks, "OG?"

"Yeah, original gangster. Damn, I forgot you from Soda Pop Florida."

"Yeah, I got ya soda pop."

The boys enjoy a few games of basketball, and Aaron wins the respect of a lot of ballplayers—both those playing as well as the onlookers.

Later as the yard closes, Aaron takes his shower; and as he walks back to his bunk, he notices that the gray-haired man with the paper has the bottom bunk next to his.

The man is sitting there with one of the young men who nearly fought earlier—Bam. As Aaron dries his feet, he can overhear the conversation.

The gray-haired old man asks if the young man was all right.

He says, "Yeah, but I can't let people think it's okay to go into my packets."

Though they both have their backs to Aaron, he can hear well; and before long, he finds himself caught up in what the old man has to say.

"Son, let me tell you something. Nothing on earth cheats you like money. You made quite a bit on the streets, didn't you?"

"Yeah," the Bam replies.

"Still, was it ever enough? To be where you wanted to be. And so you struggled on sacrificing the moment your child rolled over for the first time on his own power, or being there when he stood up on his own and began to take steps."

"Yeah, but I looked out for my shorty. I made sure he had the best: the best clothes, the best shoes, he had food…"

The old man begins to laugh warmly and says, "I tell you, these things were done for your namesake, that people may see your son's fine belongings and glorify you. Vanity is all that is. What about when he falls and is afraid? A child won't remember the Jordans on his feet nearly as much as the one who helps him to his feet when he falls down. In this manner, many are deceived. Look at the officers around you. They say come, and you come. They say go, and you go. You say, 'Yes, sir,' and 'No, sir,' and still there is not one that you could say you love. But it is your friends who you share yourselves with… Why?

"Because what they offer is precious in that they give you their time freely. Such is true with our kids, and if you're not there for them, believe me, there are plenty of people that will be. And you may object to what they are taught. Just look around you, Bam. Is there any evidence of strong family upbringing? In truth, you can always get ya hands on a twenty-dollar bill, but those moments… they are both priceless and gone. Gone forever, and you'll never see them again. Think about that when you come into your freedom again."

Bam nods and says, "Yeah, okay, I see ya point. Hell, I got more from you just then than I got from my father my whole life."

The old man smiles.

Aaron is now dressed and lays across his bunk as the old man also extends in his bunk.

The man notices Aaron and immediately reaches a hand out in Aaron's direction, saying, "Welcome to Graceville."

Aaron is surprised at how friendly he is, and there's a warmth in his eyes.

"I'm Aaron Daniels."

The man replies, "I am called All Day."

Aaron looks confused as he reads A. L. L. Day on the name tag and then confesses, "I couldn't help but overhear your conversation. I never thought about money cheating you before. So you're the guy people come to for, like, advise?"

All Day smiles and says, "Who am I? I am one who has been given over time, and now I wish to give back."

Aaron nods and says, "A man of wisdom. You may find me to be someone who has a lot of questions, if you don't mind. I'm at a place in my life where I really have more questions than I want, and none of the answers I need."

"The answers are simple. Anyone can give them. It is when you have renewed your mind to the questions you search for in truth that your heart may become informed, for in the end, we all listen to the heart." All Day continues, "Yes, the heavens suffer violence, and the violent taketh by force." He then leans back onto his bunk to greet another man hailing him.

Aaron is surprised as he remembers that scripture.

Chapter 21

Jonny's Debut

Months now have passed, and Jonny Blain has registered at the University of Florida, and there is a buzz all throughout the state as the season is at hand.

It's game day in Gainesville, Florida. Reporters usher in another collegiate basketball season.

The place, O'Connell Center, is packed with screaming fans.

The sports commentators are really talking up the starting of Jonny Blain and rumors that the red-shirt freshman will be the center of the offence. The excitement of this city is near explosion.

"It's LSU at Florida at the O'Connell Center, and it's a sold-out crowd."

"Tonight the nation will see the true freshman that's heading up Gators: the recently acquired Jonny Blain out of St. Augustine, Florida, the Yellow Jackets—a pure shooter with catlike quickness who plays well without the ball."

"His quick release has netted him Florida's Mr. Basketball, as well as national attention touted the third best guard in the country, but there are some Gators here that already take issue with that rating."

"And they may have a case. This young man plays some bold defense and is used traditionally to shutting down the opposition's top gun, still, it is college ball now. But it is no wonder Coach has him on the court from the start."

"At six feet three inches, he's an average-size guard with a forty-inch vertical and timing that lead the Class A division 1 in blocked shots among guards doing his last years of high school. To these people that have never seen him, they're in for a treat, and we'll be bringing it all right back, right after these messages."

Mickelson sits back on his Italian leather sofa, monitoring the game on his big screen TV set. He sips on a brandy and seems so excited in his own way as the game begins.

Jonny gets off to a fast start, and soon all the rumors that this kid is hype are silenced as he takes control of the game early.

Only four minutes into the game, the freshman has a blocked shot and six points.

Ten minutes into the game, he adds a steal and six more points, and LSU takes a time-out down by twelve points, and the O'Connell Center goes wild at the output and efforts of Jonny Blain.

Mickelson is amused and says, "Quite the baller, I'm sure, wouldn't you say, old friend?"

Cole slouches in an La-Z-Boy recliner.

"I've seen better," Cole answers as he turns up a scotch and continues. "I never knew you were such a fan."

Mickelson smirks and says, "Actually, I'm not. Indeed, I'm afraid my sense of adventure lies solely in the arena of commerce. No, this is an exercise in tactical warfare, and all his efforts on the court merely further illustrates my need for such a competitive spirit."

Cole rolls his eyes at his British boss, saying, "I don't get it."

"Mr. Cole, his is an exercise in futility. No, no, his place is definitely with us running our St. Augustine office."

Cole's eyes turn back to the set to watch Blain finish a fast break with a slam dunk.

"Seems to me this kid's gonna go lotto in the draft before the next commercial. Why should he want to hook up with us?" Cole asks.

Mickelson smiles and hands Cole the newspaper and directs his attention to an article heading up the sports section. Cole begins to read as Mickelson gives a narrative as he watches the game.

"It appears the NBA basketball commissioner was nice enough to lend us a hand. He made the age for the draft a lock, and some two years away for Mr. Blain. For a player of such control, one can only believe this came through discipline and hard work, a means to an end. And now to have such hard work simply put on hold. Well...while he's waiting, his need and his greed will have to be reacquainted."

Chapter 22

The Road to Come

Later at the new home of Bobby and Cricket Cox, enjoying the first day of peace and quiet in weeks, Bobby is in the study, looking over the Warrick case.

Although he has a full caseload, he finds himself captivated by this young man's claim.

"Geez, appellate law is so unfair. Imagine having to find something that couldn't be found by due diligence in the initial trial."

Penny is doing the dishes.

She comments, "Is that really difficult?"

"Well, when you take into consideration that none of these people have law degrees and building the defense is solely on their attorney, it seems unfair that this is a criteria, being that the defendant is the one that has to do the time."

Cricket turns toward the study and says, "Wow, when you put it like that..."

"Yeah, and it's just like that."

Bobby has arranged the chairs in the study and is reading the transcript of the case. He points with his other hand back and forth along the chairs.

Crick has walked up from behind him and is amused at her husband's antics.

She crosses her arms and legs and, leaning against the hallway doorjamb, clears her throat and breaks his concentration.

He turns quickly and is also amused at the expression on his wife's face.

"How long have you been there?" he asks.

"Who, me? Oh, I just walked up..."

She asks, "Who are you defending, the chair or the end table 'cause the table was with me, and we're not going down without a fight." She begins to make fencing motions.

"Ha, ha, cute, I'll have you know Jonny Cochran started this way."

Pat cuts her eyes at him.

"Okay, maybe he had a bigger room...and a blender."

"Yeah, right!" She laughs.

"So, what's up?"

"Well, I need to talk to you about something job related," she expresses.

"That's weird. I was just about to call you to ask you something job related too. So whatcha got?"

Hands entwined, Cricket begins to pace and starts, "It's a question, well, no...maybe. I guess it could be a question. I guess, since a lot depends upon the answer, this qualifies as a question."

"Crick," Bobby says, pointing at the furniture.

Crick takes a deep breath and continues, "Okay... The hospital is a little overstaffed in practical nurses, and they're starting to cut hours, and keeping in mind I'll have to take maternity leave down the line, the head nurse came up with a solution that both benefits the hospital and me."

"Which is?" Bobby asks with concern.

Closing her eyes, she quickly bellows, "Transferring me to Flagler Hospital in St. Augustine."

"What?"

"Now, Bobby, wait."

"Wait, I can see how that would solve their problem, but how does this benefit you driving all the way to St. Augustine every day?"

"I'm trying to tell you. First, it's not every day. Second, I'll be working in Anesthesiology which, once I'm certified, will mean more money. Bobby, we just bought a house."

Bobby is confused and asks, "I thought your heart was in Detox?"

"It is! It was… It is, but this is an opportunity to advance. I mean, they offered me a choice, and I haven't given them an answer yet, but man…anesthesiology… We could use the money."

"So it's already set. You're right, it's not a question."

"No, it is, 'cause if you don't want me to take it…"

"No, no, no. I want you to take it. I can see you want it, so I want it for you."

Penny jumps into his arms and showers him with kisses, saying, "Oh, thank you, Bobby, thank you."

He laughs. Suddenly the kisses stop, and Penny looks into Bobby's eyes.

"Oh, you had a question for me?" he asks.

"Yeah, this is kinda simple though… On the corner of Fifteenth and Myrtle Avenue, what's the speed limit?"

Chapter 23

Cole Calls

Back in St. Augustine, Detective Rodgers comes home from work at his Coquina Lakes Apartment on St. Augustine Beach.

"Rex!" he calls out to his pit bull, but there is no response.

He throws his jacket on the arm of the sofa and grabs the remote. He turns on the eleven o'clock news and goes to the refrigerator and grabs a beer.

He thinks to himself, *Did I let Rex out this morning? Has he been out there all day?* He sits down in his recliner and stretches out. Calling to Rex again, he begins to guzzles some beer and then takes his gun from his holster and places it on the table beside the beer.

He unbuttons his collar and gets comfortable, kicking off his shoes. He begins to drift off to sleep when suddenly there is a sharp-edged blade against his neck. He knows the aftershave, and it brings no comfort as a voice whispers in his ear.

"Relax. If I wanted you dead, you'd be someplace no one could hear your screams."

It is Cole, and the fact Rodgers recognizes his voice has dampened the seat of his pants just a little bit.

"Whatcha want, Cole?"

Cole reaches over to the gun on the table and then removes the knife from Rodgers's tense neck.

"I just wanted your undivided attention, that's all." He ejects the magazine and the round in the camber. He continues, "No sense in us risking any accidents. Besides, you should always check your surroundings before you relax. Didn't they teach y'all that in cop school?"

As he tosses the gun into Rodgers's lap, the detective asks again, "What do you want, Cole?"

Cole stares into Rodgers's eyes with contempt and says, "What I want is for you to raise your voice to me again. So I can figure you 'bout to get foggy, but why I'm here is because Mickelson has some work for you and your boy to do. He sent me to explain, so there's no misunderstanding like that Jonny Blain incident.

"Now, I know you don't like me, and I'm losing all kinds of sleep about that. So perhaps if you can manage to fuck this up, I'm sure Mr. Mickelson will allow us both to…should we say, scratch our itch? Are you feeling me, boy? Just fuck up!"

Cole pulls out the papers sent by Mickelson and explains the execution of the plan.

Rodgers is sound in his understanding, and Cole turns to leave and stops at the door.

"Oh yeah, about your dog. I let him out…of his misery."

Cole laughs as he closes the door.

Rodgers frantically looks around.

"Rex… Rex!"

Then he begins to search the house. Finally, he gets to the bathroom and sees the toilet covered in blood. He lifts the lid and immediately vomits into the sink.

Rick (Cole's driver and first lieutenant) picks up Cole. As He exits Coquina Lakes.

Rick asks, "You did the dog, didn't you?"

Cole laughs and says, "Did I!" He had some beef chunks in the freezer, I simply thawed them out in the micro wave and soiled his bathroom with beef blood and pet hairs. "Cole laughs. "I open that door though and that dog took off like a shot.…I guess even the pets know He's probably still throwing up in there ! "Coler laughs even harder.

Rick shakes his head and thinks to himself, *You're one sick son of a bitch, you know that?*

Cole takes a manila envelope. The details are very vanilla: the officer he killed, Arnold Jackson, 27, graduated high school, no college; joined the police force three years ago. Nothing jumps out. Cole tells Ricks to pull into a 7-Eleven and grab him a hot coffee. After Ricks is inside, Cole makes a call.

"Hey, I'm looking over this file my people got. I'm unimpressed. I need a deep dive into this guy. I need his dossier, birth records, high school affiliations, ex-girlfriends. I'm not believing some wet-behind-the-ears cop stumbled upon both operation and had in instinct to kill upon discovery. Something smells here. Get on it."

Chapter 24

A Real Barn Burner

In St. Augustine Tracy and Lisa are quickly becoming best friends, and before long, Tracy has invited Lisa to move in.

Lisa is a bit outgoing and animated compared to Tracy's demeanor, but Trace very much enjoys being around Lisa and witnessing her crazy antics.

Tracy is sitting on the living-room sofa, writing a letter. She's also waiting for Lisa to arrive home with tales of another adventure from what is sure to be another bad date night.

Suddenly the front door opens and shuts quickly. Tracy looks over her shoulder to find Lisa, her back against the door.

She is dressed in a layered, sequined miniskirt and matching pumps. She stands pressed against the door as to keep someone from getting in.

Tracy smiles and shakes her head, saying, "Not again!"

As she begins to laugh at the look on Lisa's face, she states frantically, "It's not funny, Trace, it's criminal, and there should be a law, ya know—ten straight things that constitutes a bad-faith date. I'm sure I could check about eight boxes."

"What happened, and should I pop popcorn?" Tracy asks with anticipation as she places the letter on the table and turns to her very animated roommate.

"Well, first, he picks me up in a monster truck! I say, *Okay, maybe the jag's being worked on.* No! It's his mother's. So now he's taking me way out into the woods of Green Cove Springs, and I'm thinking, he's cute, but is he looking to park? 'Cause even I'm not that kinky, you know? So I ask him where we are going. So he tells me a real barn burner. Okay, child, we get out there in the woods with about…two dozen hillbillies, Trace They burned a barn for real!"

"Uh, excuse me?" Tracy is now confused.

"Yeah, a real barn. I almost called 911, like, three times. I'm talking dropped calls. I couldn't get a signal. Which reminds me, we should maybe work on our smoke signal game in case one of us ever finds themself in the middle of the woods with no signal and alcohol."

Tracy raises her eyebrow, asking, "One of us?"

There is a pause, and then Lisa says, "Okay, maybe I learn to pitch 'em, and you read 'em from afar. Anyway, they had this pig… on what they called—I don't know—a spittle? The whole pig, and I just hope he wasn't alive when they rammed that thing up his ass 'cause, well, you just knew one of them was the type, ya know.

"Anyway, the darn thing kept looking at me the whole time like he was saying, 'Please tell the others…stay away!' Their doing dust out here on the farm. So then they did a Skeletor thing on this dramatically betrayed pig. I mean, you could see it in his eyes, Trace. And they ate the weird stuff. Ya know, the stuff you put into a plastic bag before you throw it in the trash can? They ate it with syrup, and this one guy took a spoon and started eating, like, the brains. And he was trying to convince me that I was really missing out."

Tracy cringes and says, "Puh-lease."

Lisa nods and continues, "Right. I went to the outhouse ta, ya know, throw up, which by the way, looking down that little hole in there…big help in the heaving process. Then I come out, and some lady offers me a chew. I'm thinking Big Red, right, I can get that taste out of my mouth. She hands me some Red Man.

"I said, 'Oh, no, thanks, I already threw up.' Oh girl, so this dude comes up to me with, I mean, one, two, maybe three mediocre teeth in his mouth, got that gap thing working the right side upper, you know. The good ones still kinda light brown, high yellow tint. Look like he used to shave until he found religion.

"So he's got, I don't know, a possum sandwich with mayo in some kinda red homemade barbeque sauce dripping off soggy bread and offers me a bite. Like for real! Like I'm going to try something that might have done all that to his mouth? I think some of the older ones pissed on the mushrooms before they make that tea. Give it that extra-green tea look. I mean, look at this dress! This dress should speak to even the countries of country boys. This dress does not scream, 'I need to get this one wasted!'"

Tracy laughs at Lisa's frustration.

"Yeah, I'm seeing it, easy access, World Trade Dead Center, yeah, I get it."

"Yeah! Wait... Okay, that was a gutter-slut joke, but at least you feel me. I caught a ride back. I figure if he misses me, I saw four or five nice-sized sheep out in the pasture, rolling their eyes like, 'Why weren't we invited?' I mean, you can only be Plan B for so long."

Tracy's mouth drops and says, "Oh that's *so bad*!"

"Girl, there's county, and there's like those people in Deliverance, okay?"

As she flops down on the sofa, Lisa asks, "Whatcha doing?"

She asks as she takes the letter off the table. Tracy quickly takes the letter from her hand.

Lisa nods and says, "Oh, you're writing Aaron again... Does he, like, not know the address here or something? I mean, you must write him every night, Trace."

Tracy gets up and starts going to her bedroom.

"Don't go there, Lis, outta bounds."

"Okay, okay," she yells down the hall at Tracy. "Hey, Trace, by the way, I met a cowpoke. I guess after a while, those sheep get old."

"That's sick, Lis!" she yells from down the hall.

Chapter 25

A Place in the Heart

The next morning Cricket finds that she has made good time on her first day going into St. Augustine. With the extra time on her hands, she decides to go through the car wash at State Road US 1.

Afterward she goes to the gas station down the street to fill up.

As she gets back into the car, she notices a man at the phone booth. His hair is stringy, and he is unshaven. He appears to be having trouble getting the money into the change slot of the phone. His hands shake as he finally starts to walk away but stumbles to the ground and begins to shake violently.

"Help!" Penny calls out, grabbing the stethoscope from her pocketbook.

She then instructs two nearby men to grab his arms and legs. They converge on the man, but he is stronger than they anticipate, and they struggle to hold him down as Pat forces the metal end of the stethoscope into his mouth and presses down on his tongue.

"Hold him!" she screams, and then just as suddenly as the shaking had started, it stops, and the man's body goes limp.

His head collapses to one side, his eyes open but motionless. Crick quickly takes the stethoscope from his mouth and checks his heart as an Indian man claiming to be the gas station manager kneels by her side.

"Do you need any help?" he asks.

"Yes." Pat spots a large ashtray, long and round, at the door of the store. "Bring me that ash can and about a one-pound bag of ice."

98

The manager takes off as she takes her cell phone from her purse and dials 911. She then hands the phone to one of the men holding the fallen man's legs.

"Tell them where we are and what's going on!"

The store manager returns with the ice and the ashtray.

Penny quickly checks the fallen man's mouth, then placing her hand under the back of his neck, she holds his nose and gives him two quick breaths. Then she goes to his chest. Finding the man's sternum, she then starts pumping the man's chest.

After she has repeated the process for the third time, the man suddenly starts to take breaths on his own.

Then panic sets in. The man becomes frightened, but Cricket is quick to reassure him.

"Hey, hey, it's okay, you're okay, I gotcha. Boy, it's hot out here, isn't it?"

She reaches in her purse and pulls out a pair of gloves and puts them on. She then begins to place handfuls of the crushed ice under the man's arms as she engages him with a soft flirtation of sorts. She then loosens his pants and takes a handful of ice and, reaching down into his pants, places it under his genitals and smiles

"Isn't that better?"

The man smiles and nods.

"You really gave us a scare." She lifts up his legs and rolls the long ashtray under his feet. "That better?"

Again, the man smiles and nods.

"So what was that?"

She slides the sleeve of his coat up and finds what she suspected, track marks.

"Ah, you've been speedballing," she says with a smile as the man smiles back at her.

She is relieved as she can hear the faint sounds of sirens getting closer and closer.

"Your ride is almost here, cutie," she assures the man.

Soon the ambulance appears and loads the man in. Penny has shown her credentials and gave the attendants his vitals, and they relay the information to the hospital.

"You guys from Flagler?" she asks.

"Yeah," one of the paramedics responds.

"Good. I'll follow you."

She gets into the car as bystanders applaud her efforts. Within five minutes, they arrive. Penny parks and rushes inside. As she enters the emergency room, she is stopped by an orderly.

"Sorry, ma'am, staff only beyond this point."

Penny grabs her key chain rope with her ID badge and places it around her neck, her eyes fixed on the speeding gurney, and she precedes.

The orderly calls out to her.

"You're new here. Hey, what department?" he asks with amused interest.

Cricket stops and turns to the orderly with intensity in her eyes.

"Me… I'm Detox."

She then disappears into the fallen man's room.

Chapter 26

The Educated Guess

Back in Jacksonville, Rollie Wade sits in his office, reading the dossier on Aubrey Mickelson, when he is buzzed by his secretary.

"Yeah?"

"Agent King to see you, sir," the secretary responds.

Agent King enters with a file in his hands.

"Rollie, I just got back the personnel file on Mickelson's staff. It's a bute."

"Give it to me!"

"First, let's start with the man himself. Aubrey Mickelson, ex-British Intelligence with ties to the CIA. Dual citizenship with England. Became an American citizen in 1980. He assisted the United States with back channels in the release of the hostages in Iran. There are some that believe he orchestrated the taking of the hostages with the intent to defuse it and win points with the US. Don't think he meant for it to take a year though. He was also an 'attaché' to the Contras at the time of his retirement.

"Then there is his righthand man. Antavius Cole. Was thought to be a rogue CIA agent. Some believe there's a file that exist that gives him a free pass from standard operating procedure involving the rogues claim. Served three tours in Nam. Investigated four times by the war crimes commission, but no indictment. The man specializes in search and destroy, and intelligence. They say he was one of the best gophers the Marines ever had. Says he sniffed out more tunnels and captured more than two hundred Vietnamese underground, but slaughtered twice as many. A real war hero. Seems he couldn't cut it off though. Since the war, he's been investigated eleven times by four different state and local police departments on suspicion of homicide. Again, no indictments. He brought along Allan Ricks from his company of commandos. The rest are hired thugs, all with military backgrounds, as you can see." He hands the file to Rollie.

Rollie looks over the file when there's a knock on the door.

Agent Steve Tyler enters.

"Excuse me, gentlemen. I've got a break in our surveillance of Mickelson's operation, courtesy of CSI."

Rollie reaches out for the file, saying, "Let's have it."

"His boy Ricks. Like clockwork, he's been making mail drops at various mailboxes throughout the city area. We noted two things: one, there were no packages, just stacks of envelopes with no return address, and two, he always wore gloves. Today they may have slipped. Riverside Avenue over by Blue Cross, his driver Ricks made the drop without the gloves. Acting quickly, we posted a sign on the mailbox, 'Out of order due to spill,' you know? Anyway, we contacted Judge Dobbie and got a warrant. Now, he wouldn't allow us to open the mail, but we could dust for prints, and we found eight pieces of mail with Ricks's prints on 'em, but more importantly, we found one with the fingerprints of both Mickelson and Cole."

"That's great!" Rollie remarks excitedly. "So, what are they, and where are they heading?" "One was addressed, would you believe, to St. Augustine High School?"

Danny looks to Rollie with concern in their eyes.

"Is he spilling into old city schools?"

Danny nods, saying, "It's not beneath him."

Rollie asks, "So who is the letter addressed to?"

Steve shakes his head and says, "The envelope said to Mrs. G. Alberry. The only problem is that she hasn't worked there in six years."

Rollie stands and goes to the window and looks out over the city.

"Maybe it's a decoy move designed to throw off any onlookers," Danny quietly interjects.

A puzzled Rollie looks back over his shoulder into the city and says, "You'd think. The whole thing could be a setup." Rollie continues, "But it's assigned to an actual person. Maybe they've been there all the time. My gut is telling me there is something there. No, let's check it out. Get Dillard, get him in the school system. I want to know why Mrs. Alberry still has a box, and who's taking her mail. Also, I want an appointment with the St. Johns County Sheriff.

"I want him to know we're coming to town. We're gonna let 'em in on this. It's their city. They should know. I want Dillard briefed on exactly the kind of people we're dealing with here. Everybody on your toes. Okay, let's get to work"

*****

Back in the Panhandle, School and Arron have just come in from working in the city of Graceville. School is excited by a young lady he saw as the work crew had job assignments near the Baptist College. He is quite animated about the ordeal as he explains what he saw.

"Man! Did you see how she kept riding by in them shorts, with that ass hanging out? Man! She knew what she was doing. She saw us out there. I bet she knows our schedule better than we do."

"She knew what she was doing. She was turned on too. You see how she kept smiling at us, okay, mostly at me!" another inmate chimes in.

"School, we're in prison. All girls' ass cheeks seem to hang out. And they smile 'cause they feel sorry us, or they glad we're in prison, the way some of us be gazing back at them with amazement."

Aaron acknowledges the inmate with a finger point.

School smirks at Aaron and says, "Yeah? You ain't so far gone. You can't size up some drawers?"

Aaron turns to School and says, "Yo, School, it was just a girl. I've seen 'em, done some too. Uh, how 'bout you? We ain't been down that long. You sound like you ain't had none in eons, dude. Hey, what was your charges again?"

They all begin to laugh.

School smirks and says, "Funny, real funny. Been long enough to know I miss it."

As they both sit on Aaron's bed, there is laughter from behind them.

It is All Day. He rolls over, and staring at the boys, he restrains his laughter.

"I'm sorry, you two crack me up sometimes."

School is visibly offended and asks, "Oh yeah, how so?"

All Day sits up and says, "While one of you says exactly what he feels, the other one never says what he really feels, and this is your bond." He begins to laugh again.

School jumps up and quickly pulls away from Aaron's hand who reaches out to him. School walks around the bunk to All Day and is standing over him.

He starts in on him. "Yo, OG, you don't know me. You don't know shit about me, so how you gonna say I don't say what I feel? I'm keepin it real, and I don't give a damn how ya take it, feel me?"

All Day looks over at Aaron and says, "He's right, you know."

Aaron looks into All Day's eyes, and then he looks at School. There is an awkward silence.

He looks again to All Day and asks, "Who? You mean me?"

All Day's eyebrows raise.

Aaron smiles. School looks under the bunk at Aaron, still visibly riled but is calming down. Now he wonders if there was something said he should know.

"What's up, Gee?" School asks Aaron.

Aaron looks School in the eye. He is speechless, slowly shaking his head.

All Day smiles and shakes his head and asks, "Tell me, Aaron… The girl at the school, what did you see?"

Aaron looks at All Day. He seems entranced as he slips into his memories. Soon he can see the girl on her bike, her young child in the baby seat attached to the back.

Then he begins to speak as he gestures with a smile.

"She had the prettiest eyes…a light green, maybe hazel. She did smile. She was beautiful, and the baby girl was too. The little girl was strapped into the seat, but she was waving her little hand too. I remembered this place Mom used to take me and my little brother out by the beach. A park. We use ta play on the swings, our heads leaning back in the wind."

Aaron smiles, and then he looks back at School and says, "That's what I saw, man... That's where I went."

School backs out from between the bunks and says, "Damn, my nigga, we still in the chain gang. You can't say that shit out loud? Shit gonna be under yo pillow like the Walmart, homie."

Again, the dorm breaks out in laughter. Aaron starts to laugh, but School continues to back away from the bunk and head out the dorm.

Aaron turns to All Day, but before he can say a word, All Day begins to speak.

"Light has come into the world, and men loved darkness rather than light because their deeds were evil. for everyone practicing evil hates the light, lest his deeds may be clearly seen."

Aaron thinks for a second then says, "So you're saying, School is in darkness?"

"Not at all. I'm saying, you are embracing the light, and there's enough light to share with your friend. Would you leave him in the dark? He is not ashamed to share his world with you. Would you deprive him of the world you have come to?"

"What am I supposed to do if he doesn't want to share in my world?"

All Day places his hand upon Aaron's shoulder and says, "You must first declare to yourself before God the world you claim. Then as you push forward in your trust in God, according to your earnest expectation, God will manifest himself in your life in such a way as to complete your joy and draw not only School but all manner of men to him through what they see him doing in you."

Aaron turns quickly to All Day, and their eyes meet.

"Kinda like something I read, provoking them to jealousy."

All Day smiles and says, "Funny how all men want the same thing even if they don't know what it is exactly...until they see it. Why don't you go see about your friend?"

Aaron leaves the dorm and spots School on the yard, leaning against the dip bar. School stares through the fence at the acres of flat green land that surrounds the prison compound.

Aaron walks up from behind him and asks, "What's up, dog?"

School just nods and continues to stare through the fence. Aaron nods as well.

"Yo, School, what is it with you and All Day? You seem threatened by our friendship 'cause with All Day?"

School's head snaps quickly toward Aaron and says, "You have a real talent for stating the obvious, huh? I mean, so that's what you see, right?" School's tone is harsh and threatening.

Aaron raises his hands and says, "Ya know what, I don't want to do this."

Aaron turns and starts to walk off.

School turns back to the fence. His head drops.

"Wait!" he calls out. Aaron stops and turns to him. School takes a really deep breath, and then he laughs. "You know what, you're right."

School continues as he waves Aaron to come back. School looks off into the horizon, then he begins to explain.

"When I first got to Florida, I moved to Pensacola, in a section of town called Shinny Town. They used to joke about Emit Smith was too bright-skinned to come up in there. But I was straight, pretty fly for a white guy, huh? Anyway, I had a friend called Tank… That was my dog. He kept me under his wing, ya know, made me one of the hood.

"Kept me in some gangster type shit too. One Thanksgiving morning Tank's coming out of his front door when a car full of crackers did a drive by on him. They had just got beat down the street an hour earlier on a dope buy. Tank made the mistake of wearing the same kinda sweat suit outside that day as the brother that ripped them boys off. Fucked up, right? Anyway, that and then hearing 'bout… my kid brother's death. Dad leaving again. Shit gets real, ya know. I just kinda withdrew, and…then I get knocked off and comin' to prison. You ain't trying to vibe with these jokers, ya know, you watch cha back. I guess I felt like for me, meeting you and you getting in ya know… I guess I was feeling like I was losing another special someone again 'cause maybe there wasn't enough of me strong enough to make them wanna stay. I guess I'm high maintenance, uh? But ya know I always got cha back, ya know that, don't cha?"

Aaron nods and says, "Yeah, I know ya do, School, and you know I'm here for you. But check this out. There is more to life than we know, or I know. I'm just trying to learn what I can in here, or else it's just time wasted. Hey, School, I don't want to come away with nothing ventured, nothing gained. That makes sense to you?"

School looks at his friend and then throws his arm over Aaron's shoulder.

"I get it. All Day is pretty cool, and maybe I wish he saw in me what he seems to see in you. Come on, let's walk the track."

Just then a voice rings out from an officer some thirty yards away.

"Hey, you two! All hugged up. Go ahead, swap some spit so I can lock ya both the fuck up! Go ahead, touch lips, motherfuckers!"

School removes his arm and whispers under his breath, "Check out Sarge with them knockoff gold teeth and that big bald spot in the middle of his big-ass forehead. If he weaved some dread extensions around the sides of his head, he'd look just like Predator."

Aaron busts out in laughter but then suppress himself as he notices the sergeant taking a double take,

He turns away and mumbles, "Yeah, yeah, I can so see that."

School and Aaron go back into the dorm, and surprisingly, School makes peace with All Day.

The next day it's the weekend, and the camp starts to settle down as most of the inmates flock to the dayroom to watch Florida at Kentucky, a basketball game in the SEC, and raking implication in terms of who will represent as the number one seed in the conference. Both are ranked in the top five, with Kentucky holding the number one spot and Florida at number three.

Aaron, School, and All Day find themselves in the back, farthest away from the TV.

As the game begins, they watch a very up-tempo and tight first half. Midway through the second half, Aaron notices that the yard is still open. There are people walking the track, some throwing horseshoes, but no one on the basketball court. He goes out and takes the ball in his hands. He begins.

He runs both ends of the court at a pace that is similar to the game he was just watching, shooting and rebounding, but also replicating defense with regard to stealing balls.

School steps out of the dayroom and surveys the dorm, looking for AD. School wonders where his friend has disappeared to, but then he sees him on the court outside. School can hear the game and finds it strange that just as the TV describes a fast break by Florida coming down the left side, Aaron is breaking down the left side of the court and making the same move; he scores the basket.

School hears the commentator announce Jonny Blain shooting a jump shot from the corner and watches Aaron pull up from the same corner.

"He hits!" the commentator announces as Aaron's shot also goes through the hoop.

As Aaron races back to the other end. School calls All Day.

"Go to the other window, okay, listen to the game, and check out our boy."

All Day watches in amazement as Aaron seems to be in lock step with the action, even scoring for Kentucky.

The game comes down to the wire, and with a one-point lead for Kentucky, but Florida steals the ball and calls a time-out with six seconds left.

Now Aaron walks in circles around the painted circle in the half court. Action resumes as Aaron runs around the half court with ball in hand. As the ball gets to Jonny Blain's hands, Aaron begins to dribble. Blain goes up for the bank shot from twelve feet out.

Aaron hits it, but quickly turns toward the dorm as though to say, "He missed the shot! Kentucky holds on to the number one seed in the SEC!"

School and All Day both turn their attentions back to their friend outside. Aaron looks dejected. His face filled with skepticism and disbelief. Now they announce the yard is close.

School and All Day look at each other in bewilderment.

Aaron walks at a slow pace, occasionally looking back at the goal.

As he walks into the dorm, both School and All Day whisper, "Big-game jitters, ya know…could happen to anybody."

Aaron just goes to his bunk and sits on his bed. There's a look on his face that says he's a million miles away.

Chapter 27

Party Favors

It's a beautiful sun-drenched morning in St. Augustine, Florida, as Special Agent Wade is accompanied by Agent King on the drive over to the St. Johns County Sheriff Office.

They arrive a little after 9:00 a.m., and the sheriff is waiting.

The agents are escorted and seated in his office as Sheriff Reese also sits in speculation of the visit.

Rollie gets right to the point.

"Thank you for seeing us on such short notice. We understand you're a busy man, but we've recently uncovered a plot that we think could possibly be overflowing from our county into your community."

The sheriff smiles and says, "I would say this is more than just a hunch, sir. You don't get a visit from the head of the Justice Department on an anonymous tip."

Rollie smiles in return and says, "You're right, sir, and I won't insult your intelligence. That's not why I'm here. We have reason to believe that a master criminal by the name of Aubrey Mickelson is looking to…"

Rollie stops as he notes the eye contact at the mention of Mickelson's name.

Rollie continues, "Sir, your reaction suggests you know the name. Do you?"

The sheriff looks at King and Rollie, then he presses the buzzer on his phone.

His secretary answers, then he says, "Get Wells from Internal Affairs. I just left him. Tell him to bring the file we were looking at along with the tapes."

The sheriff looks back to the agents and says, "I've heard the name Mickelson once before, and this morning at that. Our resources aren't quite those of the Justice Department, but as you'll find out, we do what we can. If he rears his head…"

Rollie stops the sheriff with a smile and raises his eyebrows, saying, "I'm impressed, but it will never happen. He's not the kind to come out in the open. You won't know he's here until he's in control."

There's a knock on the door, and Deputy Wells enters.

"Just place the information on the table, and I'll send for you when we're done." The sheriff takes out his tape player. Then he continues, "This is a tape made months ago on two of our detectives that we believe are working both sides. We don't have anything on them as of yet, and we were hoping this Mickelson guy would aid us in blindsiding them. But I guess they're working for him, uh? Here's the part that I think will be of interest to you."

Everyone listens as he plays the tape. The voice of Detective Rodgers comes on in conversation with Billips.

"The kid fucked us!"

"What? What kid?"

"The Daniels kid. I just went over to pull him. Seems he's already in court. In fact, on my way over, I saw the bus coming back. He pleaded!"

"He pleaded out?"

"Yeah, and get this, the state gives the Austin chick a free walk. Yeah, say they didn't have enough to convict him, let alone her."

"So they couldn't give us a little time?"

"Yeah, well, they never heard of Blain, or Mickelson, or that son of a witch's bitch Cole. All they care about is quota. Come on. Let's go."

The sheriff stops the tape.

"I'm gonna need a copy of that tape and the files and also the names Daniels and Austin. Do you know who they are? I'd like that information, and who are those officers?" Rollie asks.

"That's Rodgers and Billips, Narcotics. We suspected they were dirty for some time, but we haven't been able to pin anything on them."

"So who's the kid they're talking about?"

"To the best we can figure, it's one Aaron Daniels and his girl-friend, Tracy Austin. Daniels took a deal on a drug bust. Went up the road for three years. We haven't located Ms. Austin, and I think the other one is Jonny Blain, a ballplayer at U of F."

"The basketball player?" Rollie looks up in disbelief.

"Sounds like it. We suspected him of dealing for a while now. I was grateful that he took his talents off to school. He's a hell of a ballplayer."

The sheriff leans over his desk with a smile on his face and asks, "So how can I help?"

Rollie looks up from the brief at the sheriff then says, "You can't, sir. Aside from the Intel, you've already been compromised, and you don't know how far up it goes, and I can tell you, Mickelson has the resources to take this far beyond your control. I have to ask that you sit this one out."

The sheriff becomes outraged, saying, "Now, hold on here. I just gave you what you were looking for. I'm in."

Rollie is equally sharp to reply, "Yes, sir, you did. See, that's your job. Cleaning your house, that's my job. Now I have another job too, and it involves preserving the safety of my men. Now, we'll give you your crooked officers to do with as you see fit. They're an afterthought to me, but that's the best I can do."

The sheriff thinks for a moment and then exhales.

"So I get Rodgers and Billips?"

"On a silver platter," Rollie replies.

The sheriff reaches his hand across the desk and says, "I guess we got a deal."

Rollie shakes his hand as Danny looks through the file, making notes.

Chapter 28

Whisper Softly

Later that evening Lisa comes out of the bathroom after a shower. On her way to her room, she looks into Tracy's room; but before she can speak, she notices Tracy is smiling to herself as she composes another letter to Aaron, one of many that will not be mailed and exists seemingly only to occupy the top left-hand dresser drawer of her bureau.

Lisa, while drying her hair, began to speak, but the words elude her.

She goes back into her own room, and sitting in front of the mirror, she begins to pin curl her hair. After a while, she is startled to see Tracy's reflection in the mirror, standing in the door behind her.

Lisa stops as she observes the solemn look on Tracy's face as their eyes lock.

Tracy takes a deep breath and then begins to speak, seemingly in an effort to explain.

She begins, "Aaron and I met at the fairgrounds when he was fourteen and I was just turning thirteen. He'd come by himself and snuck me away from my parents." She smiles. "We ran everywhere all over that fairground until my parents caught up to us. I didn't know him, but somehow, I just trusted him right from the start, ya know.

"He became my best friend overnight. I guess you can say it was love at first sight." She laughs." "Anyway, years had passed, and we were spending every chance we had together, so we just thought it'd only make sense that we go together. You should'a heard that talk." She laughs. "He had football practice and basketball practice, but then he always made time to see me, even if just for a minute or two. I gave myself to him when I turned fifteen, and then one night he'd just left my house. Mom had called and left a message that she had to work late, so I'd have to cook for my stepdad.

"My stepfather came in, and I'd cooked him some pork chops like Mama told me to. He ate and got in front of the TV set, watching *Monday Night Football* with his usual tall glass of gin. I went to bed. I must've been asleep about an hour or so when I felt someone crawl into my bed. He put his hand over my mouth and used his weight to pin me down. He was saying all kind of awful, crazy, nasty, dirty stuff!"

Suddenly a single tear rolls down Tracy's cheek. Lisa covers her mouth as her eyes are filled with tears. Tracy is struggling but continues.

"And the next thing ya know…he…he was inside me." The tears stream down her face. "I tried to fight…to scream, but he was just too…just too strong. He told me if I said anything, it'll be my word against his. All of his threats seemed to make sense to me. I was scared, and so I said nothing. I didn't even tell Aaron at first, but he somehow sensed something was wrong.

"I guess it was the way I'd withdraw at his touch, sometimes even when he'd take my hand. I'd mapped out a plan, ya know, just to make sure I was never alone around the house with my stepdad, or at least not without the benefit of a locked door between us. And then just when I was beginning to draw near to Aaron again… I missed."

Lisa turns away from the mirror and to Tracy. She can see Tracy is breaking down, trying to even stand, and Lisa is up quickly to hold her friend.

Tracy takes a deep breath and continues, "I didn't know what to do, or what to think. I could only hope it was Aaron's baby, but inside… I knew it wasn't. So I told him about the rape…and the pregnancy. We cried together. He wanted blood, but I talked him down. His going to jail at a time like that wouldn't accomplish anything. Anyway, we agreed to tell his parents the baby was his. Can you believe that? It was his idea. He thought his family would welcome me with open arms, but…they didn't.

"They called my parents, and after some exchange of words over the phone, they all decided to meet at the hospital for a paternity test. We sat and waited, and then the doctor confirmed my worst fears. Aaron was not the father of the child I was carrying. Aaron's mom went off. She was all on my mother's case so hard.

"You know, until that night, I didn't even know they knew each other. But in school they were classmates. Aaron's mom brought up all kindsa little sordid tales about my mother's past. 'Like mother, like daughter,' ya know. Mom just took it all and didn't say a word. She didn't deserve that. How could she have known?

"Anyway, the only thing they both agreed on was that Aaron and I were forbidden to see each other. Later I told my mom what had really happened. She said she didn't believe me, but I think she knew I was telling the truth. She got some money together, and I got an abortion. Meantime, Aaron had devised a plan. We were to lay low 'cause we knew they'd be watching, but we were going to still be going together. Ya—I thought to myself—sure.

"Two days later, he snuck by my window in the middle of the night with cell phones. He gave me one and talked to me as he walked all the way back across town. We set it up so I could call him at certain times of the night, and whenever I'd call, he'd drop whatever he was doing to tend to my needs...even if I just needed to hear his voice.

"Sometimes I believe that's when he started selling dope. He'd kept our phones on for months without a job, and then he brought the charger, ya know. The night he got arrested, we were on our way to get married. He paid for the apartment and my car. So you see, Lisa, I just gotta hold on, ya know... Maybe I'm crazy, but I'm crazy about him, and I just can't see how that's a bad thing. He's always been there for me, Lis. How can I not be here for him wherever he is?"

Tracy rambles, and Lisa embraces her friend as tears stream from both their eyes. She holds Tracy and kisses her on the neck.

Lisa puts her hand on the side of Tracy's head, and looking straight into her eyes, she says, "Tracy, you listen to me, girl, and you listen good! Next time you write that man of yours, you give him my love, okay...okay?"

Chapter 29

That's That Loot

Gainesville, Florida, at the Oak Ridge Apartment complex, a different kind of liaison was taking place.

A Volvo S70 with tinted windows and twenty-two-inch rims eased over the speed bump, making its way near the far side of the manager's office. A tall black figure exits the car and, carefully surveying the area, walks over to the apartment mailboxes. Another man steps from behind the boxes, places a key on top of the box, and grabs the nearby pay phone.

The tall black man takes the key and examines it for a box number.

"Running a little late, aren't you, Jonny?"

The tall man places the key in the box and takes out an envelope. He then examines the contents of the envelope and smiles.

The man on the phone turns back toward Jonny and says, "You cut it kinda close there, didn't ya? I mean, for a second there, we thought you had a change of heart."

Jonny laughs with his back to the man and says, "I had to make it look real, didn't I? I mean, that's the art, feel me. I did cover the spread, didn't I? Now, if you don't mind, I got some more sympathy loving to get back to."

The man smirks and says, "Yeah, I bet you do," as he laughs.

"Be a good bet. But hey, man. These games are starting to count for something now. I'll need more for the next time…if you want us to lose. I have my teammates to think about." Jonny smiles.

The man hangs up the phone saying, "I'll notify my people."

"You do that," Jonny replies as the two men make their way.

Moments after they've gone, a light comes on across the parking lot from the mailboxes as the last of the curtains are pulled shut.

A walkie-talkie is keyed and then, "Billips, this is Rodgers. Did you get it?"

Billips picks up the walkie-talkie and responds, "Yeah, I got him, and at three angles. Hell, I even got the plate on the car. What about audio?"

"Man, come on in. This kid's basketball days are over, and we got a long drive. Besides, I'm hungry."

Rodgers laughs and says, "I feel like I just ate. I just hope Ricks didn't show up in the footage."

Chapter 30

When We Become Involved

It's another beautiful morning in Jacksonville, and at the federal building Bobby Cox is going over some papers in his office when Katie knocks and then rushes into the room.

"Ahh! I just read about Penny. You must be so proud of her!"

Bobby smiles as he reaches down underneath his desk and pulls out a *Jacksonville Journal.*

"Is she something else or what?" Bobby replies with a smile on his face.

Just then Sillenia walks in. She, too, has a *Times-Union* in her hand, then she says, "So this is the same Penny Ann Cox as is married to our newest and most impressive litigator."

Bobby smiles and says, "I wouldn't say most impressive, but I guess we have our moments."

"I'll say." Sillenia holds up a sheet of paper she begins to read, "Notice of docket call for Friday, March 19, 2003. Subject: New Trial in the Court of Appeals of one Brent Warrick. How'd you do that?"

Bobby looks shocked and says, "I got it? I didn't know. I mean, I submitted a brief…"

Katie thumbs through the mail.

"Bobby," she says, handing him a letter, "this is from Judge Shrives. This must be the notice."

Bobby opens the envelope, and quickly glancing over it, he smiles.

"Yeah! Yeah, I got him in. We pick a jury March 12."

Sillenia simply shakes her head in disbelief and says, "I've been working every angle for that boy's case for over a year. Nothing. How'd you pull it off?"

Bobby sits back with a reluctant look on his face slightly covered with a smile. He wonders how to tell the boss she overlooked the obvious.

"Sillenia, I challenged the verdict on the grounds of fundamental error. I got the idea from you while working on the Blair Case a couple of weeks ago."

Sillinia looks puzzled then says, "Yeah…but the case law Ray and Castor versus State goes to the fundamental error being the very foundation of the case. I tried the same argument…"

"Yeah, but you based the argument on the testimony given that should have exonerated Warrick, and the judge shot you down because it was a jury trial, and the jury had the right not to believe the defense witness. The finding of additional evidence should have been presented at trial."

"Yeah, that's right."

Bobby continues, "However, Sanford v. Rubin 237 of the Southern Second 134 Florida of 1970 goes to the merits of the case of action. The error must be one which amounts to a denial of due process of law. Enters *Sochor v. State*. Now the officers said they turned off Merrital Avenue on to West Fifteenth Street to observe the four men trespassing. The officer then said he noticed Warrick drop a brown paper bag from his right hand. He said he was no more than three feet away. Sillenia, I tried it. For that officer to have made that turn and to be only three feet away, he would have to have turned on the wrong side of the road coming up Fifteenth Street. Plus, he was the passenger, not the driver. The driver would have been the closest, so how come he didn't see anything? Now the State told Judge Shrives they were not willing to retry the case, but with my brief, I guess the court agreed the testimony on face value was flawed."

"Yeah, but Bobby, if that's all you have, are you ready to go back and try this case? I mean, the officer's testimony is still very damaging."

Bobby smiles and says, "Well, that just got me thinking. You think they'll stick to their guns, tell the same story?"

Sillinia nods and says, "Yeah, I know they will."

Bobby smiles and looks over at Katie then says, "I sure hope they do," as he pulls out his case folder.

Katie and Sillenia both make their way around the desk and look down from both sides of his shoulders.

Sillenia slants her eyes with a devious smile, asking, "What are you doing?"

Bobby shows her what the dispatch recorded.

*****

Back in St. Augustine, around 10:30 p.m., Tracy is watching an old movie when the door opens, and Lisa walks in with a plastic Applebee's bag in hand. By the look on her face, Tracy knows this was another one of those dates.

She laughs at Lisa's expression, and she screams, "No, Lisa, this one was cute, had a Beemer, he dressed nice. What was wrong?"

Lisa collapses on the living-room sofa with Tracy, throwing the bag on the table in front of Tracy and a leg over the arm of the sofa. She sneers.

"I've never seen anything like it. You think maybe I'm cursed? He asked me to meet him at Panama Hattie for drinks, right, so I did. Then he says, 'Let's go get something to eat at Applebee's.' I say great. But there's this smell, okay. I thought he had farted at first, ya know, one of those sneaky silent ones. Anyway, we started down 312, and I realized it was his breath. It had to be. I checked his shoes, my shoes, nothing."

Tracy's jaw drops and says, "Uh-uh, girl, I never even heard of that."

Lisa continues, "It was like he was having a chemical reaction to Jim Beam into felony halitosis. I offer him a Tic Tac and spilled, like, ten in his hand. I even told him, 'Boy that was some strong drink you had. You think they check the expiration date 'cause gee willikers? You might have a lawsuit.'"

Tracy is in tears already, begging, "Quit it, girl."

Lisa goes on, "At this point, I knew he wasn't getting laid with spinach fly, right. So now the hostess gets too close, and she's looking at me like I had to be a well-paid trick."

Tracy laughs and says, "Stop it! You know darn well you don't look like no trick. You look tricky. there's a difference."

Lisa nods and says, "Well, I think she asked somebody first if they could let us in. I told him, 'Let me do all the talking. I wanted to say, 'Don't even smile in case—you know—seepage.' Anyway, while we're waiting for the food, he's leaning into me, trying to explain... something. So I'm taking direct fire. So I say to him, 'Damn, maybe you should eat some chitins or something to get that smell off your breath, ya know? I mean I gave you the court-appointed Tic Tacs, and they didn't make a dent.'"

Tracy's mouth drops and says, "No, you didin'."

Lisa eyebrows raise as she continues, "So he's a little hurt, ya know, but now the food comes, and I'm eating, and my food looking good. So I went to the ladies' room for relief and to devise a way to tell him in a nice, subtle way, 'Ever wonder if you could maim a brick 'cause there might be money in that,' and not have to pick up the check.'

"So I thought I'd just say I got stuff to do and call it an early night, right. So I stopped by the waitress station and asked for a to-go box, okay. She nodded like, 'No shit? You don't want, like, two?' Anyway, I go back to the table, and he's, like, in the men's room.

"Girl, I'm boxing up food with the quickness, ya know, the all-new swiftness, and then he comes up from behind me, and I turn, and before I knew it, he's right there inches away, and pow! Breath like when the speakers are too loud to make out the music! I could smell the noise hair burning. I don't even know what he said, but they were swing on words."

Tracy's eyes widen.

"Oh my god! How'd you make bail, girl?' Tracy asks while half-way on the floor with tears in her eyes.

"Uh, uh, this waitress saw the whole thing, and covering her nose, she dove between us. She asked me if I wanted to press charges, girl!"

Tracy is on the floor.

"That breath musta went dancing with wolves," she screams.

Lisa nods.

"So. Then I picked up my plate and just slid everything into the box. I was seeing red, but it was 'cause, ya know, I think some got in my eyes.

Then he stepped toward me, so I'm getting ready to put these dummies on him ya know." She raises her fist in a defensive gesture.

"Ya know, get me twice, shame on me.

He says, 'What's the matter?'

I broke it down slowly, 'Your. Breath. Smells. Like. You. Gargle. Stewed. Roadkill. That's the matter.'

The waitress nods. Even the preacher said, 'Damn it, man!'

Then I called a cab."

As Lisa is talking, she reaches into her bra, takes out a folded piece of paper, and throws it in Tracy's lap.

"Oh yeah, that's for you. Try the ribs. They're baby back."

Tracy picks up the folded piece of paper, still laughing,

"What's this, the cabbie's phone number?"

"You wish," says Lisa, reaching into her top pocket. "I was very careful not to get them mixed up." She holds up a business card of the Yellow Cab driver.

Tracy unfolds the paper. It reads: Aaron Daniels DC no. 314933, 5230 Ezell Road, Graceville Work Camp, Graceville, Florida, 32440.

Tracy's mouth drops, her eyes stretched to capacity. She is stunned.

"Wha... I mean... Is this real? Lisa, don't play with me. Is this real! How?"

Lisa is chewing on a rib and smiling at her friend's expression of joy.

"Lisa! How?"

"I figure they must slow cook 'em. Now you could steam 'em, but being—"

Tracy throws a pillow from the couch at her, shouting, "You know what I mean!"

"Oh, that," says Lisa, pointing at the address. "That was easy. See, I didn't know the exact address, but I've seen the house before, so I got the driver to get me in the neighborhood till I found it. Then I got lucky.

"Mrs. Daniels answered the door. I told her how AD and I were really close friends back in high school, and I heard he'd fell, and I'd really like to write him, ya know, let him know he's got friends out here who haven't forgotten him. Oh, she ate it up. I came off like an Academy Award-winning performance. There even might have been a tear in my eyes, plus look at me... I should have ta have a license to stun 'em, right? Who wouldn't want me for their son? Maybe she thought I'd send him dirty pictures to remind him of his manhood. Ya know mothers, they wonder."

Tracy is speechless at first.

The tears in her eyes are very real, and then she says, "And you did that for me?"

Lisa stops chewing and looks again at her friend, and with a mouth full of ribs, she says, "Well...*yeah*. You're my best friend, hello! Besides, you'd do it for me if I could ever get lucky enough ta—hey! Watch the ribs, honey. Watch the ribs!"

Lisa is suddenly around her friend's neck.

Chapter 31

Who We Are

Days later at Graceville, Aaron gets off from work and is unusually quiet. He gets off to himself and tries to understand what's happening to him. There are so many different conversations and times of laughter and times of sincerity that he shared with Jonny. He was closer to him than his own brother. But basketball was sacred to them. It was the way out. And even though the time came when Aaron realized it was no longer his dream, he still dreamt for Jonny Blain.

He replays in his mind the channel of emotions that he felt on Jonny's last shot.

One question with two meanings keeps playing in his head: He missed it, and he missed it?

He tried to dismiss it, but then the thought recurs, *Who is this guy that I sacrificed so much for? Who is he really? Could he have really changed so much?*

Aaron begins to walk the track. There is a peaceful silence within his steps even as the chaos of the recreation field is all around him. He hears only the soft sound of the evening breeze. His mind's thoughts are unsure, in two words that now come with each step: *Trust* God, *Trust* God. Now his thoughts are on Jonny again, and he realizes his betrayal.

Lesson learned.

He notices the birds at the tree line near the fence.

He sits at the end of the track, and his mind is now on Tracy. He so wants to contact her, but he fears that then Rodgers and Billips would find her.

His mind also wonders about the people of his past.

He becomes concerned with the things that he knows go on, and he thinks of ways to fix them, practical things that not only make sense but lead to other remedies, and ways to at least offer hope to an out-of-control situation.

Aaron sits along the grass at the end of the track. He gazes off into the skyline, watching as the orange-and-blue rays deflect against the clouds.

The rays stream from behind them as the sun is gone from view. He notices a bird off in the distance at the tree line nearest the gate (some fifty feet away). Sitting there, he begins to talk to *God* aloud.

"Father, why have you given me these things that I should think about them so much? When all my peers would think about women and the ways of the world and how they may prosper, here I am in torment with my soul. I am made ashamed before you by the reading of your word that does, oh, to, well, describe me even in thoughts as well as deeds…and so now I wish to change and to make amends all that which was wrong by my doing, and yet I don't know where to begin or…or even if it's really me or…just a phase brought on by loneliness and guilt. Is this my spirit or just my mind's way of making sense of this time by telling myself I'm getting better?"

He thinks, *Am I alone in this (my thinking)? Surely there are others who have seen the same things and wonder what if… Who am I that I should say these things before all of them? I am but a boy, you know. Who I am—I've done things in darkness, even things I wouldn't tell Trace. What can I do?*

But then a voice comes up from behind him

"Funny thing, though. Even the gutter needs a priest."

He looks back to see his friend All Day.

With his hands in his pockets and a warm smile upon his face, All Day says, "Aaron, long ago there was another in which the Lord said, 'Before I formed you in the womb I knew you; before you were born… I sanctified you; I ordained you a prophet to the nation.' And ya know what he said to the Lord?"

Aaron remembers his grandfather's teachings. He and All Day begin to quote verbatim:

"He says, 'Behold I cannot speak, for I am but a youth,' but the Lord said to him, 'Do not say that I am a youth; for you shall go to all to whom I send you.'" All Day looks off unto the tree line. "That youth's name was Jeremiah. I think *God* for his obedience and his letter to the captives. 'I know the thoughts that I have toward you, thoughts of peace and not evil, to give you a hope and a future. Then you will call upon me and go and pray to me, and I will listen to you. And you will seek me and find me, when you search for me...with all your heart.' Who knows the millions upon millions of people that turned from their ways, the things that held them captive because of Jeremiah's willingness to do what was right before *God*? How many shall find him because of you? Understand something, Aaron, they'll not be your words, only your willingness."

Just then All Day is surprised by a young man who comes up from behind him. He has an envelope in one hand, a letter in the other, and tears in his eyes.

"I'm going back!" the man yells as he hands the letter to All Day and hugs him.

All Day holds the letter behind the man's head as he is being hugged and reads. Soon a smile comes to his face.

"This is good, this is very good, and you have a new attorney as well."

"Yes." As the man lets go, he searches the envelope for a name. "Yes, Bobby Cox. He must be good for Ms. Daniels to give him my case. I mean, he got me back. He must've argued the case you made."

Aaron is confused, so he asks, "All Day, you do legal work?"

All Day nods and says, "Oh! I dabble. Aaron, this is a good friend, Brent Warrick of C Dorm. He's from around your parts, as a matter of fact."

The two shake hands.

Then Aaron hears his name and looks across the yard near the dorm.

He sees School calling out to him, "Hey, AD, you got mail."

Aaron excuses himself, and just before he can leave, he notices the birds again—like hundreds of them all going to the one tree line nearest the fence.

"They've never done that before, not that I've noticed in almost two years," Warrick responds.

"No. They usually find shelter across the field," All Day answers.

Then Warrick laughs and says, "I bet they figured there's more food dropped on the ground by inmates out here as well as over by the kitchen. I guess there are pretty smart birds, uh?"

All Day looks at Aaron who is now entering the dorm. He looks then to Warrick and says, "Perhaps," but in his thoughts, *Or maybe they gathered together to hear a man earnestly talk to* God. *I guess they are pretty smart birds.*

Aaron goes to the front desk and receives his mail. First, his attention is caught by the *Sports Illustrated* cover showing Jonny Blain's last-second missed shot and the caption: The Fix in the Mix.

Aaron walks to his bunk, thumbing through the pages as he drops one of his two other letters. He picks it up to see the name Tracy Austin and is stopped in his tracks.

He rushes to his bunk and quickly opens the letter. As he reads, tears swell up in his eyes, soon accompanied by laughter.

All Day comes in and sits on his bunk. He looks over at Aaron as Aaron wipes his eyes as though he's trying to see.

"That must be a letter from that pretty little girl I've seen in your album?" All Day asks.

Aaron smiles and nods, saying, "Yeah, she found me."

All Day lies back on his bunk, and reaching into his locker, he pulls out the Bible.

"Yeah, you know what they say, 'When praises go up, blessings come down.'"

Aaron looks up at All Day again and just nods.

Chapter 32

The Connection

In St. Augustine early on a Saturday evening, Detective Rodgers walks out to his car, gets in, and leaves his parking lot. He heads across the 312 Bridge.

Behind him is an unmarked car.

"Okay, we got Rodgers turning right on US 1, heading north."

Another car responds, "I'll pick him up at King Street."

The other car falls back at King Street, and they both note his speed.

They follow him as he turns left on Highway 16, going west. Soon he is out of the city limits. The first car responds to the second.

"Go ahead and pass him, take I-95 north, and if he does you, stay ahead of him and take the Orange Park exit. I'll call Rollie."

"10-4."

As Rodgers turns onto I-95, Rollie is contacted. He then calls Danny.

"Danny, we may have a meeting. Get everyone together. Tell them this is not a drill. We may not get another shot, so let's get it right. Also, get Hutch and Duke ready. We've got about forty minutes, so let's move!"

Some thirty minutes later, Rollie contacts Danny.

"Are we ready?"

"Yeah, Boss, everyone is in place. Duke and Hutch are in the van at the US 1 exit by the Avenues."

"Good."

"We have two more cars tailing him and one in front of him watching his turn signals."

"Okay, stay alert. Rodgers drives on past the Orange Park exit, and the van with Agent Hutch and Duke gets behind him."

"Rodgers just turned off on Emerson. His blinker indicates he is turning west," the tailing car reports to Rollie."

Another transmission comes in, "Rollie, he's turning into McDonalds, and he's parking."

"Is he going in?"

"Affirmative."

"Hutch, you've got the ball."

Rodgers goes inside to the counter as a van drives around to the other side of McDonalds and stops.

The side door opens, and a blind man and his dog exit. The man is led to the front of McDonalds by his dog and stops. The blind man wears dark shades that are thick and completely go around both sides of the agent's face. The shades are both infrared cameras on the front and sides, as well as a transmitter and receiver along the nose and earpiece.

Rollie calls for a systems check.

"Hutch, can you hear me?"

Hutch's back is to the McDonalds, and the dim of night acts as a shield.

"Yeah, Boss, I hear ya."

"Okay, I'm coming off the 95 exit. I'll set up in the Sam's parking lot with a visual soon."

Rollie gets into position. Using binoculars, he can see Rodgers inside eating a Big Mac and fries. Danny gets into the car.

"That's our man?" he asks.

"Yeah, that's him. He came a long way for a burger and fries, huh?"

"I'll say. I count at least three Mickey D's he passed to get to this one."

"It's definitely a meet of some sort, Danny. This guy checked his watch three times already."

"So where's Hutch?"

"He's right in front, sitting on the outside patio with his back to the perp."

Just then a black Mercedes pulls into the McDonald's parking lot and parks between Rodger's car and the restaurant. Rollie notes the car.

"This may be it. let's get Hutch into position."

Then Danny taps Rollie on the shoulder and points to a sign near the parking lot.

"Whaddya think?"

Rollie turns his binoculars to the sign, *Bus Stop*. He then picks up the transmitter.

"Hutch, okay, now don't move yet. Are your glasses on zoom?"

Hutch smiles as he checks out the blond across the street in the really tight short skirt and the V-neck blouse.

"Oh yeah, and they're working just fine."

Rodgers begins to move out from his seat. Rollie is alert.

"Hutch! He's on the move. Go ahead and start getting yourself together. Then go toward the bus stop, and on the way, get us a good visual on the Mercedes. Angle for whoever's in the back seat if the window comes down, or stationary at the stop for an in-and-out-the-car quick pic. We need to get a picture of who Rodgers is meeting!"

Rodgers moves through the door and reaches under his shirt. He pulls out a folded large envelope and makes his way over to the Mercedes rear window.

The window comes down, and Cole is in the back seat. He is at first a little distracted by the man and the dog in front of them walking toward the bus stop but then turns his attention back on Rodgers. Rodgers hands him the envelope.

"Is this it?" he asks Rodgers as the detective leans over into the window.

"That's it. We got the kid dead to rights, and the story's been leaked. These photos should insure his cooperation."

Cole looks again at the blind man standing at the bus stop now and squints.

"Are you sure you weren't followed?" Cole asks.

Rodgers grins and says, "No, I wasn't followed."

The window starts to go up, and Rodgers quickly removes his arm.

"Drive out. Turn left," Cole commands the driver.

As they pull out, Cole again looks at the blind man as though he may have seen him before. Just then, a bus rolls up, and Cole is on the on-ramp.

"Something's wrong," Rollie says to Danny as he watches the Mercedes roll out of sight.

"Like what?"

"I don't know." Rollie grabs the radio. "Keep a tail on both cars." Then he grabs the transmitter.

"Hutch, get off at the next stop. We'll have the van pick you up. Meet me in my office in twenty."

Back at Deerwood Estates, Cole walks into Mickelson's office and drops the envelope Mickelson's desk.

"Here's the shots," he says.

Mickelson watches as Cole goes back to his desk, and sitting down, he sets off a teeter-totter, puts his feet up, and stares into nothingness within the frame of the office walls.

Mickelson opens the envelope while observing his companion.

"Anything wrong?" he asks.

Cole stares with a squint in his eyes.

"I'm not sure...probably nothing."

"You have concerns nonetheless?"

Cole stands and walks over to the picture window overlooking the garden.

"There was a blind man. I saw him when we pulled up at the McDonald's. He and his dog...they were waiting for a bus. Now, I can't quite..." As he plays the encounter back in his head in slow motion, Cole shakes his head and smiles. Then he continues, "I was going to say, put my finger on it, but then, neither could he." He laughs.

Mickelson stares and is obviously confused as Cole walks over and leans on Mickelson's desk.

"I'm watching this guy, see, and then I notice he's blind. Ya know, seeing-eye dog, the whole bit. But as we're sitting there, he gets up and starts toward the bus stop, and he intersects with Rodgers and me like he had a spotter, now that I think about it. But ya know what's weird?"

Mickelson smiles as one entertained by Mr. Cole's paranoia

"Please don't tell me you are so out of touch with the city's transportation system that you didn't know they let seeing-eye dogs on the bus."

Cole laughs with a touch of sarcasm and says, "Ha, ha. No, but I do question how he timed that bus without a watch?"

Mickelson slowly sits back in his chair as his smile fades.

"Actually, there could be a number of reasons why he knew the bus was coming."

Cole nods and says, "Yeah, but only two worry me. Either your Keystone Cops have been made, or someone's setting us up."

Mickelson knows Cole's dislike of the detectives, but he also trust Cole's instinct.

"Those are two very good reasons that we can't afford to overlook. What's your take? I mean, you were there."

Cole walks back into the center of the room and says, "I'm thinking he was followed… Yeah, that was my first instinct."

"Very well, let's find out. Tell Ricks to take four men in four cars and watch Rodgers and Billips as well their surroundings. The first car will act as a spotter to see if they're being followed, but they are not to be lost. Also, I want documentation of their activities, as well as photos."

Cole starts out toward the door, but stops. He turns to Mickelson.

"Hey, what if they're not being followed?"

Mickelson gives Cole a stern look and says, "Then we'd better come up with the reason your blind man caught that bus. In fact, put someone on that bus stop. Perhaps he'll catch it again."

Cole turns slowly as Mickelson continues to examine the envelope.

"Don't worry, Mr. Cole. You'll get to kill them soon enough, but right now they still have a usefulness about them."

This news brings a smile to Cole's face as he exits the door.

Chapter 33

Guesswork

Back at the federal building, Hutch hurries down the hall, quickly making his way to Rollie's office.

"Boss, you're not going to believe these shots. I mean, the lab won't have them ready until morning, but—"

Hutch stops as he notices the sentiment is not shared. The expressions on Rollie's and Danny's faces gives Hutch reason to feel concerned.

"Okay, what?" he asks.

"Rollie thinks you got made," Danny replies.

Hutch grins and says, "No way, guys. I mean, that bus showing up when it did just set it off. This was a perfect shot." There are only looks of skepticism. "Come on!"

Rollie gets up from his chair. He walks a circle around Hutch and then sits on his desk.

"Danny, do you see it?" Rollie smiles. "To the average Joe on the street, yeah, you got him up close and personal, but to a seasoned pro, trained to detect, to assess situations, this man taught himself to read foreign soil, to profile an enemy with foreign characteristics in a foreign culture. To him, we may have made a mistake, and with the stakes so high, well, you can understand my concern."

Hutch looks at Rollie and Danny. They smile.

He smiles back and says, "Okay...you guys aren't just messing with me, right?"

Rollie smiles and says, "That's it, kid. You can go."

"Boss, ya just messing with me, right?" he says, looking back as he leaves the room.

Rollie starts back behind his desk with a grin on his face. Danny stares with an amused look of confusion.

"So you want to let me in on it? What did you see that I didn't?"

Rollie sits back in his chair and says, "What was Hutch doing when you called him to come to work?"

Danny thinks for a moment then answers, "He told me he was working out, pumping iron."

"Yeah, I bet he was working his forearms…wrists."

Danny looks where Hutch was standing. A mental picture comes to mind of Hutch's appearance.

"He wasn't wearing a watch, was he?"

"No, he wasn't."

"So you think that Cole could have caught that?"

"I noticed Cole checking out Hutch both on the move and at the stop. It would strike me as odd that a blind man caught a bus without the aid of a timepiece, especially if he wasn't waiting at the stop. No, Danny, I wouldn't bet my life he missed that."

"So you think they'll double-check the bus stop. Maybe we should have Hutch do another performance?"

Rollie walks around to sit on his desk directly in front of Danny.

'Wait, let's think this through. Mickelson's calling the shots—a great thinker—so let's think like he would. We put a blind man back out there. You almost have to try him, follow him home, where does he go during the day. That puts my man at unnecessary risk. No, I think we need to shake 'em up a little, but in their own backyard."

"Rollie, we do nothing. If they are suspicious, they'll be suspicious of their own crooked cops. Rollie, they'll take 'em out."

"I don't think so, Danny, not right away. From the profile I got on Mickelson, he's got his use for them. He won't risk other crooked cops banding together in retaliation. No, I think he'd watch them, though, at least for a while, so we'll watch them, see where they take us to work in the old city. Tell ya what. I want to pull back surveillance on Rodgers and Billips. I want the telephone repairman just outside Coquiina Lakes moved to the mayor's office. That'll give us

Main Street one way and the cable guys outside Flagler, and that'll give us all directions.

"They'll be our spotter. I want four teams at least a mile off the markers. We'll stay in front of them and then keep coverage on their location. We'll need their dispatch log tied in to our communications tonight before they move, just in case Mickelson orders a hit. I want each of our agents to have photos of Mickelson's men.

"We'll play it by ear for now, and maybe we'll find an opening, which cops Rodgers and Billips are meeting, are they dirty, something. Also, get me an update on where we are on Mickelson's mode of communication. I want to know what those transformers can do. Are they a specialized item? I'm also waiting on the paperwork surrounding Jonny Blain, Aaron Daniels, and… Tracy Austin. We need to get in front of these guys, Danny, and I'm thinking they have to many fronts to cover them all."

Chapter 34

The Verdict

It is the morning of March 19, and Bobby makes his way into the courtroom where Sillenia is already waiting—to his surprise. He smiles and waves at the jury already assembled in the jury box. He places his briefcase on the table and speaks softly to Sillenia under his breath as he removes his paperwork.

"Hiya, Boss. Thought you'd come by for moral support?" He smiles.

"Actually, I thought I'd second chair on this one...if you don't mind?"

Bobby smiles and says, "No, not at all. You have a rapport with Mr. Warrick, and that's always a benefit."

Their attention is turned to the side door as officers bring in the defendant. He is brought over to the table where Bobby and Sillenia sit in the center of the table between them.

"Brent Warrick, Sillenia Daniels. She's the chief public defender."

Warrick turns to her and smiles, saying, "So finally we meet." Reaching over and shaking her hand, he continues, "Ms. Daniels, I gotta thank you for a year of keeping me abreast of what was going on with my case. You can't know what it's like to put your fate in the hands of someone you've never even seen and then have ta wonder if they're really doing all they can, or even what they say. Thank you very much."

Sillenia smiles then gestures to Bobby.

"Mr. Warrick, I wish I could take credit for getting you your day in court, but I can't. The man you should be thanking is Mr. Cox."

Warrick turns back to Bobby, who laughs and says, "Don't thank me yet. So far, all I've done is get you a weekend pass, and maybe some visitation."

They turn their attention to the entrance as the DA and her team comes through the door. They also greet the jury and acknowledge the defense table.

Sillenia makes her way over by Bobby as he sets his papers in order.

"That's Tamika Ramsey."

Bobby looks over Sillenia's shoulder.

"Cute, she's got a nice smile."

"Yeah, well, so does a piranha, and they'll both tear flesh from bone if you're in the water. She's real nitpicky, and she likes to play that smile for the judge."

"Sounds as though you know her well."

Sillinia rolls her eyes and smiles and says, "Let's just say we don't do brunch."

Bobby raises his eyebrows and returns the smile, saying, "Ah, so she the reason you're here?"

Sillinia mouth drops open, sputtering, "No! Not exactly… I'm here for support. You have a good case. Just don't blow it." She smiles.

"Hear ye, hear ye, all rise for the honorable Judge Shrives."

The bailiff gives notice as the judge enters. After everyone is seated, the judge calls the State to present its case. Ms. Ramsey makes her opening statement. She talks about how three years ago Mr. Warrick, while in the act of trespassing after a warning, was detained and found in possession of a paper bag containing twenty bags of crack cocaine, twenty bags of powder cocaine, and twenty bags of marijuana.

She told how the arresting officer witnessed Mr. Warrick drop the bag from his right hand, from just three feet away. She told how Mr. Warrick was with three other people in his crew and how one of them even came forth to claim the bag in an attempt to get the charge off of Mr. Warrick.

She points out that a jury then didn't believe the defense. She asked that they not be fooled now. The defense makes its opening statement.

Bobby points out that the higher court had found factual basis that fundamental errors had occurred in sustaining that conviction and that the facts will exonerate Mr. Warrick.

The State calls Officer Prosper first; he's one of the two arresting officers and the one who saw Mr. Warrick drop the bag. Ms. Ramsey examines the witness.

"Officer Prosper, will you give us an account on what happened on the afternoon in question?"

The officer clears his throat and begins.

"Me and my partner Tilly—ah, Officer Tillman—were on our patrol, ya know, the usual sector of town we are assigned to patrol, when we turned off Myrtle Avenue on to West Fifteenth Street and saw the defendant and his friends standing in front of an area clearly marked no trespassing, so we pull them over."

"So then what happened?" Ramsey asks.

"Well, we got out of the car, and as we did, I saw the defendant drop a bag from his right hand and try to mix into the crowd. We put everyone against the wall and patted them down. We knew we had them on the trespass, so we cuffed them. I asked my partner to check out the bag, so he did. That's when we found the dope."

"No further questions."

Ms. Ramsey takes her seat.

Bobby approaches Officer Prosper.

"You stated my client dropped the bag and then tried to mix into the crowd of three? Tell me about the crowd."

Ms. Ramsey stands, saying, "Objection, Your Honor, may we approach?"

The judge nods.

Once they are in front of the bench, Ms. Ramsey begins.

"Before Mr. Cox begins, the State has conceded that in their initial statement the officers did omit three people who were present during the initial stop, but in the context that their presence was incidental, contacts as bypassers and not witnesses, only the four men who were arrested were considered because they, in effect, had already been warned about trespassing in that area—"

Bobby interrupts, "Your Honor, the law states the rules of evidence 90.104 that a court may predicate error, set aside, or reverse a judgment on the basis of admitting or excluding evidence."

The judge responds, "It also says when his substantial rights have been adversely affected. Mr. Cox, we're giving him a new trial."

"Yes, Your Honor, and I don't want the same injustice to happen again. I'm just trying to declare to the jury the actual occurrences. I'm just trying to walk them through it."

The judge again nods and says, "Proceed, objection overruled."

Bobby goes back in front of the witness as Ms. Ramsey takes her seat.

"Officer Prosper, how many people did you stop there that day?"

Prosper hesitates then answers, "There were four...no! Seven, but only four had been warned."

"So why did you detain the others?"

"Security. We wanted to make sure they weren't armed."

"Okay, you pat 'em down, call 'em in for outstanding warrants, that sort of thing."

"Yes, sir."

Bobby walks over to his table and picks up a sheet of paper. Then he walks back to the stand.

"So Pamela Marks, Lameta Marks, and Tommy Marks were released because they had no weapons, or warrants, no drugs?"

Ms. Ramsey stands and objects, "Objection: asked and answered."

The judge agrees, "Sustained. Next question."

"No more questions, Your Honor." Bobby starts back toward his table and then turns around to the stand. "Oh, one more question, Officer Prosper. Were you the senior officer on this arrest?"

"Yes, sir. I have eight years on the force. I had five then. Tilly was the rookie."

"Thank you. No further questions."

Ms. Ramsey stands up and calls her next witness.

"The people call Officer Tillman to the stand."

Tillman walks in from the witness room and takes the stand.

Ms. Ramsey begins, "Officer Tillman, would you explain to the court what happened on the morning in question."

Officer Tillman composes himself then starts, "Well, I was driving down Myrtle Avenue when we turned on West Fifteenth Street and observed the defendant and some more people standing in a posted area. We pulled over and stopped them. We then searched them and ran a check on them. Four of them had been warned about that corner, so we decided to take them in. Officer Prosper said he'd seen the defendant drop a bag and asked me to examine it."

"Will you tell the court what was in that bag?"

"Yes, we found twenty baggies of crack cocaine and twenty baggies of marijuana and twenty bags of powder cocaine."

"Your witness."

Bobby approaches and asks, "Officer Tillman—or would you rather be called Tilly?"

The officer smiles and says, "I'll answer to either."

"Okay, tell me, Officer Tilly, is Officer Prosper a good cop?"

"Yes, sir, he is."

"Is he a good friend?"

Ramsey stands and says, "Objection. Relevancy?"

"Your Honor, I'm simply asking if the two officers are close."

The judge nods and says, "I'll allow it. Objection overruled."

Bobby asks again, "Is he a good friend?"

The officer thinks then says, "Yeah, he is. I mean, it's not like we get together after work and drink beer or nothing. He's single, I'm not, so, ya know…"

"Okay, thank you. You Honor, I'd like to reserve the right to recall this witness at a later time."

Sillenia makes eye contact with Bobby. Her eyes seem to say, "What are you doing?"

His says, "My job."

The judge instructs the State to call their next witness.

Ms. Ramsey looks down the table at her team and asks, "Does he have something on the cop I should know about? Who's he got on his witness list?"

An associate answers, "Just Mr. McKenzie, the guy who testified he dropped the drugs three years ago, and we checked both cops' credibility. They're good cops."

She continues, "Did you check to see if the witness showed up?"

Another associate answers, "I saw a black man wearing a Jaguars Starter jacket and some Jordans in the witness box."

Ms. Ramsey smiles and says, "That's him." Then she stands. "Your Honor, the people rest."

The judge looks over to the defense table and asks, "Very well. Is the defense ready to present its case?"

Bobby stands and answers, "Your Honor, we are. We'd like to call Officer Tillman back to the stand."

Ms. Ramsey looks at Bobby and then to the corridor to see the doors open and a very confused-looking Officer Tillman slowly making his way to the stand.

Bobby walks up to the stand with large tablets in each hand. He hands one to Officer Tillman.

"Officer Tillman, these are the transcripts of the testimonies given about three years ago. I figured you wouldn't remember the events today as clearly as you did then, so I took the liberty to help you through. Now, where I have it marked is where your testimony begins. You see it?"

The officer thumbs through it, finding the marker.

"Yes, sir."

"Please turn your attention to page 243, line 4. Question: How many people were in the area in reference to the building? Answer: Just those four. Now, being that we know there were seven people, which four were you talking about?"

The officer sits up in his chair and answers, "I was concentrating on the defendant and his guys, I guess."

"Okay. Could you please not guess so much here? There were five guys. How did you determine, assuming all of them could be armed, that Mr. Marks, one of the five men there, wasn't with Mr. Warrick?"

The officer takes a deep breath and says, "I guess… I mean…it was the way they were dressed."

"Oh, okay, you assumed, so Mr. Warrick and his boys were dressed nice?"

"Yeah."

"And I guess Mr. Marks and his daughters looked like they shopped at the Goodwill?"

Ramsey stands, stating, "Objection! Leading the witness!"

"Sustained!"

Bobby thumbs through the transcript.

"So although you knew the Mark's weren't part of the defendant's posse, you still questioned them?"

"Yes, sir, I made up contact cards and ran their names for priors."

"You did. You did that with all of the detainees, isn't that true, Officer Tillman?"

"Yes, sir, I did."

"Now, while you were talking with Mr. Marks and his two girls, did that pose a bit of a danger to your partner?"

"No, sir. We had secured Mr. Warrick as well as his associates."

"Handcuffed, zip thighs?"

"That's right, sir. I mean we had them on the trust pass, and we sat them down, and Officer Prosper stood observation while I ran the checks."

"Now, I don't understand something. They were being stopped for trespassing after a warning, but there is no record of that warning. Why is that?"

"I'm not sure."

"Did you recognize them from a prior stop?"

"No, sir. Officer Prosper did."

"He did?"

"Yes, sir."

"And he's a damn good cop to know everyone he's ever warned about trespassing and where. Wow! How does he do it?"

Ramsey stands and says, "Objection: calls for speculation."

"Sustained."

"Okay, tell me, Officer Tillman, the charge of resisting without violence, did you witness that?"

"Yes, sir."

"How did that happen?"

"The defendant was very vocal with his objection about being detained. He was very animated and obscene."

Bobby smiles and says, "Pissed you off, did he?"

Tilman smiles, saying, "Well, he wasn't talking to me at the time."

"According to these transcripts, this was before you called in on the Marks, wasn't it?"

"Yes, sir, we took care of the Marks first."

"Do you remember what my client said?"

The officer begins to think then says, "Something about how he knew how much money Officer Prosper had taken off him."

"Oh really, do you remember how much it was?"

Again, the officer pauses then says, "Well... I believe it was north of five hundred dollars."

Bobby shows the officer in the tablet the dollar amount.

"The transcript shows five hundred sixty-seven dollars thirty-seven cents. Is that about what you remember?"

"Yes, sir."

Ms. Ramsey stands and says, "Objection, Your Honor, does the defense have a destination with this line of questioning?"

Bobby interjects, "Your Honor, I'm almost finished with this witness, and I ask the court to indulge just a few more questions."

"Very well, Mr. Cox. Overruled."

Bobby walks over to the defense table and asks, "Okay, you didn't see the bag until your partner told you to pick it up, right?"

"That's right, sir, I missed it."

Bobby reaches into his briefcase and pulls out a brown paper bag.

"I went to a head shop in town and bought some of those little baggies. I filled them with salt, except for twenty of them—those I filled with oregano. I compared them to the State's exhibit A. Is this about the size of the bag you personally recovered?"

The officer looks at the bag and says, "Yeah, looks right."

Bobby then hands the bag to the jury. After they have examined it, Bobby picks up the bag, takes three steps away from the jury box, and drops it.

"Now you see, that's what's been bothering me about the facts of this case. This is a pretty nice-sized bag dropped in front you and what you describe to be a good cop from three feet away, and yet..."

Bobby goes back to the defense table and picks up another piece of paper.

"According to this police dispatch, there is no mention of the bag of dope for some twenty three minutes after, I repeat, thirty three minutes after the initial stop, almost like a, 'Hey what do we have here? This must belong to the guy with the gold teeth and roll in his pocket.' You see that, don't you, Officer Tillman?"

Tillman's eyes go straight to the jury box and then back to Bobby.

Ms. Ramsey stands and says, "Objection. Your Honor, does Mr. Cox have a question, or is he simply going to testify?"

The judge nods, saying, "Sustained. Mr. Cox, please refer your cross-examination to questions."

Bobby picks the bag up again and drops it again. He then kinda kicks it toward the jury box.

He shrugs his shoulders and shakes his head.

Then Bobby lights in, "Four dope boys, you're watching them for weapons, oops, they drop a bag in front of you, and you question them about trespassing, you're taking the time to count the money? I don't know if I wanna believe that! You're doing contact cards on little girls over there, and you're not even curious about this bag that's been lying here for ten, fifteen minutes over here? Is that what you're selling us over here?"

Ramsey objects, "He's badgering the witness."

But before the judge can rule, Tillman shouts back, "I never said I saw him drop the bag, my partner did!"

Bobby rushes up to the stand and looks Tillman right in the eye then says, "Yeah, well, do you believe 'em?"

Tillman hesitates but answers, "Yeah."

Bobby goes over to where the bag lies in front of the jury box.

"You say my client had five hundred dollars, I believe that. You said he was verbally abusive... I can buy that. Call him a dope boy!"

Bobby looks over at Warrick. Warrick smiles, the gleam of his twelve gold teeth sparkling.

"Yeah, he's certainly got that smile. But why should we believe something that you yourself just showed us all you are hesitant to believe?"

Ramsey stands, objecting, "Objection. Asked and answered, Your Honor?"

"Sustained."

"Here's a question for ya. You ready? First call was at eleven thirty-one p.m. You called in the stop. At eleven thirty-eight, you called in about warrants on seven suspects. At eleven forty-six you called in to ask for transport. At eleven fifty-four, you reported." He kicks the bag over by the witness stand. "That's when you reported the discovery of the drugs your partner says he saw a man drop. Now, do you really expect us to believe your partner saw the defendant drop this bag twenty-three minutes earlier?"

Tillman looks over at the jury again, but gives no answer.

Then Ramsey stands up and says, "Objection, Your Honor… asked and answered."

"Sustained."

Bobby looks over at the jury, then he looks at Tillman. He picks up the bag off the floor and turns to Ms. Ramsey.

"Your witness, Counselor."

Ramsey is quick from her seat.

"Officer Tillman, these seven people that you drove up on in the dead of night, may be thought to be drug dealers, is there a standard operating procedure when officers are outnumbered more than two to one?"

Tillman responds quickly, "Yes, ma'am. We use our own judgment to call for backup, but safety is always an issue."

Ms. Ramsey is clearly leading the officer to a way out, but within the confines of legality.

"So sometimes securing an area may take longer than others. Is that a true-enough statement?"

"Yes, ma'am."

"No further questions."

Bobby stands now, saying, "The defense rests, Your Honor."

The judge nods and says, "I'll hear closing statements in ten minutes."

At closing, Bobby begins. He steps to the judge, handing him a sheet of paper. He then puts one on the States table, and then he addresses the jury foreman.

"There was a list of instructions to remind you of case law, your rights that you have as the jury as granted by the Supreme Court. They have upheld this decision and recognize this as the law of the land. It is Paul vs. State of Criminal law 394.6(4).

"The key being, and I quote, 'District Court did not have to believe police officers testimony even when it is the only testimony offered. They went on to say in Paul vs. State that even though State's witnesses are uncontested or un-contradicted, the jury does not have to believe them.' Play the whole night over in your head. On paper, it sounds just like another drug bust, but in reality, this is exactly the kind of case Paul vs. State was written for.

"Ask yourself, is it reasonable to assume that bag sat there all that time…after an officer saw who dropped it? Or maybe a man— just like you and I—just got a little tired of seeing people make a comfortable living off of the pathetic illness of others and said, 'I found drugs, and big mouth's gonna take the rap.' Could that have happened? 'Cause, ya see, if that could have happened even in your mind, that's reasonable doubt. You look at my client, even in passing, and you think, no, he doesn't have a nine to five. No, he doesn't have to answer to an alarm clock or a boss whose trippin' 'cause she didn't get any the night before!"

He points toward Sillenia at the defense table and says, "He's got my whole paycheck in his smile! Is that his way of saying screw me? Or catch me if you can? Or maybe…it's just his *God*-given right as an American to express himself. Maybe he doesn't have a job—I don't know. What…what do you know him personally? 'Cause the only thing that's important about this case is, do you see this guy, with those teeth, in that neighborhood, dropping that bag in front of any cop uncontested for twenty-three minutes before *any cop* would have walked over and said, 'Hey, you dropped something, what do we have here?' and I believe you are pretty sure of that too. It is the State's job to present proof beyond a reasonable doubt as to the guilt of my client. Honestly, is what they're asking you to believe all that reasonable? Thank you."

Before Bobby can sit down, Ms. Ramsey is on her feet.

"The defense council is pretty good with smoke and mirrors, but what he's asking you to *not* consider is, you don't know what you don't know: the drama that goes along with being a police officer on a day-to-day basis in Jacksonville, Florida, and what are the procedures in these circumstances. As an officer, you want to do your job, but you also want to go home at the end of the day. Yes, they took twenty-three minutes to secure a crime scene. Hell, that might be a record for all we know when officers who are outnumbered more than two to one, but I don't think it changes the fact that Officer Prosper saw Mr. Warrick drop that bag. He's asking you to believe that, oh, that bag of drugs just happened to be lying there just as these guys just happen to be standing there and that his defendant was just carrying his income tax money 'round in his pocket.

Mr. Warrick was convicted in the first jury trial because it walked like a duck, and the first jury was not going to be fooled. Officer Prosper—he had a rookie beside him, and he took precaution. He secured the suspects. I think that says a lot about just how good a cop he really is… He's the kind that makes sure he and his partner go home at the end of a day. Thank you."

Bobby and Sillenia stay on hand after court in a lounge at the courthouse. Warrick is also being held in a waiting or holding cell.

Sillenia walks over and offers Bobby a cup of coffee.

"So what'd ya think?" she asks.

Bobby looks at her and then kinda stares into space.

"I don't know… I thought I had her on the ropes, but she pulled off one hell of a closing statement, didn't she?"

Sillenia raises her eyebrow.

"Why didn't you call McKinny to testify? He dropped the bag."

"Couldn't find him."

Now Sillenia is puzzled then asks, "So who was that inside the witness room?"

Bobby sighs and says, "That was my brother-in-law, Charles, I paid him $40.00 to sit in for an hour or two. I was trying to keep her concentrating on cross-examining him. The timing inconsistency of the dropped bag would catch her off guard."

Sillenia laughs, saying, "So that's why you spoke so loudly about there being seven people at the stop and not four."

"Yeah. I wanted Tillman to run with that mindset of defending that error. I figured he'd try to impress upon the jury the reasoning behind excluding the Marks family, and in doing so, he was constructing my case of what all was happening during the time the drugs lay dormant. The timeline would surprise him as well, and he'd realize he'd committed to it. I could get him to admit his partner's story was hard to believe, and he was there. Surely the jury would kick it out. But that Ramsey's good, and she didn't use the smile all that much either."

"That smile. What smile! I'm telling your wife about you!" She smiles.

"Cricket, she knows I'm a sucker for a smile, but I'm a slave to her eyes and in particular to her heart."

Sillenia also interjects, "Oh, and another thing, when did I ever come in as though I was…doing…without?"

Bobby laughs and asks, "We gonna go there?"

But his laughter is cut short by the sight of the bailiff standing in the lounge door.

"Attorneys, the jury is back."

Bobby and Sillenia enter the courtroom to find Ms. Ramsey and Mr. Warrick both already there. Ms. Ramsey signals to Bobby, and he goes over to her table.

"Mr. Cox, listen. I'm prepared to offer your client a deal before the verdict. I'm offering him time served on the possession. Deal's good for five minutes."

"What makes you think he wants a deal? The jury looked like they were leaning in our direction if you ask me."

"I hear ya, Mr. Cox, but I believe your client should have the final say on this being that if you lose, he goes back to Jackson CI for the next sixteen months and not you. You now have four minutes." She looks at her watch.

Bobby turns and hurries back to the defense table and Warrick, Sillenia standing by as he tells him.

"Look, Brent, the State has put time served on the table. This whole thing was about going home, son. I think you should take it."

Bobby looks at his watch.

"You've got three minutes to decide."

Warrick looks to the ground and then around the courthouse.

"I'd have a felony conviction, won't I?" Bobby nods. "And they get to say I did something that I really didn't do. Yeah...yeah, I'll take the deal."

Bobby turns to her and gives her the okay.

Shortly after the judge is announced. As he takes the bench, the DA informs him of the deal made by the State. The judge accepts the plea, and Warrick is shortly taken back to the county jail to be released.

Chapter 35

When We Dance

Back in St. Augustine, Lisa is home after a hard day at work. She opens the door, ready to tell her roommate of all the fun-filled events she missed on her day off.

Lisa turns the key to find Tracy in the middle of the living room, vacuuming and dancing to a song on her Walkman.

Lisa is pleasantly surprised with Tracy's rhythm. She sneaks in and closes the door unannounced to Tracy. The music is Outkast's hit song, "The Way You Move."

Lisa maneuvers herself by the hallway and near the sofa, just inches away as Tracy turns to see Lisa and screams,

"Ah!" She falls backward over the sofa. She lays spread out, yelling, "You cunt!"

Lisa is beside herself with laughter.

"Hell, that's as close as you've ever been to a cuss word. I'll take it."

Now Tracy is laughing

"Lisa. You have a dark side, girl! There's a place even the Easter bunny won't visit!"

Lisa looks puzzled.

"You've been talking to my mother?" Lisa replies.

Tracy nods and says, "Next time you check your medication, don't just check the date, make sure all the pills look alike!"

Lisa helps her up, and then they both sit and laugh.

Lisa tears into her, "So you dance good. How come you don't ever want to go dancing!"

Tracy takes a letter from her back pocket, saying, "I might be inclined."

Now Lisa screams, "Ahh! Aaron?"

"Yes!"

"Ahh, did you tell him I said hello!"

"Yes!"

"Did you tell him all about me?"

"Yes, yes, I did!"

Lisa's laughter digresses to a smile, then she says, "Wait, you... didn't really tell him, like...all about me...did you?"

"Oh, I cleaned you up, a lot, but without really lying, ya know."

Lisa nods then asks, "Them true lies?"

"Ya heard!"

They laugh.

"Hey, ya wanna go out?" Tracy says.

Lisa's eyes show the surprise.

"Uh, yeah, yeah, I'd love to. Where'd you have in mind?"

"I don't know, what about All Stars?"

"All Stars! I was there about two months ago. Girl, it was hot, you'll love it, and if not, I'll love it for ya."

Tracy nods, saying, "Say, we'll leave around nine. My treat."

Later that night the girls arrive at the sports bar.

The bar features two very large dance floors upstairs and down, TVs for the sports enthusiast, as well as pool tables and dartboards. The place is packed on most Friday nights, and tonight is no exception.

Tracy is dressed in designer jeans and a blouse, yet she is getting looks at all angles. Lisa is wearing a tight short skirt in keeping in character.

A man sends a waiter over to the table where the girls sit.

He informs Tracy that the man at the bar would like to buy her a drink.

Tracy smiles and declines, "No, thanks, but tell him I said thanks anyway..."

Lisa grabs the waiter by the hand and looks to Tracy, saying. "Girl, that's being rude. Tell the gentleman you're drinking a sloe gin fizz. I gotcha back." She smiles, and so does Tracy.

When the drink arrives, Lisa takes it, looks over to the young man, waves, and begins to sip the drink.

"See, Trace, he won't bother you now, seeing I'm the one with the drink."

"Yea, but what if he bothers you?"

"Don't worry." As she looks back over at the young man, she says, "I hope he wants to bother me. I've got my fingers crossed, girl."

"You oughta quit."

Lisa smiles and says, "Watch, Tracy. Next he's gonna come over for a dance, ya know that right, see if he can warn me up."

"I know, I know, and when he does, he's gonna find you don't even do cooled off."

Lisa's mouth drops open, saying, "Did you just call me a whore?"

Tracy's eyebrows raise with laughter

Lisa squints and says, "Oh no, trust me, he'll pay. If only a few more of these drinks. Oh, and by the way, if you get any more offers for drinks, they're called sloe gin fizz, ya got it?"

Tracy shakes her head and adds, "You know there's a name for me too. You have a designated driver."

"Girl, it's a good thing you wore those jeans."

The young man now approaches and asks Lisa to dance.

Tracy sits for the most part, drinking a Pepsi and watching Lisa dance and flirt.

She gets up to use the restroom. On the way back to the table, she bumps into an old friend.

"Tracy?"

She turns and looks at the table to find Jonny Blain sitting at the table near hers. He is with another guy and a girl.

"Tracy, that is you! How are you?!"

Tracy smiles and says, "Hi, Jonny, been a while, uh?"

"Yea, please sit with us for a moment."

Tracy checks over her shoulder to Lisa still on the floor and says, "Okay, but just for a minute."

Tracy sits, and Jonny introduces her to his friend and his date.

"This is Funk and Tish." Tracy just waves. "Wow, Tracy, you look great. I haven't seen you since…"

"Since the night Aaron went to jail, Jonny," Tracy interjects.

Jonny drops his head and exhales, "Yeah...yeah, since then You heard from AD?"

"Yeah, I got a letter from him today, as a matter of fact."

"So how is he?"

"He's good under the circumstances."

Jonny expresses major concern and says, "Look, if he needs anything, if you need anything, please let me give you my new number."

He takes a pen and pad from his blazer pocket. As he writes, he looks over to Funk.

"Funk, get the ladies something to drink. Tracy, what'll you have?"

Tracy looks over at Lisa who is now sitting at the table with her new friend.

"I'll have a sloe gin fizz."

Funk jumps up and is off to the bar. He returns shortly with drinks. He places everyone's drink in front of them but then calls Jonny aside.

He whispers in Jonny's ear and then points to some people across the floor. Jonny and Funk excuse themselves for a moment. Tracy can sense its some kind of drug deal. Lisa takes that opportunity to go over to the table where Tracy is sitting. She brings a glass almost empty with her. She places it in front of Tracy and takes the full one and drops her straw into it.

She smiles and jokes, "You seemed in need of assistance."

"Yeah, how 'bout you?" Tracy asks.

"Girl, he's got a 5.0, and my attention gotta go."

Lisa hurries back to the table with her new friend.

Tish grins as Tracy explains, "I'm the designated driver."

"Oh!" Tish responds.

"So, you know Jonny and Funk long?" Tracy asks.

"No, I just met them tonight. I go to school at Flagler."

"Oh! Really?"

Tish began to drink her drink. Tracy observes Lisa listening to her friend as she sips on her drink.

Tracy turns back to Tish and asks, "So what's your major?"

Tish doesn't respond. Tracy figures it's the music; it's too loud.

She raises her voice, "So what's your major!"

Tish kind'a turns her head toward Tracy with a blank expression on her face.

Tracy grins, saying, "Damn, girl, what you drinking?"

Tish still has no response. She just stares. Now Tracy's smile leaves her as she can see this could be something seriously wrong with her. She looks at the glass, and it's half empty. She turns toward Lisa who appears to be hanging on her new friend's every word. She studies Lisa.

Jonny and Funk come back to the table. At first, Tracy's attentions are still on Lisa, but she hears Funk's grin.

"See, check 'em out, dog. They're gone, baby. We can do anything we want to these whores."

Jonny smiles and kneels down in front of Tracy. She's fixed her eyes on Lisa and doesn't let on.

Jonny begins to smile and says, "Man, I been wanting to dig into her for years!"

Funk grins as he leads Tish to her feet and says, "Hey, man, now we still gonna switch, right? I mean, I want some of that myself."

"Yeah, yeah, but we gonna need pictures too. AD was my best earner, but she always fillin' his head with dreams of that work life. I'ma need something to keep her in check. She ain't gonna want nobody to see pictures of how I'ma handle her ass tonight ever never!"

Now Lisa's friend is waving his hand in front of Lisa's face and snapping his fingers. Lisa is unresponsive. Tracy quickly snaps to her feet and slaps Jonny in the face and pushes him into Funk. They fall.

Tracy screams, "What did you drug her with, Jonny! Get away from us!"

The people nearby have stopped what they were doing and observed some come to assist as Jonny and Funk try to play it off like the girls are fronting on him. Tracy grabs Tish by the hand and quickly leads her over to the table where Lisa is sitting.

She grabs Lisa's hand and asks the young man to help her.

As Lisa gets to her feet, there are now people between them, and some of them begin to intervene, giving Tracy and the girls a head start toward the exit.

Lisa's friend helps her get the girls in Tracy's car. Ten minutes later, she arrives at Flagler Hospital's emergency room.

Chapter 36

Aftermath

The girls are taken inside for treatment as Tracy waits in the waiting room. She is nervous and scared. Soon a nurse comes out and sits beside her.

"Excuse me, Ms. Austin?"

"Yes," Tracy answers.

"My name is Nurse Cox. I'm here to tell you your friends will be just fine."

"Oh, thank you so much." Tracy is relieved.

"Okay, but I'm gonna have to ask you some questions. How did they get like that, I mean, do you know what they took?"

Tracy shakes her head, saying, "No, but wait... Didn't you say they'll be okay?"

"Yes, yes, and they will, but...well, they had a controlled substance in them, and the method they ingested—it matters. The way it was introduced into their system can be important. It's policy for us to turn over cases such as these to the police. Now, I've got a feeling this wasn't self-induced. I mean, the way they are both dressed, I'm feeling like they were at a party or maybe a club, and maybe... someone put something in their drinks?"

Tracy is confused and scared. She doesn't trust what the police may do to her, especially after Aaron's warning, but Lisa's her best friend.

"Look, Nurse Cox, if I could help, really, I would. I went to the restroom at this club called All Star. I came back, and they were like...that, like zombies or something. I didn't see anything."

"Are you certain?" Cricket asks.

"Yes, yes. If I knew anything, I'd tell you."

"Okay. But you'll still have to write out a statement for the police, Ms. Austin. We had to notify them."

Tracy's head drops. Nurse Cox can see the anguish in Tracy's eyes.

"Is there a problem? Look, talk to me, Ms. Austin."

There is no response.

"Tracy, isn't it? Is there some reason you don't want to talk to the police?"

There is no answer as Tracy's eyes begin to survey the entrance door.

"Okay, Tracy, is there some reason why maybe...you can't talk to the police?"

Tracy's eyes are clearly fighting to refrain from tears. She nods.

Nurse Cox puts her arms around Tracy and asks, "Look...will you trust me?"

Tracy looks into the nurse's eyes. They seem sincere. Then she notices two uniformed policemen entering the hospital door. She jumps, but then then nurse gently restrains her.

"It's all right. Okay, I got you. Okay?"

Nurse Cox gets up and calls the two officers over. She folds the paper with Tracy's name on it and puts it in her pocket

"Officers, I'm the one who called."

"Is this the person we need to talk to?" the one officer asked.

"No, she's here for someone else. The young lady that brought in the two girls left already. She told me that she saw the girls in a nightclub called All Stars. They seemed ill, so she brought them here."

The cops look at each other.

"So you didn't get a name, an address, a plate?"

"I'm sorry, Officers, I was more concerned with the girls."

"What about the orderlies. maybe they saw something?"

"Actually, I was coming off break when the girl stopped me. She'd already set the two girls in the chairs by the door, gave me her story, and left."

The officers nod and asks, "So do you have a tox report of what was used on the girls? Have they been assaulted? Can we speak to them?"

"I'm afraid the report won't be ready till morning, and the girls are resting. You can see them in the morning. Now, at the risk of sounding rude, I really must get back to my patients. Would you excuse me?"

Nurse Cox turns and takes Tracy by the hand and leads her toward the double doors leading down the corridor of the hospital.

She leans Tracy's head on her shoulder and says, "Your grandmother is in a better place now."

Tracy fights to contain her joy. Once they are out of sight, Nurse Cox confronts Tracy.

"Now, ya wanna tell me why I just did that?"

Tracy is stunned by her candor. She stares at the nurse with eyes and mouth wide open.

"Tracy, please. Don't lie to me. I've lied enough for the both of us, okay. I simply feel that anybody who would take a chance on giving up their own freedom to help friends, you just may be worth the risk I just took for you. You seem like you can be a good friend. So can I. Talk to me."

Tracy exhales and says, "Yeah…you're right… You took a chance on me, and you deserve the truth. I haven't even told Lisa the truth. I don't really know where to begin, Nurse Cox."

"Well, why don't you start by calling me Cricket. My friends call me Cricket."

"Cricket?"

"It's a long story, but let's hear yours first. Okay, why can't you talk to the police?"

Tracy is hesitant but tells Cricket all about Aaron and the night he got arrested; how Aaron had told her to avoid the police.

The two talked, and a friendship unfolds. As morning approaches, Cricket goes into an empty room where Tracy sleeps. They have talked and decided that Lisa should disappear at the earliest safest possible time to avoid another confrontation with the police.

She has heard Tracy's story and has compassion for one so young and yet mature. Hours later, she awakens Tracy, and the two go upstairs to Lisa's room. Upon entering the room, Cricket directs Tracy to the closet where Lisa's clothes hang as she awakens Lisa.

"Hey...hey." She gently shakes Lisa.

Lisa begins to push Cricket away, saying, "Uh...hey! Okay, okay, I'm awake. Damn, I got a headache. Call me in, Trace. Tell mom I lost a pillow fight. It's code. She'll know what it means."

Cricket gives Tracy a look of surprise and asks, "Aside from the headache, how do you feel?"

Lisa looks around the room and at the IV in her arm. Then she looks up at Cricket and Tracy.

"*Okay*, what happened?" she asks.

"You were at a club... You got drugged," Cricket explains.

"Drugged!" she says with a confusion in her eyes. But then she smiles. "That skirt was killing it! Were there like three of 'em? I saw these three guys checking me out. Please tell me they use protection?"

She looks under the cover as though to check herself, and then she looks at Tracy.

"Did you get any phone numbers?"

Cricket covers her mouth in shock.

Tracy grins and says, "Yeah, she's okay."

Penny look back to Lisa and explains, "You were given Rohypnol, or as it's more commonly called Roofies. Your friend here saw you were in trouble and, at what could have been her own peril, fought to get you here safely and without harm."

Lisa looks up at Tracy and then at Crick.

"So you're telling me... Yeah." Lisa looks again under the cover then turns from under the cover to Tracy. "Yeah, that sounds like something you'd do."

Then she shakes her head and continues, "Kid, how many times I gotta tell ya timing is everything."

Cricklet jaw drops, and they refrain from laughter as they watch Lisa get dressed and mumble to herself.

Tracy smiles and says, "Yep, she's back to normal."

Cricket rolls her eyes toward Tracy and laughs.

Cricket tells Tracy to get the car and meet Lisa outside. She tells Lisa to come with her, and she'd sign her out so that there would be no communications with orderlies.

Chapter 37

The Dye

It's Monday at St. Augustine High School. Hundreds of kids scatter the hallways and their lockers and going to class.

Special Agent Dillard is undercover as a custodian and has observed the mail lady drop off the mail to the secretary in the principal's office. He studied her routine of going to the teacher's lounge and placing the mail into the individual mail boxes in the teacher's lounge.

The teachers are gathered together before class, socializing with each other.

He has created a spill close by to observe the lounge in hopes of seeing who'll exit with the letter from Mickelson. The letter has been treated with phosphorus dye. Agent Dillard is wearing sunglasses that are able to pick up the dye.

The teacher leaves the lounge before the bell, but no luck.

Once the lounge is empty, he goes in and checks the boxes. The envelope is not there. He takes the trash bucket and sees the open envelope. He then places the trash bag into the bag on his cart to retrieve it privately.

Just then the principal, Mr. Strikland, comes up with another janitor. He orders Dillard to follow him and leaves the other older janitor to finish Dillard's work.

He then leads Dillard to a mess left in the boy's bathroom. He explains the older man has seniority and so he'd be expected to take on the brunt of the work.

Elsewhere in the school, a man reads the coded message sent by Mickelson. He then writes a brief letter and, walking to the teacher's lounge, places the letter in the box of Mr. Fells, the English teacher.

Fortunately, there is trace residue on the new letter, and Dillard now has a name.

Chapter 38

The Intersection

Later that night, Cole and Ricks sit inside a sedan parked along the A1A Interstate Highway. They have been sitting there for some time.

There is mostly silence as they listen through the static of a police scanner, monitoring police activity in the area.

While Ricks sits under the wheel, Cole's phone rings.

"Cole, it's me."

Cole raises the window between the front seat and the back for privacy.

Cole asks, "What'd ya got?"

The man on the other end sounds confused.

"Okay, ya got be straight with me, Cole. Is this some kinda test?"

Now Cole is confused and asks, "What are you talking about?"

The man says, "He was one of ours, Cole."

Cole is silent, and the man asks again, "Did you hear what I said? Cole, he was one of us."

Cole responds, "Yeah, yeah, Mickey, listen. Talk to nobody about this. I'ma need you to be careful Okay. But I need to know, what's his origin? Who did he work for, and what division?"

The man agrees, "I'll do my best."

Just then, Ricks voice come in over the speaker, "He's on his way."

"Good," Cole responds as he hangs up.

Cole then nods to Ricks, who flashes his headlights twice.

"Hey, this looks like our boy," says Ricks as he turns into A1A.

The vehicle is a royal-blue SUV turning into the gated community of Ocean Palm's.

As the SUV stops, the window comes down, and the driver reaches over to punch in his code. Suddenly there's a tap on the passenger-side window. The driver turns to see a sawed-off shotgun pointed at him.

Then another man opens the driver's door and presses the unlock button.

A man jumps into the back seat and pulls the driver into the back seat with great force.

A second man quickly jumps into the driver seat as the man with the shotgun jumps into the passenger's side and continues to train the shotgun on the man pulled into the back seat.

The new driver then backs the SUV up and drives back out onto A1A.

Ricks passes in front of the SUV which follows them down the street under the cover of night.

The two vehicles turn off a deserted dirt road.

The road is a closed-off state park. Another man in the road removes the chains that seal off the park.

As the vehicles pass, the man puts the chains back in place.

The vehicles stop, and Cole gets out of the sedan and gets into the passenger-side back seat of the SUV, carrying a brief case.

Then he addresses the young captive.

"Good evening, Mr. Blain. My name is Cole, and though we've never met, I'm a fan of yours." Cole smiles.

Jonny's speech is stammered.

"Hey, if this is about that scandal, look, I'm innocent. They want me to come back, and I'll be there next year!"

Cole laughs as he looks around at his men. Pointing at Jonny, he says, still laughing,

"You believe this guy? No, you're not. We made damn sure of that, but damn...the composer. The delivery of such a mammoth lie in the face of adversity. Truly impressive. Hell, if it wasn't me paying you off, I might have believed you, but who gives a shit about basketball anyway? No, I'm a fan of your extracurricular activities."

Jonny looks around the vehicle and says, "My what?"

Cole looks him directly in the eyes.

"Aw, come on, Jonny, you're a dope dealer, and a rather good one, I might add. And you've been recruited to play for our all-star team. We even have a signing bonus."

Cole pats his hands against the briefcase.

Jonny looks into Cole's eyes and says, "I don't know what you're talking about."

Cole nods at the man in the driver's seat. He jumps out and runs back to the sedan.

"Look, Jonny, we're not getting anywhere like this."

Just then Ricks climbs into the driver's seat and looks back at Jonny, saying, "Hiya, kid, remember me?"

Jonny's eyes stretch, exclaiming, "What the hell!"

Jonny looks at Cole who reaches across to the front passenger side, pushing the sawed-off shotgun away from Jonny's face.

"We're the ones who set you up, Mr. Blain, but they don't have enough to convict you or even to kick you out of school—truth be told—that is, not unless they get pictures, recordings, sworn testimonies. Your dream's not gone, Mr. Blain. We can give you back your dream in one year, and you'll be old enough to go Lotto, but first, you goin' to work for us."

"What do you want from me?" Jonny asks.

"We just want you to sell dope, but on a grander scale. You tell us who the competition is, we kill 'em." Cole laughs as he looks around the vehicle. "We leave you the sole source of distribution for the city, and we even provide police protection. You get a house just down the street from your mom's right there in Ocean Plains and a front job to explain your lavish lifestyle, so what da ya say, kid? You in?"

Cole smiles then continues, "Or do you want to look behind door number two where we just take your ass apart for a few hours before we put one in your nose?"

Now Cole's smile is gone. Jonny looks into Cole's eyes and can see he's serious.

Jonny begins to smile, so does Cole. "Yeah, hell yeah, I'm in."

Cole then puts the briefcase in Jonny's lap.

"In here"—Cole opens the briefcase—"is the key to 4143 Casta Verda, your new home."

Jonny looks down into the briefcase, and his eyes stretch as he looks at stacks of fifties and hundred-dollar bills.

Cole can see the greed in his eyes.

"Yeah, kid, I told you, you get a signing bonus. That's fifty thousand dollars for openers."

You can hear Jonny swallow as Cole continues, "There's also a key to a front real estate office on A Street off A1A. The secretary will call you Monday with directions. She'll be expecting you Monday, so you have time to make some phone calls, buy some suits. Inside the house you'll find up in the fireplace some packages. You can start our work right away. Now, remember, we can give you back your career, if you still want it, but if you fuck us, I'll do ya mother in front of you—slowly, by the way—and then I'll do you, and we'll simply replace you with someone else. Got me?"

Jonny nods then asks, "So how do I get your money to you?"

Cole smiles and says, "Good question, smart question. I like that. We'll let you know on Monday when you go in to work. 9:00 a.m., suit and tie, don't be late."

Cole gives a head signal, and they all exit the SUV, leaving Jonny in the back seat with the briefcase.

Chapter 39

The Lending Hand

In Jacksonville, Bobby Cox has just had a long day at work and pulls into his driveway. He parks his car and leans back to rest himself and stare at his home in relief. He makes his way to the door, and as he enters, the aroma of something cooking is a pleasant and welcome surprise.

He throws his briefcase on the sofa and calls to Penny, "Crick! I'm home!"

"I'm in the kitchen," she replied.

Bobby walks down the hall and turns into the kitchen where Penny is standing in her robe with her back to him, attending the stove.

"Hi, honey, something smells…"

He stops in his tracks as Penny turns around. Her robe is open, and she is almost wearing his favorite nightie.

"Good," he continues.

She smiles, and while reaching behind herself, she turns the knob on the stove until he hears a click, indicating the stove is turned off.

She replies in her sexiest voice, "You're just in time. Everything's ready."

Bobby smiles as he loosens his tie and walks toward her.

"This seems planned."

She begins to walk toward him.

"Attorneys…" she says as she reaches over the counter to hit the remote.

Suddenly Bobby can hear Seal's musical rendition, "Kiss From A Rose."

As she looks into his eyes, she continues, "You're so suspicious."

They walk slowly, almost passing each other as their shoulders rub. They turn a slow circle.

Then she says, "Well, I guess not everything is ready," as she turns her eyes to his coat.

He rears his shoulders back as she reaches across him, sliding the jacket to the floor as they move in slow circles, softly rubbing their cheeks against each other's.

He then pulls her gently to himself as though they begin slow dancing.

The music plays and they are in perfect rhythm with each other as she begins to unbutton his shirt. Now their faces meet each other's, lips barely touching as to brush against each other's. Now their cheeks softly touch. There is the scent of her hair that is enticing.

Their tongues meet as to savor each other's flavor. She begins to kiss him on his neck.

"Crick, when was the last time we made a day of this?"

She runs her tongue up his throat, reaching his chin.

"Way too long," she replies as he takes her bottom lip into his mouth and begins to suck softly on it, and then they kiss.

Now she is reaching for his belt buckle, and he has unrobed her.

"Can you make a day of this? I mean, in your condition and all?" he asks.

"Oh yeah, baby, I can do this for another month." She smiles.

Bobby's pants drop, and he steps out of both pant legs and shoes. Then he scopes her off her feet, their lips locked in passionate embrace. He turns toward the bedroom when, *ding, dong*, the doorbell rings.

They stop kissing, and their eyes meet. Then they laugh.

Ding, dong.

Bobby looks in the direction of the door and then to Pat.

"What da ya think?"

Cricket sighs and says, "Well, both the cars are out front. It may be important."

Ding, dong.

"So is this!" He laughs as he puts her down.

She grabs her robe.

"I'll get the door. After they leave, put the cars in the garage, okay?" she says laughingly.

Bobby rushes to get dress while Pat opens the door.

There stands a well-dressed young black man who asks, "Ah, hi. Does Attorney Bobby Cox live here?"

"Yes, he does. Who's calling?" she asks.

"My name is Brent Warrick. He represented me."

Now Bobby comes to the door.

"Mr. Warrick? It's been a while. How are you?"

The two shake hands as Penny steps behind her husband.

"What can I do for you?" Bobby asks.

"Well, no, I'm good. I mean, I'm all right. See, when I was in the courtroom, they wouldn't let us take anything in there with us but our own court stuff, ya know. But I promised someone back in the Graceville Work Camp that if you were the real deal, ya know, a good man, I'd give you this."

He hands Bobby a manila envelope. He looks at it and hands it off to Cricket.

"The same guy who done my work did this one for this guy too. It's a surprise the guy doesn't even know he's got an appeal in. Anyway, I hope you don't mind me stopping by like this. I got your address out of the book."

"No, no, it's okay." Bobby nods.

"Okay, well, look, I'll be going. Looks like I might have come at a bad time."

He smiles. Bobby smiles too.

"Okay, Mr. Warrick. I'll take a look at it. See what I can do."

"Okay, and hey, thanks again too for what you did for me."

"Okay." Bobby starts to close the door as Mr. Warrick turns, but then he turns back.

"Oh! Mr. Cox."

Bobby catches the door. "Yeah?"

Warrick drops his head for a second but then looks straight into Bobby's eyes.

"Those things... I really didn't drop that dope...ya know."

Bobby nods and says, "Yeah? I believe yea, so what are you doing these days?"

Warrick drops his head again. He looks off, and then back in Bobby's eyes.

"You really want to know?" The look in his eyes says it all.

"No...no, I don't think I do, Brent." Bobby smiles.

Warrick smiles and says, "It won't be forever, ya know. Some'em got to give. I made some mistakes, and they still fresh on my record. I made some bad choices, and they all in my grill. In time though, right? Right though... Still got to pay them bills, ya know."

Bobby nods, saying, "Yeah, I know. Well, good luck to you, and good night."

Warrick starts down the sidewalk.

Penny holds up both set of car keys and smiles.

"Yeah!"

Bobby grabs the keys. He rushes out to put the cars away. After a while, he rushes back inside.

He's beelining for the bedroom, unbuttoning his shirt, when he catches a glimpse of Penny in the living room as he passes by. He turns back to see her sitting in a chair, the manila envelope on the floor and papers in both her hands. There is a look of concern on her face.

Bobby assesses the situation. "You're kidding, right? This is you messing with me right now, right?"

"Uh?" Penny looks up at him.

"Since when are you so interested in my legal briefs?" He smiles, eyebrows raised.

She looks at him with a solemn look of surprise.

"Bobby, I know this guy... Well, I don't know this guy, but I know somebody who knows him. I know this case!"

Bobby can see she is serious.

"What, like, from school or something? How do you know the case?"

170

Penny begins to tell him about meeting Tracy and Lisa and everything she told her about that night.

"Bobby, ya gotta get him out of prison."

Bobby nods and says, "I'll see what I can do, babe…in the morning."

She looks into his eyes and then, "You're right." She puts the brief on the table, and Bobby pulls Crick from the floor into his arms. Now her eyebrows raise. "But promise me you'll give him top priority, Bobby. Like next of kin, okay?"

Chapter 40

Tanked

Rodgers and Billips put into the Dairy Queen on San Marco, and once inside, Roger asks Billips to order him the combo meal.

Rodgers takes a seat.

Some thirty minutes later, as they both finish their meals, Rodgers become fixated on something out the window. Billips turns as suddenly a man gets off his bike and heads inside the restaurant.

The man passes by and drops a piece of paper down by Rodgers's feet. Rodgers then knocks a spoon of the table and reaches down to retrieve both the paper and the spoon. He then begins to read it aloud.

"Blue town car, parked just next door. No one exited the car."

Billips is confused and asks, "Who was that? What's going on?"

Rodgers calmly finishes his shake and tells Billips, "This is me keeping us alive. We're being tailed, and they've never seen them before. I don't think the cops are on to us, so I'm guessing Mickelson's men. No telling what kind of poison Cole has put in his mind. I told you how paranoid he was at the last meeting. Man sees spooks everywhere. We're gonna need to be on our game from here on out. They won't bother us now. They need our connections, and they don't know who all they are. While we have time, partner. Start saving ya money, buddy. We may have to leave abruptly."

Chapter 41

The Redirection

Tick, tick, tick, tick. The metronome's metal balls hit against each other in the office of Mickelson in Deerwood Estates.

The metronome is on Cole's desk as he lays his head along the desk, watching the balls in play as his mind wanders.

Mickelson reads the paper and occasionally studies Cole.

"I had a thought concerning that off-duty policeman from Putnam County that was murdered. So close to St. Augustine and all. One would think, being so close to St. Augustine, the ground-work for our friends in St. Johns County to befall—what is it you Americans call them—serials is ever increasing."

Cole smiles but doesn't take his eyes off the metronome.

Mickelson continues, "So have you uncovered any suspicious activity with those two. Heard of any suspicious after-hours long-term meeting with internal affairs?"

Cole eyes don't move when he responds, "Naw."

"Well, it's been a week. Surely, they would have slipped up by now, don't you think?"

Cole takes a big breath and exhales. He pulls himself off the desk and walks over to Mickelson's desk.

"Ya know, this rock we call the earth is supposed to be moving at six feet per second. Now, that's pretty damn fast, if you ask me. But just because we are not all falling all over each other, wasting our coffee, doesn't change that fact."

"The point being…"

"Why take chances? I say, let's throw 'em a body."

Mickelson sighs and says, "Good lord, dear boy"—he laughs—"which one did you have in mind?"

Cole sits on Mickelson's desk.

"Now, that's what I was thinking about. See, if they are connected to Billips, Rodgers, and us, the only way to know for sure what's there is through the school. So I say we get a record of the most recent employees going back the last six months. One of them is probably a plant. We watch 'em, and the one that's most shady, we take 'em out and watch what kind of people come around the body."

Mickelson sits back in his seat. He folds his hands together before his face.

"That's very good, Mr. Cole. I like it. And if our cops are clean, we don't bring any unwarranted heat on us. If they're not, we send them a subtle message. I'll get us a printout tomorrow, and we'll begin from there."

"Yeah."

"But about Rodgers and Billips. I mean, if they are being followed, it means perhaps they have other interests that are presently bringing attention to themselves."

Cole smiles and says, "That would make them hot. Hot is hot."

Mickelson turns toward the window in his revolving chair.

"I suppose you're right. They would indeed have a bargaining chip in us, don't they?"

"Yes, they do. It's just too bad there's some maniac out there, killing off-duty police officers in the tri-county area." Cole smiles.

"Quit." Mickelson smiles and continues, "Of course, this maniac hasn't killed two of them at the same time before, but I suppose there's a first time for everything."

Cole smiles again.

"I suppose so."

"Yes, well, let's first see who's watching. That way, we can best determine what it is there looking for."

Cole looks confused and asks, "I don't follow."

"Well, seems to me that they've been on a stakeout for the better part of the week."

"So?"

"So if you were the local police and watching some dirty cops, why not loosen their reins so that they may go out freely and do something…dirty?"

Cole lights a cigar and says, "I see ya point."

Chapter 42

And Baby Makes Three

Back at the federal building, Bobby Cox is working a little late. Kaddy has decided to stay with him and take notes as she studies Bobby's tactics in working cases.

They have both become worn and decide to call it a night. Kaddy takes her notes back to her desk as Bobby closes the files.

He begins to put it all away when he sees the Daniels file underneath, a file he'd promised his wife he would work on... *Like next of kin*, he thinks to himself.

He'd laid it out hours ago with the intent of researching it and hopefully taking home some good news. He presses his office phone as he opens the Daniels file.

Kaddy answers, "Yeah, Boss."

"Kaddy, you go ahead. I'll be another half hour or so."

"You found something?"

"Uh? Oh, no, no, it's just something I promised Crick."

"Oh, okay. Hey, I'll be another fifteen minutes or so, getting stuff together out here. How 'bout I make us both a cup of coffee for the road?"

"Kaddy, I love ya."

Then he buzzes, "*No raise*," and he smiles, as he can hear Kaddy's laughter in the other office.

Bobby opens the police affidavit and begins to read, but then the phone rings, and shortly Kaddy buzzes in, "Bobby, it's Crick."

Bobby picks up the phone.

"Hi, honey."

"Hi yourself. So you are coming home tonight?"

Bobby smiles and says, "Yeah, honey. I won't be much longer. I'm working on the Daniels kid case as we speak, but if you want me to stop…"

"No, no, I… I just kinda missed ya."

"You missed me? Since this morning? Uh-oh, this sounds like the part where you ask me to bring home some pistachio, peppermint ice cream, and artichokes. Please don't make me watch that again."

"No, silly. If you must know, I was about to do laundry, and I picked up a sweater of yours, and I got all caught up in your scent and…"

Bobby stops her, "Penny, Penny, I can't hear you. What's all that racket? Sounds like a siren?"

"Oh yeah! That's why I called. I guess I got so excited that my water broke!"

"What!" Bobby is shocked.

"I knew there was something else I meant to mention!"

Bobby becomes excited.

"Could have lead with that one, honey! Yeah, that's like something else! Wait! Don't panic! I'm on my way! Kaddy just made coffee, okay!"

Crick laughs and says, "Bobby, I don't think they'll let me drink coffee."

"Yeah, you can't drink coffee!" Then he yells into the outer office, "Kaddy! We can't have coffee! Penny, look, don't panic. They'll be no coffee!"

"Bobby, calm down. I'm getting into the ambulance, as we speak. I'll meet you at Baptist Hospital, okay. Don't—come—home. I'm not there, okay?"

"Yes, okay, Baptist Hospital! What room?"

Penny laughs and says, "I don't know what room, just ask for the maternity ward. I'm sure you'll find me, okay, baby. I'm leaving now"

"So am I. I'll beat you there!"

"If you do, Bobby, promise you won't start without me."

"I promise, babe, I swear! *Kaddy*!"

Within twenty minutes, Bobby and Kaddy arrive at Baptist Hospital.

They rush into the hospital to the front desk as Bobby promptly gets the attention of the on-duty nurse.

"Hi, my name is Bobby Cox. My baby's having…no, wait, my baby's…my wife, do you have a Patricia Cox here? And I'm her husband, Bobby Cox."

The nurse grins as she checks the registration.

"Yes, sir, she just arrived, and she's in the delivery room 3."

The nurse calls in an orderly, "Would you show Mr. Cox to the delivery room 3 and inform the doctor that he's here."

Within minutes, Bobby is dressed in a surgical gown and mask. He is escorted into the delivery room and later would witnesses the birth of his daughter, Charlie Parker Cox.

Chapter 43

Blain Thang

The next day finds Jonny Blain giving birth to a baby of his own. This real estate business is his dream come true. Though he doesn't have a license, the organization has him with a bogus test score, and he's already grasping the concept.

The organization supplies his company with seemingly wealthy prospects looking to buy homes. They buy a series of houses already owned by other questionable clients. Then they take the property value of the house up as the house is purchased each time for more money after they submit a bogus renovation. Each buyer deposit moneys through their prospective relator to clean the drug money through the real estate company. The other monies from the bank go back to the organization. Where is unknown to him.

He's also reestablished himself in the streets of St. Augustine through supplying more and more street dealers. He's met with Mr. Fells (the St. Augustine High School teacher), and they put together their setup to distribute to street dealers and at the same time keeping the heat off himself and the real estate company. He doesn't know that Mr. Fells has always been a part of this organization or that Fells is how he became known to Mickelson.

To Jonny Blain, this life is a dream come true. Not only does he get a percentage of the profit, but he also gets a pretty healthy paycheck.

Chapter 44

Territory

Back at the justice building, Danny King walks the corridor to Rollie's office with files and a manila envelope under his arm. Shortly he enters.

"Rollie, we got a break on the drop wire theory of execution. Your friends at Counterterrorism got a complete signal. There's a house at an address 1440 Blanding Boulevard. We sent Hutch and an undercover unit to take a look. They report a single-story house with three bedrooms, two baths, and there's a six-foot privacy fence, motion detector, and indication of heat sensors."

Rollie smiles and says, "See, now that's interesting."

"I thought so too. I asked the counterterrorist unit to use their satellites and take a peek. There is some kinda supercomputer transmitting data and acting as a switchboard in there, complete with a scrambling unit. We know it's the reason we haven't been able to trace the phone line at the Manson, but that kind of tech isn't being generated for privacy issues only. There's got to be something more."

Rollie looks as though his mind is moving with thoughts of possibilities.

"Even the wealthiest of South American drug lords don't have this kind of infrastructure in protecting their product. What else is Mickelson involved in? We need to get a good look. Can we get inside?"

Danny shakes his head and says. "I don't know, Rollie. Even a federal judge would have to see we're fishing for evidence to bring against a license attorney. And the security devices were the ones we detected outside of the house. Who knows what measures they took to protect their privacy inside, and bear in mind, Mickelson can't be tied directly to this property on paper."

"You're right, and being that's a residential neighborhood with that much security, the house may be rigged to take the whole block up."

"Oh, on another note," Danny says as he's reaching inside the envelope. He places some photos on Rollie's desk. "These came out of St. Augustine today. We made some of Mickelson's men watching Billips and Rodgers. I guess you were right about Cole's eye for details."

"That's not good. Did we get made?"

"Oh, no way. We stayed off sight and used a sniper's scope lens to detect them."

"Good, Danny, but that still doesn't give us much time to work with. If they're watching them, then they're worried about 'em, and they are not the type to lose sleep for very long."

Danny nods in agreement and asks, "You wanna pull 'em in?"

"No, not yet. What would we do with 'em? They are not going to incriminate themselves on speculation. They'd just lawyer up. Now, from the profile I read on them, Billips would be the one to go after. But we need something on them. We need to tie them to something so they'd consider the prospect of certain death was inevitable and they'd need our protection."

"Yeah, but having that bargaining chip kinda puts them on the hot seat. Rollie, how much time do you think they can afford?"

"I don't know. We need to"—Rollie pauses—"wait...okay. Let's look at this from another angle for a minute, Danny. What if we could increase their worth?"

Danny smiles and says, "Increase their worth... Okay, but how?"

Rollie stands and walks around the desk.

"The best thing about having crooked cops on the payroll is the vast amount of info they can provide, yes?"

Danny nods and says, "Okay."

"So we need something big, a leak, straight drama, something to go through the St. Augustine narcotics department, something that would be verifiable. Mickelson will have to both buy it and swallow it. Something he'd want to monitor closely and would require a man on the inside to do so."

"Okay, what do you have in mind?"

Rollie smiles and says, "Well, I'm thinking…what if there were suddenly word of competition coming into St. Augustine, ya know, heavy weights. The kinda name that gets an eyebrow raised. Someone MicKelson couldn't just push around. What would he do?"

Danny thinks for a second.

"He'd wanna keep tabs. He might even wanna speed up on the hostile takeover of whatever he's looking at to make sure he's established and had to be dealt with, or he could feel as though my cops had made a deal and were trying to set me up."

"Exactly!" Rollie clutches his fist and continues, "Now you get the picture. The press is on. They'll have at act, and act now, and since they'll still need their cops long enough to check out the information, Rodgers and Billips are still on the board. Get me a DEA report on a major drug dealers who's been out of arm's reach a while. I'm talking big like Michael Jackson, and twice as hard to interview. We'll need associates. I want to know this someone is not an old affiliate of anyone in that house or in that orbit."

Danny takes out his pin and pad as Rollie continues, "Also get with Sheriff Rease. We're going to need his help. If we're wrong, then he needs to know two things: one, his two dirty cops are dead, and two, their replacement are probably staring him right in the face."

Danny nods and turns toward the door.

Then he stops and asks Rollie, "Oh yeah, I meant to ask you, what do you think about this? Mickelson has goons on his payroll with various degrees in something or another. That guy Ricks has a degree in computer science."

Rollie looks confused and asks, "Degrees?"

"Yeah, a couple of these guys graduated from the likes of USC, Alburn, Ohio State, Ole Miss, and Georgia Tech. They're all ex-military, and they all used their GI bill."

Rollie looks over the file Danny hands him.

"Interesting. They never disband. They all got their degrees on line right here in bold city. Did KOAS give us anyone that could be connected to Mickelson or Cole at St. Augustine High? I mean, maybe we need to go back deeper. I'm thinking sleeper status. Mickelson's been here for years, but we just recently discovered his drug organization. Yeah, go back about ten years and see who was at the school then. That's still there. Now we know about the teacher's name, Fells, but not enough. There's nothing there to indicate he's more than a go-between, probably never even met his handler."

Now Danny is thinking and says, "Okay, Rollie, I'm with ya. This guy probably picked Fells from among the staff. He'd be smart enough to profile the character flaws to turn his man without actually exposing himself to the target. Guys like that don't grow on trees. I'll get right on it."

*****

The next day the chief of police calls a meeting at the sheriff's department for narcotics officers. Rodgers and Billips are there along with undercover agents and vice. They sit in the squad room as Sheriff Rease reads a prepared memo handed down to him by Justice.

"I have just received word of a possible syndicate organization interest in relocating their organized crime family into the St. Augustine, St. Johns County area."

The sheriff holds up a picture, and both Rodgers and Billips are at first stunned, but they are pleasantly surprised as the sheriff continues.

"This is a picture of Antwon Vega, a known drug lord out of the Argentina. He's believed to have ties with the Africans syndicate as well as the Columbians. He is considered dangerous in his own right. Now, this guy's supposedly has access to some pretty advanced hardware, and a small army to boot, so bulletproof vests are no longer optional. We're gonna try to collect some photos of some of his hitch men in the near future. I'll keep you informed as the information comes in to me. That's all. Hit the streets."

Before long, Rodgers and Billips are off in their patrol car, and Rodgers is on his cell phone.

Cole answers, "Yeah."

"We got a problem."

"What's up?"

"Have you ever heard of a heavy name Antwon Vega?"

"Vega…yeah, I heard it. The question is, how'd you hear it?"

Rodgers looks over at Billips and smiles as they drive along US 1.

"Well, it would seem he's also expressing some interest in the real estate business in our little town."

Cole looks over at Mickelson, who is looking at Cole with concern. He knows who Vega is as well.

"So where did you hear this?"

Rodgers explains, "We just got briefed by the sheriff himself. I figure this guy's gonna make trouble. Maybe bring a bit of attention to what we're trying to do."

"Yeah…yeah, you did good. We'll get back at ya." The phone hangs up.

Rodgers screams with laughter as he turns to Billips.

"Ya missed it! Cole's scared! I could hear it in his voice! Boy, I'd pay good money to see his face right now."

Meanwhile at the mansion, Cole looks at Mickelson.

"I don't buy it. The timing's all wrong. I believe they are being busted, and they're trying to buy time till they can set us up."

Mickelson turns and glances through the picture window.

"Maybe. We can't afford Vega, or to be hasty on this. No, let's solidify our standing in St. Augustine, get Ricks ready. I'll have some mail to send in the morning for him. In the meantime, get me some people in the streets over there and continue to shadow our officer friends and monitor their activities."

Chapter 45

At First Glance

At the Graceville Work Camp, long after the sun has gone from the sky, all is quiet as the inmates have long since been put to bed.

Aaron tosses and turns in his sleep as an uneasy feeling (like the rush of the wind) invades his dream. He is suddenly somewhere beyond the gates, just off in the woods, in the dead of night. He feels he is not there, but he can see the still of the night within the woods, and yet he can feel the disturbance of peace.

His eyes begin to scan the forest. Suddenly he sees a figure of a man walking through the woods toward him. He is seemingly walking unimpeded right through the trees and brush of the forest.

Aaron can hear his footsteps of a ghost as each step echoes this crushing sound of leaves beneath his feet. Now the specter is making his way across the field of the restricted area around the gates outside the prison. In a matter of moments, he has passed through the gates and across the recreation yard to find he is now standing at the side of Aaron's bed.

Aaron looks up at the dark specter. He has no face. He is caped and wearing a floppy brim upon his head. There is only the white of what appears to be a priest's collar about his neck, a white of brilliance and gleam. His clothing seems old and tattered. The whites of his eyes seem to almost glow through the dull void that is his face.

Aaron is uneasy but not afraid. The specter reaches out his hand to Aaron. Aaron is at first reluctant, but a warm feeling of trust comes over him, and he takes the specter by the hand. As he stands, he looks to his bunk to see himself still laying in bed. Then he looks back to the specter.

"Am I dead... Are you Death?"

"Come and see what I see," the specter replies.

Suddenly they're off through the ceiling and into the rush of the wind in the cover of night.

Aaron holds the Spector's hand and then looks upon the city lights and the maze of buildings and tree lines that make up the city of Graceville.

In an instant, he can feel a great shift, and he sees mountains, valleys, and great rivers. Aaron's excitement far exceeds anything he's ever felt before. Never had he even imagined such in expressible feeling of freedom.

Now they are circling the Stature of Liberty as the lights radiate her massive beauty that has illuminated the darkness for decades with visions of hope and light unto all her shores.

Aaron screams with excitement, and now suddenly he sees the Liberty Bell and the Justice, the cascading night lights brings to the great bell of glory.

Aaron looks into the specter's face without form.

"Show me more!" Aaron pleads.

The specter turns his head back toward the city, and Aaron can feel the descent in speed, and he turns around as they both start back toward the city.

"You wish to see more? Then you shall," the specter replies.

Suddenly Aaron can see a girl in an alley being held down by six men. Her mouth is covered by one man's hand, her hands held down, her legs held apart. They are as so many rodents savaging a trash bag of fresh meat.

Her screams are muffled, and she whimper as her resolve to resist has been taken. She has come to an inflection point where she cannot decide if she cares to survive, holding the memory of this for all her days, or simply die in this moment.

Her eyes seem to look right into Aaron's. He can hear her screams within his mind and is horrified at the emptiness of her eyes and the lifeless expression that befalls her face.

"Oh my god, stop them!" Aaron screams.

Suddenly he is startled by a shot so close beside him. He looks quickly to his right and sees a man falling slowly in what seems to be in another part of what must be another city.

The man's eyes are still open as his lifeless body falls limp toward the ground as his killer reached into the dead man's pockets. He quickly counts out thirty-two dollars and fifteen cents as he surveys the area. He then takes off with the dead man's watch and runs into the shadow of the night.

Now suddenly Aaron hears a gargling sound just behind him, and he's in an apartment bathroom; just inches away, he sees a man holding a small child from behind, pushing the child's face underwater.

The child fights, but he is no match for the adult man. The child's body grows tense and then suddenly...limp. The killer takes the lifeless child's body, laying him across a bed, begins to undress the boy, speaking the vilest of language even among the living to this child that now visits among the dead.

Now Aaron feels agony in the tears that stream down his face as he trembles with rage.

He hears a crashing sound just behind him and the voice of an elderly woman as she screams for mercy, "Please! Please!"

Aaron looks over to his right, and there is an old woman. Her house is being ransacked and she herself thrown around. Her frail body crashes into wooden table, one eye dark and swollen, and bleeding from the mouth.

A young man stands over her with tears in his eyes and screaming at her, "You're lying, Grandma. You always got more money than this in the house. Now where is it! Don't make me break something else!"

With every direction, with every turn of his head, Aaron witnesses the worst of unspeakable atrocities and horrors until he places his hand over his eyes, now sore from the agony of crying so much, so hard.

"Please! *No!*" he screams. "I...can't take it! Please!"

But now his is the only voice he hears. Suddenly Aaron can feel the wind no longer against his face nor does he hear the sound of the winds of pain and anger.

Slowly Aaron removes his hand and yells at the specter, "*What the fuck was that?*"

The specter now stands in front of him and asks, "What is your understanding?"

Aaron looks around as he tries to understand the place he now stands. He is in a place without form, likened to a living cloud that swirls, changing colors into faces.

Aaron opens his mouth to speak.

"Understanding? Understanding what?"

The specter speaks, "*It is written: we fight not against flesh and blood but against principalities, against powers, against rulers of darkness of this world, against spiritual wickedness in high places...* What is your understanding?"

Aaron opens his mouth to speak.

He trembles, and his breathing is erratic. But then there is a calm, quiet confidence that comes over him as he can see their faces again. He's seen them before, both perpetrators and victims. He's seen their younger selves, but now... He has seen their futures.

He looks to the specter who claps his hands with a thunderous clap, and all is a swirl again. A single scripture is revealed within his consciousness.

It is from the book of Romans 15: 34 Aaron speaks the words, "Bad company corrupts good character... There are some that know not the word of God... I say this to my shame."

Suddenly there is a gust of wind, and Aaron finds himself back in his bunk, slumbered by exhaustions.

All is silent and still. He is emotionally spent and rolls suddenly in a deep sleep.

Chapter 46

Dark Cover

Meanwhile in St. Augustine, the cover of darkness finds agent Dillard is making his way through a different set of woods. This assignment as a custodian has an interesting familiarity to actually being a custodian in one of the largest high school in the state.

The events of being the new guy has led him astray of his actual duties as an investigator, but a situation has presented itself again as word from the bureau has confirmed another of the mysterious letters has been mailed and are heading his direction. The duties of the high school has put him once again out of position to retrieve the documents for fingerprint analysis, but Dillard has gone after hours old-school as he surveys the dumpster area and the security guard that patrols the area around the school at night.

Just north of the St Augustine football field, he is dressed in black and a hoodie. He's carrying a small bag over his shoulder as he reaches the fence along the tree line. He reaches into his bag and retrieves a set of mini binoculars. He surveys the area around the track and ball field. He pays special attention to the dumpsters and distance.

Speaking to himself, he says, "Rollie, I just really can't thank you enough for this assignment. Oh boy…the words escape me. But perhaps here I'll find something that truly conveys my appreciation."

Then a voice comes in over his com unit, "Dillard, you got incoming Bogie at nine o'clock."

Dillard checks in, "That's affirmative, fellas. Got 'em."

He then marks the time on his watch.

Soon that security car will come around, making another check near the dumpster. The car doesn't stop, and soon as it's out of sight, Dillard moves into position.

Some twenty minutes later, the car comes around again. Once it is out of sight, Dillard checks his watch and climbs over the fence. Staying close to the fence, he makes his way into an area close to the dumpster and then across the field.

He puts on his special-made goggles to detect the dye through the clear and dark plastic bags. The first two dumpsters are a bust, but he gets lucky on third. The residue is clear and on more than one document.

Dillard checks the area to make sure he's left no trace of his visit. He packs and is quickly backed across the fence.

The next day Dillard's findings are forwarded to Rollie's office.

The crime lab lifts the prints of an unknown due to smudge, but because of traces of residue on another piece of paper, they determine that a note had been handled by the teacher named Fells.

His prints were also on another piece of paper he'd handled that seems of interest.

Trace residue had been transferred to an invoice from the real estate company that Jonny Blain works for.

Rollie is sure there's a message encoded in plain sight and sends the contents to encryption.

So now Dillard's focus is on Fells in hopes of getting a line on his connection—someone with no arrest, no fingerprints in the system, and old enough to be Mickelson's sleeper.

Chapter 47

Beware the Gates

In Graceville the day is particularly warm.

About twenty-five men, some standing, some sitting, most with their Bibles in hand, have gathered in the yard.

As they listen, All Day begins to read from the book of Matthew chapter 12, verse 25.

> Every kingdom divided against itself is brought to desolation…and every city or house divided against itself will not stand… If Satan cast out Satan, he is divided against himself.
>
> How then will his kingdom stand? And if I cast out demons by Beelzebub, by whom do your sons cast them out?
>
> Therefore they shall be your judges.

He glances toward Aaron. Their eyes meet, and then he continues to read.

"He who does not gather with me scatters abroad."

Then All Day closes the Bible and looks around the group of men and asks the question, "What is your understanding of what I have read?"

Aaron is taken back at the statement, remembering the specter in his dream.

Just then Aaron is touched on his shoulder. He turns, and School is kneeling down beside him.

"Yo, AD, you got legal mail. They callin' you up at the control booth."

Aaron is perplexed and asks, "Legal mail. Me?"

He gets up and goes inside. The desk officer spots him coming in.

"Daniels! Get up here!" As Aaron hurries, the officer continues, "You got a court date in Duval County day after tomorrow. Get ya shit packed, get my clothes over to laundry, and hurry up!"

As he hands Aaron the letter, Aaron hurries toward his bunk, reading the 38.50 appeal that he had no clue existed.

School is walking hurriedly right beside him, trying to read over his shoulder.

"Damn, AD. You sprung dog!"

Aaron shakes his head and says, "Wait, man, it's just a court date, doesn't mean a thing."

School pushes his friend in the back.

"Yo, dog, what about this walk-by-faith stuff you been talking to me? Now you trippin'?"

Aaron smiles as he gathers his laundry.

School continues, "Ya know they want even bring you back 'less you had a case, so you know they'll offer a deal or something, and you got here short."

Aaron just smiles harder. He then drops the letter on the bunk for School to read. He takes his bundle and walks through the door to the yard on his way to the laundry.

He sees All Day walking cross the yard. Their eyes meet, and there is a warm smile on All Day's face.

"I got an appeal," Aaron says to him.

All Day nods and says, "As do we all, young priest."

Aaron laughs and says, "I don't suppose you know how that came to be, do ya?"

All Day laughs and says, "Young priest, is it not written, not even a sparrow falls from the sky outside the will of God?"

Aaron drops his bundle and hugs All Day.

"Thank you," he whispers in his ear.

All Day returns the hug and then reaches down and grabs Aaron's bundle.

"Come, young priest. You are not far from home. Behold, there are the ever-increasing dangers of the world beyond these walls of protections. Tonight we shall pray for you."

Then Aaron stops and says, "You know, I promised myself I wasn't going to ask you this until I had time to figure it out for myself."

The look on All day's face is curious when he asks, "Figure what out?"

"The kingdom of heaven suffers violence, and the violent taketh by force. Here goes. The violent force being spoken of is the war we wage against ourselves. When we in our own conscious have accepted that we should do right—repent, change, or whatever. After we have done wrong for so long, we concede that it is all that we know. And that every day we battle to grow more conscious by growing closer to *God* who strengthens us to take back a piece of the life he intended for us every day. That spirit within us all, a warrior of God."

All Day looks at Aaron sternly and adds, "But it begins with that wonderful freedom that comes over an individual once they decide that they want and will pursue a deeper and more profound relationship with God above all else. Then there at that point they will know the essence of the scripture as it is written, when Jesus sets you free…you are free indeed."

Chapter 48

When Death Calls

Later in the week in Jacksonville, Rollie is in a conference with the chief of the city of Jacksonville Duval County Police.

The discussion is on a set of car tire tracks his cops had found near the scene of the killing involving the off-duty police officer out of Putnam County.

The chief and Rollie agreed that until a motive is established, every branch of law enforcement should be on alert and privy to the information in this investigation.

There are also components of soil that are found in sites that may indicate a specific area that has more in common with Duval County than Putnam.

During the meeting, Rollie's cell phone rings.

"Rollie, this just came over the wire. Thought you'd want to hear this. A car accident on Highway 95 north out of St. Augustine with one fatality. One Yoko Ming, age thirty-one. Two years military as a 95 Bravo. Former military officer. Wife, Sharon Ming, one child, Evan Ming, age three months."

"What's the catch, Danny. How did he land on..."

"Rollie...he was presently employed at the St. Augustine High School as a substitute teacher, English."

Rollie turns away from the chief and asks, "So, what da ya think? Who is he?"

Danny sighs and says, "I'm hoping he's someone we didn't just get killed."

There's a silence over the phone for a moment.

Rollie takes a deep breath and then, "Find out everything we don't know about the accident, and Danny, I want you to check out the widow Ming. I want phone records, the works, who he talked to, where he went after work. Maybe he was a loose end...at least... that's what I'm praying."

Danny nods his head, and he takes notes, saying, "I understand. I'm on it."

A few hours later, and Danny is leaving the widow Ming's home.

His thoughts are only of the possibility this young father's death may have been collateral damage, and could they have done something different that may have prevented it.

Traffic is slow as a city crew tries to shut off a fire hydrant just down the street of the widow Ming. Danny thinks about his own child and how Mr. Ming will never enjoy the special moments that goes with raising a child.

Chapter 49

Joy Cometh in the Morning

The morning is bright and sunny in St. Augustine. Tracy gets up and slowly makes her way out of bed and into the shower.

The smell of bacon and coffee reminds Tracy that Lisa is also off today, and she's glad she woke up to do breakfast.

After the shower, Tracy opens the door with her robe on and towel on her head. Lisa comes out of her room in her robe. She looks at Tracy in passing.

"Good morning."

"Good morning," Tracy replies. Lisa is entering the bathroom, and just as Tracy starts in her door, she asks, "What all did ya cook?"

Lisa looks at her with a smile.

Tracy asks, "What? What's so funny?"

Lisa gives her a look and says, "Yeah, okay, I knew it was my turn to cook, so rub it in. Go ahead, brag about the fantastic breakfast you hooked up. I know that's what you wanna do. Smells great, by the way."

Tracy laughs and asks, "No, really, what did coo…"

Suddenly they are both silent, and their stare is frantic as they can hear the sound of silverware striking plates and glasses striking their wood table.

Lisa reaches inside her room and grabs a mini bat as they both start walking toward the living room, and just as they turn the corner, they find Cricket sitting at the dinner table with her baby in the basinet, asleep. She takes a bite of bacon and notices the girls stop in their tracks. Cricket says good morning.

The girls both reply, "Good morning."

Then Lisa asks, "Uh…why are you in our kitchen, and who let you in?"

Pat takes another bite of her eggs and points toward the kitchen, saying, "He did."

Bobby walks from around the corner of the kitchen with a plate of salmon croquettes and eggs.

"Good morning, ladies. I'm Cricket's husband, Bobby. I hope you girls are hungry. We got bacon and eggs."

Bobby starts back toward the kitchen when Tracy asks, "Uh… Bobby? Why are you in our kitchen, and who let you in?"

Bobby looks at the girls, and then he and Cricket look at each other. Then they look to the kitchen and point.

They both respond simultaneously, "He did."

Slowly Aaron walks out from the kitchen.

"Hope we didn't scare you. You were both asleep, and we've been on the road for hours. I thought I'd make everyone some break-fast. I haven't done that for a while, ya know. The key was still in my property."

He looks at a shocked Tracy whose hands are covering her mouth as tears began to stream down her face.

She says, "Lisa?"

Lisa nods and says, "If he's not real, I'm saving that bud."

He asks, "You still like 'em sunny side up? I made some bacon too."

Lisa is even speechless as Tracy walks, almost stumbling over, slowly and embraces Aaron and melts into his arms, their eyes flooded with tears.

Their lips meet and lock in a kiss that is reminiscent of two people gasping for air.

"Oh god," she says. "If I'm dreaming, please let me die in this dream."

He pulls her head to his and whispers, "Then here I die with you."

Now Lisa speaks, "So you on the run or something, I mean… how?"

Penny laughs and gestures at Lisa.

"I wish we had timed this. That's the longest she ever been speechless since I've known her, and twice she was unconscious."

Then Cricket turns to Lisa and explains, "It's really quite simple. My husband's a genius, and the bomb! Which, by the way, for future reference, that whole withholding-sex thing has its merits." She laughs.

Bobby clears his throat and says, "Really, it was quite simple. You see, when Aaron entered his plea, he was supposed to be sentenced as a youthful offender. He should have gone to a git camp for about eight months for his first offence and released. I don't even know how they screwed that up and sent him to a work camp. The judge agreed with me, and the State had no grounds for objections. Time served. Walla!"

Aaron reaches into his pocket and pulls out a box with a ring in it.

"This was also in my property too. Still belongs to you…if you still want it." Now there is seriousness in his eyes. He continues, "You were right that night. Ya know, when you're behind those walls, it's strange the different ways life replaces things that are the makeup of our lives. You got the boys. Canteen gives you statis. if you're a baller. It feeds your need to feel the rush of superiority. Some just work.

"But we all of us, different as we are, we all seem to share the one thing in common—we mostly see our family in our dreams. We all lay there and stare into the ceiling, and it is there where we find the strength to take on the next day. The hope…a day closer until we can be with them again. I have shared every moment of every evening with you. You are my family, Trace.

"And ya know what? There was nothing that we shared that required the use of money in my dreams. We were just us being us. And the moments were priceless…and you were wearing my ring, and so I'm asking you, Tracy—no, I'm begging you, Trace. Would you give me my dreams? Will you be my wife?"

Lisa looks on at the ring and then in Tracy's eyes and says, "You're so done! I'm done for you! Yeah, we're getting married! Aren't we?"

Tracy nods franticly with tears in her eyes, saying, "Yes, yes, yes!" She then grabs Aaron by the hand. "Come on, baby. We got to talk, and I got to get dressed."

Lisa rolls her eyes as Tracy pulls Aaron by the arm down the hall.

"Get dressed! Yeah, good luck with that! At some point, I'm sure it will make the to-do list."

Bobby's mouth drops open with surprise at Lisa's comment, but Cricket doesn't even blink. She just looks at Bobby and smiles.

"You thought I was playing?" Cricket asks.

Suddenly Lisa pauses and asks, "You guys hear that?"

Now Bobby and Cricket pause.

"It's trash day!" she yells.

Lisa goes to the window and looks out, saying, "Oh god, there he is. Bobby, grab the trash out of the kitchen, would you?"

Bobby rushes and grabs the plastic trash bag. He ties it and starts toward the door when Lisa stops him.

"Ooh no, I got this."

Undoing the tie in the front top of her robe, Lisa grabs the bag and starts through the door toward the curb casually just as the trash truck gets to the front of the apartment.

Bobby and Crick rush to the window to observe. The man at the back of the truck is tall and dark. His shirtsleeves are torn off. His biceps bulge. He is lean, muscular, and unshaven. Bobby looks down at Penny as she is peaking through the lower blinds.

"She has no shame, that girl?"

Cricket smiles and says, "Not unless it's a perfume."

Lisa is now talking with one man as the driver is now halfway out of the passenger-side window, chatting as well.

Again, Bobby looks down at Pat and observes, "She's quite the charmer, isn't she."

Cricket smirks, saying, "Bobby, please, she's half naked. They start making men different since I woke up?"

He mumbles, "Yeah, I guess...that helps."

Later that day Tracy and Aaron are married. Bobby was best man, and Pat and Lisa acted as maids of honor. They celebrated and then came the moment of truth.

Aaron and Tracy surprised Aaron's mom and dad with both his freedom and news of his wedding.

They are so delighted all is forgiven, and Tracy and Aaron's moms are like old friends. Aaron calls his father off into the kitchen so that they can be alone.

Aaron's father can only imagine what is on his mind (being freshly married).

"Dad, I got to ask something of you, and I really don't know how."

"Well…if it's about money you're a little late at—"

"No," Aaron stops him. "Dad…what I have to ask isn't about money, it's really an issue of trust.,See I feel like I've betrayed the trust you may have had in me. I'm sorry, and I want to get it back."

His father smiles and says, "Son, I love you. But I've made some mistakes too. Jesus once said, confess your sins, and I did. But now I have to wonder if I should have been confessing them to you."

Aaron is confused and asks, "To me? What could you have to confess to me?"

His father smiles warmly and explains, "In all my getting, I was supposed to get wisdom, my son. But I forgot what it was to be a young black man growing up in a country where you weren't always going to be seen for who you are. And what was the example I was showing you? That a man was to make money and be a provider… but as you grew further, I realized that I had not brought forth character to bare. To teach you to be a principal individual. But I remembered the promise, and I prayed that as for me and my house, we shall serve the Lord. I see the boy that once stood before me, but I also see the man before me now. I trusted God, son. I ask you now, my son, to place your trust there, and I will always be proud of you. So tell me then, Aaron. What's on your mind, son?"

Aaron smiles and says, "Church."

His father smiles as well, saying, "Well, ya mom never stop paying ya dues, so technically you're still a member."

"Great! Now, as a member, can I be allowed to say something… at the church?"

His father looks with concern and asks, "Something like what, Aaron?"

Aaron shakes his head, saying, "I don't know, Pop. I just know I have to speak. Would ya set it up for, like, this weekend?"

His father nods and says, "This weekend? Sure, sure, son. I'll clear it with Reverend James. Turns out, I was supposed to give the sermon this Sunday anyway as a deacon. Funny thing though. Nothing came to mind… Perhaps this is why."

Aaron smiles and agrees, "Yeah, perhaps."

Chapter 50

Fun and Games

Somewhere on State Road 16 just off Highway 95, Danny King is driving into St. Augustine. He's to meet with Agent Dillard at the conch house on Anastasia Island, but Danny's cell phone rings.

"Yeah?"

"Danny, Rollie. We've got a code yellow alert at Dillard's house."

"I'm fifteen minutes away."

"Make it ten."

"What's the situation?" The agent accelerates.

"They've got men on Dillard. I've just been informed there are two men about a block down the road watching the house. Our surveillance picked them up about twenty minutes ago. They're Mickelson's men. We did satellite surveillance sweep of the car. We got two men carrying heat and something in the trunk that could be a M72, A2."

"A what?"

"A handheld rocket launcher."

"Damn! So what da ya think, the teacher, now Dillard, they're both fairly new at the school."

"Yeah, I'm thinking the same thing, and that house has a gas stove. Cops wouldn't even think to look for a rocket. Listen, if I know Dillard, he'll want to stay in the game, he'll want a shot. What da you say we give him one?"

"What da got in mind?"

"Two of ours just called in at both corners. I'm gonna pull one off and send him to the Oldest House, you know the spot?"

Danny laughs and says, "So much for dress rehearsal. Do we have time?"

"Yeah, I think so. You know your part. Dillard will be playing it by ear, and they may be listening. You may only get one shot, so make it count."

"Let's do it. I'll see him there."

Dillard is setting in front of his TV set, waiting for Danny's call when the vibration of his watch tells him he's being watched and he has a supporting team.

The yellow light blinking on his watch tells him he's not in any immediate danger.

Dillard places a receiver in his ear the size of a small hearing aid. He doesn't say a word in the event that the house is bugged.

Suddenly he hears, "Dillard, this is Rollie. We're gonna take you for a ride."

Dillard smiles. *That's my boy*, he thinks to himself. He gets up and grabs his coat. He then makes his way to the car.

Rollie calls again, "We got cha outside. Now drop the keys if we're still transmitting and you can hear me."

Dillard drops the keys as he's unlocking the car door.

"Okay, Dillard, now we know what you can do with a car. Okay, try not to lose them."

Dillard smiles as he starts his engine.

"You're going to the Oldest House parking lot. That briefing tonight just went real time. You're already their new person of interest. Make it interesting, would ya. You'll be met in the car by Danny. He's your supplier. Just park and wait."

Shortly after Dillard parks his car in the Oldest House parking lot, Mickelson's men pass by the parking lot and proceed to the elementary school next door and watch.

Ricks is in the passenger seat and says, "Okay, he looks like he's waiting for somebody. Get the voice amps. I'll get the inferred camera. Let's check this out."

Soon they are out of the car and making their way to the fenced-in area under the cover of darkness and the thick shrubbery that masks the fence.

They begin to survey Dillard's car when they notice a man coming from the other end of the parking lot on foot.

There is a transmission from a sniper overlooking Mickelson's men from the roof of the school.

"Dillard, be advised they got sneak-a-peak equipment, so they'll be listening."

Danny, dressed in a hoodie and a South Pole jacket, is soon across the dark parking lot and in the passenger-side door of Dillard's car.

Dillard looks surprised. He reaches into his middle console and pretends to hand Danny something.

"Here's the take from the school."

Danny looks at him and then pretends to count money while Dillard plays along, monitoring the area.

"Okay, yeah, good haul, but it ain't St. Joe. You think you got the school crew locked down? You see any players I need to know about?"

Dillard seems nervous and says, "I got it. I just got there, but this is the good stuff, and the size is like nothing they used to. I mean, it's a big school. I'm sure I'm not the only fish swimming these seas, but I'm making friends, and with friends come info. I think Mr. Vega would be encouraged by its potential. Hey, maybe through me a little some some for playtime. I mean some of these chicks, ya know... They young, but they in school to learn, right? Besides, the more of them I get hooked, the more I can put 'em to work, right?"

Ricks reacts to the name Vega and takes out his cell phone.

Danny reaches inside his jacket and hands Dillard some drugs, saying, "That's for you. We'll meet at the Tuesday night place tomorrow at 9:45. I'll set you up then." Danny jumps out the car.

Ricks and the other man make their way to the car with new instructions.

An hour later in Deerwood Estates in the mansion's library, the door opens, and a silhouette stands in the door of the darkened room.

There is a flat screen projecting picture after picture of law enforcement officers.

The silhouette speaks, "Any luck, Mr. Cole?"

"Yeah, all bad," Mickelson exhales.

"It appears that the competition is already at St. Augustine. Ricks witnesses a meeting from a small-time player who has a rap sheet for sales and distribution sealed by the state. I'm thinking. What if it's not Vega himself that's feeling out the area but his front man? He's pretty hot even though St. Augustine does offer a certain obscurity. What if Vega is just using someone and setting up the turf?"

He hands Cole a picture and continues, "Check this guy out. Ricks taped a meeting with this guy and our school janitor."

Cole thinks on the info as he listens to the recording.

"So you don't think Vega, I mean in the flesh, is even in the city yet?"

Cole shakes his head and continues, "Well, Jonny's people have pretty much took the streets and flooded them with our product, but this guy seems to have something different by what was observed, but I haven't heard anything 'bout any new stuff on the streets. I'll tell Jonny to run down the area it's most prominent. Nail down the source."

"So should we worry about the shores?" Mickelson asks.

Cole grunts, "Well...the thing about a rash—it sometimes spreads."

"Quite true, dear boy. Keep me abreast."

Cole nods, saying, "When I know, you'll know."

Mickelson leaves the room, and Cole looks at the picture of Danny King in the car outside the Oldest House. Then looking over his shoulder to make sure he's alone, he takes out his cell phone and makes a call.

"So, Mickey, what are we looking at here? The info I picked up on this Officer Jackson seems very vanilla to me, I mean almost too vanilla."

"Yeah, that's what I was thinking. Could somebody be running an op on us from inhouse? You think we been made?"

Cole is silent for a moment then asks, "How did it play out with known associates?"

"Generally, good old boy's from around the way, but he has an uncle that seems to have conflicting histories. Can't tell if he died or if he's Russian."

"Russian? What's the connection?" Cole asks.

"I'm not sure if he's the same man or if there two men, but, well...chatter, ya know. They seem to be in communication with each other, but then nothing. Like they just stopped."

Cole asks, "And this bothers you why exactly?"

"Because he's a blip on the screen. One minute he's there, the next minute nothing, no address, no phone number. Just your dead cop and only kin."

"So where does he keep blipping on your screen at?"

"See, that's the thing, Cole. He's a little bit everywhere and no place at all. I'm telling you, I'm running into death certificates, yet he's attending political galas in Virginia."

"Start there, Mickey. Follow the power until you find ya way back to me, okay?"

"You know I will. He spends quite a bit of time in Virginia but he doesn't seem to have any ties there, no close friends, no apartments, not even a woman on the side. I'll be in touch as soon as I know more."

Cole hangs up the phone and opens an envelope that he picked up earlier from a drop point from his friend Mickey. He already recognizes one of the pictures from his own surveillance. The picture of Agent King from an unmarked police car passing the home of the widow Ling and the oldest house. *Gotcha*, Cole thinks to himself.

Chapter 51

Let the Boy Speak

Now it's Sunday morning. Aaron sits in the back and listens for the announcer to call his name. Bobby and Cricket have driven down from Jacksonville, and Lisa and Tracy sit in the congregation. They don't know what will be said but only that it is important for Aaron to have support.

At this moment, Aaron isn't even sure of what he should say. He sits, he listens, and he prays. Suddenly he hears his dad's voice. He's announced and goes out before the congregation. Aaron stands in the pulpit and waits in silence.

He stands there with all eyes on him, and then he says, "May I come among you?" He is assisted freeing the microphone.

He makes his way down with the cordless microphone.

"I know it's been a while since you seen me here... And I guess that, too, was necessary to come to this point in my life. Ya see, today I'm kinda on a mission... I... Do you remember when you could go to sleep at night with your screen door open, and it was safe, or when having your car door unlocked and your windows down, all you had to worry about was rain mostly? I've heard my parents talk about those days, and at times I have to wonder, what happened?"

As he makes his way up and down the pew, a feeling of warmth and comfort comes over him. Suddenly he is not alone.

"Well, I got an answer. It kinda came to me. We have not occupied as the Lord had instructed us. We as a people—a Christian people—we have not carried on the values and principles in trust and faith that were given to us by our forefathers who instructed us to learn and preach the Gospel to our children."

People began to mumble and shift in their seats, but Aaron continues.

"In 2 Corinthians 13:5 the Bible says to examine yourself to see as to whether you are in the faith. Well, I believe it's time. Let's look at this as a pop quiz, and we're well overdue for this quiz."

Suddenly there is no nervousness but a great feeling of calm, almost as though he, too, were one of the listeners.

He asks, "What is your understanding?"

The congregation looks puzzled.

"Some of us barely ever even ask ourselves this question because it is put off by where we appear to be to our neighbors. There is where we are defined. We can say we are better than some and not as bad as others because what they believe about you has become much more pressing and urgent than what God knows about you.

"It allows us to be busy with our own true selves. And in the course of events, we forget that with all the people that press against the Lord Jesus as he walked along the streets, there was only one that touched him that day. Sure, the others had walked and pressed beside him—I'm sure some for miles—and they had be seen as walking with the Christ! They were among those seen side by side walking with the Messiah.

"But when the woman with the issue of blood just touched the hem of his garment, we as Christians then realized it's bigger than that. It's a personal thing to our Lord. Is it bigger than the way we don't see those who are homeless, or rather helpless, a slave to the lack and left behind by a generation of Christian soldiers not willing to take on the war we were fashioned to win through faith?

"Why don't we engage the streets or at least bring that which is formidable to combat what we know is problematic, to take back the streets that make us afraid? Could it be that we have all of our nice things secured inside our houses, everything that we've worked for. And if the streets should take even our family away from this which I have built, then so be it! It has, you know, taken your family, enslaved them.

"You have brothers and sisters, uncles and aunts, mothers and fathers out there. Mostly hooked on drugs or drink or pills or something. You say, 'I tried and all they do is take. They took my TV, they took my rings, they took my credit cards, they took my car.' What you're really saying is, 'They took my heart! They took so much of all my nice things.'

"Ya know, one could argue that God gave up a little bit more than a TV set when he gave his only begotten son to bring us back to him. Have we forgotten the reason we are here? I'm here today to say to you take back your own! Your daughters who lay down with strangers just to get enough money for a twenty-dollar crack rock—don't be ashamed. Take her back even as Jesus took back Mary Magdalene. Your sons who were once the pride of life to you, now you know him a slave to a world known as the game. It's not a game but a war, and these are the traps that present themselves to the streets. How is this your fault? Because the fact that you thought to yourself that you were excused meant you needed forgiveness, and so God took you back. You were out building a way of life, a fine home, and nice clothing to wear to school. All of this is vanity. Ask yourself, IF it was really all for them, then why not give it to them? 'Cause they'd give it away to feed their addictions? Ah, so the addiction is the enemy? So why not make it the combatant? You say their grown. I ask, will they ever be not your kids as they live? As you live? So this was really about...you.

"Kids need character. They don't need Nike, but they sure look nice, and people talk about you. But didn't that first develop their character, and let's be real, not as Christians. Maybe like you had it growing up? But you turned out all right! But we just established that. Those things, the kingdoms of the world in all their slender, they were not always before our eyes, and so we cherished our children.

"But now the time has come to take back your own! Oh, don't you know that they, too, were formed in the very image of the living God that you have proclaimed to serve just as Jesus did? That needs to mean something to you inside if you're gonna touch him from here, 'Take 'em back!' For in truth, don't you know that if Christ came today (as he did then), who would be the poor in spirit, and who would be the Pharisees? Who would be those who thought they were godly. Ask ya self, does your righteousness exceed theirs?

"Jesus said to us the harvest is plentiful, but the laborers are few. Paul said there are those who do not have the knowledge of God. I say this to your shame: Where is your understanding?" Aaron screams.

As Aaron walks between the rows in the center of the church, he continues, "Say, which of you have that in which you did not receive? Uh? Who among you have the knowledge of the word of God by his own doing? Indeed, the gift to believe in God came from God. I tell you to be given to others, and so you share it with strangers because they go away and do not see the truth of who you really are after they're gone, but that's okay. They weren't supposes to see you shinning. They were supposed to see salvation. Does not the word of God also say in the book of Romans 10:20,; I was found by those who did not seek me; I was made manifest to those who did not ask for me.' How do you suppose such a thing happens?

"Do you remember the story the Lord told of Lazarus and the rich man? Two things jump out at me when I read Luke 16:19 through 31. One, that the rich man could see Lazarus in Abraham's bosom, but the second thing was a question to me. Could Lazarus see him…in hell? So what if God would not only have you to look upon strangers but those you would have contact with in life and show you how your reluctance or lack of empathy lead them down these roads? Seems there is that possibility. Tell me, who do you know that you wouldn't mind if they should fall into hell? And then what does that say about the love in your heart? What is your understanding?"

Just then an older man stands up from the middle aisle on the end of a bench.

"Now you just hold on a minute!" The man is visibly out raged as he continues, "I know you, boy. Yeah. I know your whole story. Now, who do you think you are to ask us about our understanding of the word of God?"

Tracy makes her way up from her seat and rushes toward Aaron. He puts out his hand as though to tell her it's okay, and she stops. She can see he is fixed on the man who is still shouting at him. She slowly makes her way to him and takes his hand. Now his head turns to her, out of a daze. He looks into her eyes, and knowing her as he does, he can see in her eyes she only wants to stand beside him. So she does.

Now they are both turned and listening to the older man's complaint when a voice resonates from the very back of the church.

"Oh, shut up, Silas, and sit down!"

The old man stops to look back as the rest of the church does also because they know that burly voice. An old lion of a man makes his way up the opposite aisle. He wears a full-length jacket with a fur collar, a fur hat, and a chain with a large cross around his neck. Aaron recognizes him instantly.

He whispers under his breath, "Grandpaw."

He then turns back to see his father who smile with approval and nods his head.

As the pastor gets to the row of seats that Silas is standing, he repeats himself, "I said…sit down as well as shut up, Silas, before I tell the congregation what I have observed of you throughout our upcomings." This seems to sharply send the man to his seat.

The pastor then starts again toward Aaron and Tracy.

He begins to quote scripture, "It is written in the First Corinthians 3:7, 'It is neither he who plants nor he who waters is anything, but it is God who gives the increase, and each one will receive his own reward according to his labor.'"

The man is Reverend Mason, the former minister of the church and a much-respected man in the community.

"This boy is making a plea to you that should not offend you, but indeed it should quicken your very soul. How long shall we sit silent and do nothing while the very God we serve, or claim to serve, is being stripped from our schools, our courtroom our currency, even the very holiday as we sit aside to honor our Lord's birth? How long will we agree to do nothing as we pretend to be laborers in the army of God. The Lord has said, 'If you would deny me before man, I will deny you before my Father. This doesn't scare you? Do you not fear the Lord your God? Have you already done so much? What is your understanding?"

Then the pastor walks over to Aaron and takes him by the hand.

"Young man, you look like a man with a plan."

Aaron can see the support in the eyes of the onlookers.

"As a matter of fact, I do. It's just a little…off glass."

"Excuse me?" The Reverend looks confused.

"How would you like to go to a barbecue?" Aaron asks.

A few days later, just over the railroad tracks from a place called The Bottom by the Georgia Market is a strip where most of the Westside drug dealers hang out. Across the street from them is a field and a tree line.

Some of the young men and women from three different churches observe their classmates on the street. They are accompanied by an older man with a cell phone. The kids began to tell him the names of some of the youths selling drugs from their school. The man then calls the civic center where there are collected a large number of parents and just concerned citizens from different churches.

In the front of the center is a man with a cell phone in one hand and a microphone in the other.

He begins to call out the reported names, and as he does, people from the congregation stand and shout, "Yeah, I got that one," "Yeah, he's ours," and "I'm his uncle."

As they sound off, they line up at the door; and then as they are all gathered, they enter a bus and are off.

Pastor Mason smiles and turns to Aaron.

"I feel like I'm back in the army. Phase one is under way, and now."

Aaron turns to his cousin Pookie and says, "Okay, Pook, you got the ball."

Pookie laughs and says, "And you know I can run it—run it."

Then he goes into another bus that is empty, and they take off.

Aaron turns to Pastor Mason and asks, "Now, we have all the generators we need?"

"Oh yeah, I'm just interested to see how well this goes off. Quite frankly, I wish I had thought of it myself."

"Well, all glory to God, Grandpaw, but we still got work to do."

"I agree. Let's get these people paired off and into these busses."

"All right, ya got to send the cooks next."

Soon a bus pulls on the back streets just behind the dealers on King Street, and the first bus lets it soldiers off. They walk up from behind the dealers on four different corners.

They begin to call out names, "Eric!" "Timmy!" "Carl!" "DeShawn!" They are all family members who are respected by this assortment of dealers and have their devoted respect.

They begin to explain that in the field across the street is where the church is about to set up for a BBQ, and they need some helping hands. Unable to refuse, the youths quickly start unloading the trucks that seem to come out of nowhere. They are followed by the truck containing grills and food.

A sound system is set up quickly, and while they work with tables and chairs, an all-female youth choir (an assortment of talented singers from all the different churches) begins to harmonize some spiritual, upbeat music.

The smell of the food cooking fills the air as some have been prepared early for effect, and each of the youth are now talking to each other about getting something to eat for their troubles.

Pastor Mason, Aaron, and others walk through the youths, explaining that this picnic is for them. They also walk along the streets, inviting people to come over and have a free plate of food.

Meanwhile, Pookie's bus is filling up also with those who are the drug's victims: the users, the boozers, the judged. Pookie (also being a user himself) knows all the dope holes and houses in St. Augustine. He's been given a driver with a tank of gas and at least two hours before the festivities are on the way. He also receives a lot of help by those who know people, friends who can more than likely use a meal.

Back at the field, long tables are set up, and some of the most legendary cooks in the hood are unknowingly pitted against each other as the young dealers proclaim who makes the best eats. Ringing cell phones are soon shut off as the majority has already decided to take the day off. With that, Aaron has noticed some good has already been done.

Soon Pookie pulls up, and everybody is being seated. Dealers with families and users are the order of the day as everyone there are now seated or standing in line to be seated.

Pastor Mason takes a microphone and begins to speak, "Thank you so much for accepting our invitation."

The crowd laughs as many of them didn't have a choice.

The pastor continues, "We came here today because we wanted to say to you, we're sorry. We got lost, so caught up in the world around us and making money to survive that we forgot what it was we were trying to survive for.

"We began to get away from what is our real purpose—one another. We are failing you, and to be honest with you, somewhere down the road, we stopped caring, or worrying, about you. That is not who we really are inside. We ask your forgiveness, and we'd like to ask if you would take us back?

"As Christians, we still fight daily with an adversary that has only one good thing about him. He's very good at what he does, and that's evil. He would have us to believe that you don't matter because you're not like me, but the Bible tells me plainly I should consider myself of less worth than you. You see, you know pretty much where you are...spiritually. We had somehow become deceived as to where we were.

"It is written, 'A man who knows the way and will not share it with his brother is worse than an unbeliever. Aaron Daniels has compiled some information that we hope many of you would find interesting. It's a guide of free schools and classes in which you have a right to learn skills, to get jobs to go after more, to build dreams and homes. You're only wasting your time out here. Nobody at this level ever retires a rich man from selling drugs in the street, but I tell ya where you can find thousands who've tried. They're at work camps, on road crews, making Florida a more beautiful place to see. They're at work release programs, doing a full day's work and giving more than 45 percent back to the state. You're going to have to work for someone you'll find in this life. The choice is up to you. Many of you have the mind and capability to really be something special, to own the street corners you're so content to stand upon. Let us help you as God gives us that we may.

"God will not be mocked. What you sow, that you shall surely reap. That includes the good stuff too. God loves you. We love you too. What you're doing right now is simply missing out on your youth."

Pastor Mason begins to move through the rows of the tables, occasionally shaking hands with some of those young men that he'd remembered from years ago.

Suddenly Aaron takes note of a man staring at him like an old friend. He's in his mid to late forties, well shaved, well groomed, and very well dressed.

"Do I know you?" Aaron asks.

"Do you?" the man replies.

Aaron looks harder and says, "You do look familiar. Where have we met?"

The man smiles and says, "I was lying facedown in a puddle of water in a parking lot on a very rainy night."

Aaron eyes are widening with disbelief.

"You!"

"Yeah, the drunk. You didn't know me, and I didn't know you. Good thing God knew us both. He seems to have a flair for the dramatic. I'm Derrick Philmore."

"Yeah, now I remember your name."

Derrick smiles and says, "Anyway, when my pastor told me about what your church was proposing, and I heard your name, and in all that haze from my drunken days, I somehow remembered your name. I knew what it was that I must do."

Aaron nods and says, "You have a testimony."

Derrick nods, saying, "Yes, but then again, *no*."

Aaron is confused and asks, "No. I don't understand, then what?"

"Aaron, do you remember that lottery ticket I tried to give you?"

"Yeah, I…"

Suddenly there is an awkward silence.

The man nods and explains, "Yeah, twenty-six million dollars, give or take, after Uncle Sam took his share, but the point is, the money is rightfully God's, and I believe he meant for you to be entrusted with at least a tenth of it. Call it my tithes."

Aaron is stunned and says, "Wait, what? Are you for real right now? That's like two point six million dollars!"

"What do you want to do first?" Mr. Philmore asks.

Aaron turns to Pastor Mason who is still speaking to the people. Then he turns to Mr. Philmore.

"We'll see what Pastor Mason says after he's finished," Aaron replies.

Then they listen as Mason continues, "You are strong, but you can be stronger. Yes, you must be strong enough to observe your own frailties. It takes a great strength for one to go to his knees. Despite your profanity, despite your lustful thoughts, believe your ever-present helper is not only with you but for you. Pray earnestly to God."

Paster Mason, Aaron, and Mr. Philmore get together and discuss a central location for an opportunity center. They decide on the name Insert.

Meanwhile, they observe some representatives pull together an impressive list of those interested in school grants for the junior colleges and vo-technical schools in the Duval and St. Johns County area.

There are questions about convicted felons and what is available to them. Some of the young people even find jobs offered to them by people with private businesses that day. Some of Jonny Blain's gang observe the gathering as well.

"Man, ain't this a trip. Jonny's gonna trip when he hears some of these losers think they can hold a job and that Aaron done went all Billy Gram up in here."

Hours later, two of Jonny's main men, known as Chain Gang and Lil Boy on the streets, go by Jonny's home.

They walk through the door, laughing. Jonny is sitting behind his desk in his study. These are two of his most trusted friends from the streets, and he decided they should have access to his home in the event that he needs some product delivered somewhere while playing office manager.

He recognizes their laughter and calls to them, "In here!"

They walk through the door of the study.

He amuses himself with their laughter then asks, "So what's so funny?"

"Man, guess who's back in town!" Chang Gang replies.

"Who?" Jonny asks with anticipation.

"Aaron Daniels, AD!"

"What? My cousin jumped? My AD? Hell naw! Where'd you see AD?"

Lil Boy smirks and says, "Oh yeah, dog, get this... He's helping in getting a ministry started, him and yo grandpaw."

Jonny rolls his eyes.

"Now I know ya lying!" Jonny replies.

Chain Gang adds, "No, straight up, and he's trying to congregate the streets. Nigga was signing 'em up to like he was touchin' something deep inside."

Lil Boy interjects as they break out in more laughter.

Then Jonny cracks and asks, "No shit? Y'all didn't sign up, right? I mean, y'all here to break the news in person?"

The two look at each other with an almost-straight face.

"Now he tried us," Chain Gang says, looking over at Lil Boy

"Right, I guess 'cause he know people now, so he can try us like roll ups."

Chain Gang nods and says, "Yeah, that must be it."

Jonny laughs as the two clowns pull out large amounts of money. Jonny smiles.

"I guess everybody didn't join, y'all got all this!"

Jonny takes three glasses from the bar."

"Let's bust this yak. We gonna get loose. To the Reverend Aaron Daniels and his dopehead congregation," Jonny jokes, but deep down inside he's proud of his cousin's decision.

Later, hours after the Jonny's boys have gone, his bell rings. He opens the door to find Aaron.

"AD, *ahh*! Welcome home, come in." They embrace.

There is a silence as Aaron follows Jonny into the living room. Jonny turns quickly.

"Yo, cousin, you might have heard about something going down between me and Tracy. What happen—"

Aaron interrupts, "Was exactly what she told me, Jonny, but that ain't what I'm here about."

Now Jonny is defensive.

"I see, so, what, you came here with the hopes of bringing me into the fold?"

Aaron looks at him with a smile and says, 'Stranger things have happened."

"What? AD, you know what I do. Look at how I'm living. You think I'm… Ya dreaming and that dumb shit you trying ta bring to the streets. Okay. Remember how we use ta play basketball almost every day, how we would pretend to be all these famous people, how one day our star would shine? Cousin, my star is doin' just fine, and yours is too for a minute, but even if you could get them junkies home, for how long? They gonna taste that dope all in their sleep, AD. Them white girls you trying to save"—he grabs the crotch of his pants—"boy, they been hit correctly, and with that vigor from a from a hood nigga. They trembling in they sleep now, thinking about how to break up with a brother who don't even know they dating." He bursts out in laughter.

"Now what they gonna do about that, uh? With some Austin Collin lookin' motherfucker? You can have 'em…for now, my brother, but the numbers in percentage say they most of them are gonna be coming back to me. And so will you. Help me carry this loot."

Aaron slowly shakes his head.

"I do remember those games, and I remember those stars. They were going to make us enough money to build a hospital in Hastings and lights for the playground and a skating ring and a civic center. Are those the dreams you talking 'bout, Jonny? 'Cause they're still on the table. Now, maybe I am dreaming, but then those dreams are what gives me hope because I'm closer to them than I ever knew I could be.

"Maybe you're right. Maybe those junkies…maybe they want stick. But then if just a few of them do, Maybe they'll fight through and make it to a place where they'll find others. Maybe someone who has lost their battle will begin to believe again there is something to push on to 'cause they've been there before, and they'll believe it again.

"You seem to have arrived, Jonny, good for you. Someone once told me nothing cheats you like money. He never told me it could steal ya dreams. I really just came by tonight to see you because I love you, man. Now I'm just trying to respect you."

Jonny head saps in Aaron's direction.

"What, you? Yo I got ta get up in the morning, so respect that and come on and get the fuck out my house."

They walk down the hall, and as Jonny opens the door, he says, "Oh, and they probably watching me, so if you and Grandpa gonna do this, you might wanna stay away from my house."

He slams the door.

Chapter 52

Bait

Dillard is set up at the Tuesday night place, and it's 9:40 p.m. Just off US 1 South and 315, Dillard is browsing through the CDs at Best Buy.

The store is almost empty.

Danny walks in with his South Pole jacket and hoodie on. They make eye contact from across the room, then Dillard walks back to a secluded area of the store. Danny makes his way toward him.

As they both browse, Dillard begins to speak softly, "Two of 'em at three o'clock from the door."

Danny drops a package in a bag by Dillard's feet.

"Same guys?"

"Naw, it's the locals."

"Damn, did you get the plates too?"

"No, but one of 'em has a mustard stain on his tie."

Danny giggles and asks, "How serious are you right now?"

Dillard just looks at him without expression.

Danny nods, saying, "Okay, look, you got the dope, so who do you think they'll pull?"

"You. They know where I live." Dillard walks away.

"Sure know how to make a guy feel warm and fuzzy, don't cha?" Danny replies.

Dillard walks out.

After renting a tape, Danny leaves. He's in his car and heading south for the Shores. He notices a car behind him suddenly coming up fast. Then the police light come on, signaling him to pull over. He does.

The two officers approach from both sides of the vehicle as Danny lets his window down.

"Good evening, Officers. What up? I wasn't speeding, was I?"

"Naw, nothing like that, sir. We thought your tag light was out, but it's just dim. You really should have it checked."

"Okay, ah, I'll have it checked tomorrow."

Then the officer asks," You mind if we see ya license and proof of insurance? I mean, since we're being all friendly and all."

Danny smiles and says, 'Sure, Officer, since we're being all friendly."

Danny hands it to him.

The officer calls his partner, "Billips, run a check on this guy." Billips takes the license.

Then Rodgers asks, "You mind if I take a look inside ya car?"

Danny smiles and replies, "Ya know I would. I would feel so violated, letting anybody search my car, even my friends, so I gotta say yeah, a lil bit."

"Why, you got something to hide?" Rodgers asks.

Danny shakes his head and says, "That must be traffic stop one-oh-one. I mean, every time I get pulled, someone wants to search my car."

Rodgers becomes serious, "Stop being cute, it's not becoming. 'Sides, I thought we were being all friendly and all."

Billips comes back and says, "He's clean," as he hands Danny his license.

Danny smiles and asks, "So may I go now?"

Rodgers nods.

Then as Danny puts the car in gear, he calls out, "Oh, Officer… you got some mustard on your tie…since we being friendly and all." Then he pulls off.

Rodgers looks at Billips and asks, "So what do ya got?"

"His name's Ronnie Clay. He's out of Atlanta."

"Atlanta, uh. I guess Mickelson was right about this guy. You got a local address?"

"Yep, he's out in the Shores."

"Good. Maybe we'll see if he's got any other friends we should know about."

Later Danny is at the home in the Shores, a government front house. He sits at his computer and marvels working with Dillard for the first time. Rollie had spoken highly of him, but he is much more than Agent King expected.

Out of curiosity, he uses his access to look into Dillard's background. He's quite fascinated by Dillard's Gulf War escapades. He's also stunned to find his oldest son died of a drug overdose, and he can see when Dillard transferred to narcotics, it coincides with his son's death, and he's presently raising another son who is deaf. Then the phone rings.

"Yeah."

"Danny, it's me, Rollie. Can you talk?"

"Yeah, I'm clean."

"So how are we progressing?"

"Well, according to our eyes, I've been very popular. There're like five cars that tailed me, including Rodgers and Billips, and Mickelson's men."

"Okay, so are they ready for us to push 'em into the game plan? Make them move before they're ready. Got any ideas?"

Danny smiles and says, "As a matter of fact, they won't imagine we'd go after what they've already got. They see us as flying under the radar."

"Talk to me."

"Suppose we go to their realtors and express interest in some houses in different parts of their turf around St. Johns County?"

"That would raise some eyebrows for certain, like a shot across the bow. Okay, Danny, make it happen. I'll set you up a bank account, something offshore. With your name being linked to Vega, they'll have ta see that as an intentional act of aggression on their planted flag They'll make a move one way or another."

"My thoughts exactly."

"I'll get back with you tomorrow with the details."

Chapter 53

Game Face

That same night at the Deerwood Estates, Ricks delivers some information off to Mickelson in his office. Cole is sitting at his own desk.

"This just in from St. Augustine."

Mickelson looks over the paperwork.

"Just what I was afraid of, dear boy. It would appear that this man, Ronnie Clay, has been linked in a number of accusation and indictments with our Mr. Vega. However, neither were convicted of any wrongdoing which indicates they are protected. This is getting messy. I mean, who's to say who is protecting who, and so who is really protected?"

Cole sneers and says, "As usual, your boy's a day late a dollar short, and you do realize that all of this intel is coming from two cops whose creditability suck, if you ask me."

Mickelson nods in agreement and asks, "But you've look into it for yourself?"

"And I'd be willing to leave it alone?" Cole says with concern on his face.

Mickelson express concern and says, "Now, that's not like you to stray away from a fight."

"You know me, I don't just walk into a setup either, and I'm betting Rodgers is setting the whole thing up. But if we walk away, what does he really have on us?"

"I'm aware of your mistrust, but suppose all the dirt down there could only be traced to them. We can still use them, just keeping ourselves at a safe distance."

"There is still Fells who they can tie to Jonny who they can tie to your whole organization!" Cole says with raised eyebrows.

Mickelson is now stern when he says, "And yet they haven't, have they? I mean, they have always had that, and since our eyes haven't seen anything to alarm us concerning Fells that their still holding that."

Cole goes to the bar and pours himself a drink.

"I think you're playing a dangerous game."

"All the more reason to be meticulous in our assessment of the playing field."

Cole, sitting at his desk, laughs and says, "Okay, okay, let's try this. We approach this Clay guy…maybe we can interest him in making a little extra money maybe a partner, and we use your Keystone cops to keep the heat away from us and on this Ronnie Clay dude?"

Mickelson leans back in his chair with his hand against his chin.

"I'm not sure that's not a bad idea, oh boy. Of course, then we'd tip our hand."

Cole shrieks, "I was being sarcastic!"

"And I made that distinction. Still, perhaps you may be on to something."

"Jeezus, I was on ta something when I got the claps too. I still don't know if it was worth it."

Mickelson has a look of vulgar on his face and asks, "Dear boy, must we? You can admire a picture in the distance, but you cannot appreciate the broad strokes until you've come close enough appreciate it."

Chapter 54

The Damn Thang

The next day a car pulls up in front of the Forts parking lot in the middle of the day. It's very busy downtown in the tourist district of St. Augustine's bayfront along the St. John's River.

They are two people short on money and long on addiction. The man—a black, well-dressed, neatly shaved, young man. The girl—well-dressed, young black woman. They borrowed a car from a girl back at his place who happens to be jonesing and had a car with Dade County tags.

He's experienced and explains, "Okay, Lyn, check it out. See all these people? They come from Wisconsin, Detroit, New York, and Texas. The one thing they have in common—they didn't come here broke. Now, check it out. We're from Miami. We were on our way back home from Elizabeth City, North Carolina, but we had car trouble in Brunswick, Georgia. We got the car repaired, but it took more than we expected, and now we're in need of twelve gallons of gas to get back down south."

Lyn, using the mirror on the passenger side, nods and says, "Okay, I'm ready. Let's go."

The man, Darryl, grabs her before she can exit the car.

"Go? Baby, you just sit tight. That's just so you'll know the story. Baby, this is art, okay, you just don't go out and take home the Oscar. Takes talent, baby, and I ain't saying you ain't talented. Just not at this. But don't worry. I'll make us a quick forty, and we'll get some slugs, and then when we get back to my place, I'll give ya a chance to get ya talent on, feel me?"

She smiles and says, "Just hurry up, babe!"

Darryl jumps out and runs across the street. There is a restaurant. He stands out front as people pass from every direction. He gets himself together. Now he is poised for the task at hand.

Just then Aaron walks by and glances into the restaurant window, trying to see if his mom's inside the dining room. Suddenly his attention is drawn to Darryl who is unaware that Aaron is watching him. There is a sense about Darryl…something off.

Aaron gazes back into the window and is at first stunned by what he sees in the reflection.

This young man (Darryl) seems to have a demonic monkey on his back. The monkey is dressed like that of an old organ grinder's monkey, but his eyes are large, and his teeth are like knives. The monkey has one arm around the young man's neck; the other hand he holds a pipe of glass. He puts nothing into the pipe, but the monkey sucks hard upon the pipe. Aaron can see the clouds of smoke flowing with a fury though the glass stem of the pipe.

He then looks directly at Darryl who is now talking to a family. Aaron can hear the conversation. And as he turns toward Darryl, he can see nothing around his neck, only in the reflection. He also notices that he seems to be the only one who does see this beast around the young man's neck. Darryl is at the end of his speech as Aaron taps him on the shoulder.

Darryl jumps (fearing police), and Aaron says calmly, "I couldn't help but overhear your story. Would fifty dollars cover your needs?"

Now Darryl is pleasantly surprised and says, "Oh my god, yes, sir. You don't know how much my wife and I appreciate this, sir!"

He smiles.

As the other family eases away, Aaron goes into his wallet.

"Ya know, Jesus once said, a man should give unto Ceasar that which is Ceasar's, and give unto God that which is Gods. Just make sure somewhere down the line, you thank God for his forgiveness for even this moment. For this day, blood was spilled so long ago that you may have the life you only dream about. Not this pretend life of following suit. Sometimes we get so caught up in the moments that we forget we even have choices. Even if we don't honor them."

As he hands Darryl the money, but before he releases it, he says his name, "Darryl."

Darryl is shocked. Aaron is just as surprise he called the man by name. Aaron looks over to the car where Lyn is sitting. Aaron can see the spirit of anger and frustration just behind her as she gets out and stands beside the car, smiling and waving.

"Lust, I get it. Darryl… I offer you a choice. If you show up here tomorrow, I'll have you a job. I'll work on getting you a place to stay with people you can talk to. This way of yours won't last for long, and it'll end badly just as surely as I knew your name."

Darryl looks back over toward Lyn who is smiling from ear to ear, then he looks at Aaron and asks, "Who are you?"

"Somebody who cares, Darryl. I'm just someone who cares. Right now, you'll do what you do. Hold on, my friend… Joy cometh in the morning. Start tomorrow off right, and take God with you. Starting now."

Darryl nods and begins to makes his way through the traffic.

He gets back inside the car as Lyn waves at Aaron and smiles.

She boasts, "You work the shit out of him, baby. I can see the jack from here! Damn, you're good, baby. Let's go get some dope so you can lay back and let me show you that talent you were talking 'bout, baby."

Darryl is slow to start the engine and looks again across the street into Aaron's eyes.

Then he takes a deep breath. He looks at her, smiles, and says, "Yeah, I told ya, baby, I got skills! Now let's go do the damn…thing."

His smile leaves his face as he examines his choice of words.

Chapter 55

By Proxy

The next day Rodgers and Billips are on patrol when Rodgers's cell phone rings. The call is short, and Rodgers mostly listens. He hangs up and turns to his Billips.

"Seems we're coming up in the world. We have a delivery to make."

The patrol car U-turns and speeds away just off of Highway 207. They zoom by as a Greyhound bus pulls into its station.

The driver announces, "Welcome to St. Augustine, Florida, the oldest city in the United States."

The bus door opens, and a lone person exits the bus. The bus station is in a very rural location just outside the city limits, and the passenger is a bit stunned.

"Damn...show looks small." Then he looks back at the driver and asks, "Yo, you got any more St. Augustine's, yo?"

The driver smiles and replies, "Nope, this is it. Just grab ya self one of those cabs, and they'll take you into the city."

The passenger looks to the cabs and says, "Yeah, some things never change. Cabs, they take you all right. Ya think they can tell I'm not homegrown?"

The driver observes the passenger's New York Knicks jersey and T-shirt, the sag of his baggy jeans, and the slightly sideway tilt of his baseball cap.

"Naw, you'll fit right in."

"All right?"

"All right."

The passenger makes his way over to the cabs while examining his address book.

Meanwhile, on the highway just off to the right, Danny's undercover SUV is also passing by.

Danny is on his cell phone.

"Hey, you guys with me?"

"Yes, sir, we are tracking you down State Road 207."

"Okay, control be advised, I picked up a tail."

"Yes, sir, we have a man covering you. He has advised us of the situation. We are now confirming the tag, sir. Okay, the car is registered to the St. Johns County Sheriff's Department to an Officer Rodgers, sir."

"Patch me through to Special Agent Wade."

Within seconds, Rollie is on the line, "Danny?"

"Yeah, Rollie. I visited the realtor today, and now Rodgers and Billips are on my tail. How do you want to play this?"

"You know what, the fact they're still above ground means Mickelson's fishing. Take 'em somewhere secluded yet safe. See what they do."

"I got a place in mind."

"Good. Advise dispatch and keep them in the loop."

"Ten four."

Minutes later Danny, pulls into the Flying J off highway 95, and as he exits his vehicle, Rodgers and Billips walk up quickly.

"Mr. Clay," Rodgers calls out. "We'd like a word with you if you don't mind."

Danny looks at the two officers with contemp.

"And if I do mind?" he replies.

"Then we'd have to insist," Rodgers replies as he pulls his cuffs out.

Danny smiles and syas, "Now, there's no need for that. What happened to us being all friendly?"

The detectives take him by the arm and lead him to their car. Billips gets into the driver's seat as Rodgers and Danny both sit in the back seat where he pats Danny down. Billips starts the engine and pulls out.

"Where are we going?" Danny asks.

"We just want you to meet someone."

"So what if I got enough friends?"

"He doesn't, so that's the real point," Rodgers says with a fake smile.

The patrol car travels across the 206 highway bridge and turns left. Soon they reach the gates at Ocean Palms.

Rodgers presses the code, and they go in. Soon they are at the home of Jonny Blain.

Jonny opens the door, and Danny looks confused.

"I know you," Danny states with a puzzled look on his face.

"Yes, Mr. Clay, we saw each other briefly at my office. You had some dealing with one of my realtors, which is why you're here."

The four men walk into Jonny's living room and sit down as Jonny continues, "You see, we know your scouting for Antwon Vega, and we are…impressed at how quickly you got in and established."

Danny looks around at Billips and Rodgers.

"So our intel was right. I'm listening," he replies.

Jonny continues, "We would like to make you a proposition. See, I believe you're a man who can see when you're looking a gift horse in the mouth, and so I'm thinking, what if you could put aside a few hundred thousand dollars for yourself by selling our product. You could always assure Mr. Vega that the market is slower than expected, and his product would be visible so you couldn't be called a thief. You could help us fortify the Shores and Southside, maybe even advise him that Gainesville would be a better location to set up going forward. I could help you there too. If he feels you are not trying to beat him, you won't be sweated, and we'll cut you a deal to compensate your delinquency. What da ya say, Mr. Clay?"

Danny stands and looks around the room.

"So I just betray a man that's been very good to me for years?"

Rodger stands up and exclaims, "You don't get it! You don't do this, you don't exist, friend! Make ya self a few dollars for ya self or go home! If you're lucky."

Danny looks at Jonny and says, "So that's your position? Big Boy style."

Jonny taps his fingers on the table and says, "Look, what if you moved both of our products, just mostly ours. Your take is 5 percent, and that's on the side action. We both know shit sells itself, and we'll be using my men. You don't even get your hands dirty. That's what I'm trying to say."

Danny grins and says, "Vega pays me 7 percent."

Jonny nods and says, "Vega can't move your product like we can. We're talking 5 percent of a fortune, as compared to 7 percent of a ticket back home…if you're lucky."

Danny looks around at the men facing him and decides, "Okay, I'm in. What can I say? I like the city. Besides, if Mr. Vega were to feel he was not welcome here, that could be messy, and nobody wants messy."

"Good. Welcome to the team." Jonny extends his hand, and they shake.

Shortly Rodgers, Billips, and Danny exit the house and back to the car.

Off in the distance, a transmission goes out, "Now they're leaving, sir. Our boy seems intact, and in no present danger."

"Good. Contact me when he's back in his vehicle."

"Will do, Agent Wade."

Chapter 56

Off Glass

Aaron sits at his desk, going over some paperwork, when his mind drifts into thought. Tracy opens the door, holding a large grocery bag.

"Hi, honey," she says as she motions him to stay seated. She continues, "I just stopped by Mom's on the way home. You should hear her. She is so proud of her son-in-law." She kisses Aaron on the top of his head. "She says that you can visibly see a difference in the blocks in the hood. Says, in the last three months, the buzz in the City Council and PTA have been the taking back of our own."

Tracy looks over as she puts away the groceries. She can see her man's in another land.

"Mom's also growing a third leg. She's thinking of naming it Carlton. What do you think?"

Aaron turns, smile, and says, "Okay, don't do that...wait, what? I was in my thought, babe, ya got me. So what was Mother Austin saying?"

Tracy reaches in her bag and pulls out an art pad, saying, "Check this out."

She shows Aaron a poster.

Blue background with large, wide lettering that says, "Man's best friend is *dog*." At the bottom of the poster, there is a pair of hands holding up a piece of glass behind the word *dog*, which reflects backward the word *God*. In small caption at the bottom, "Turn it all around now." Aaron smiles and is pleased.

"She's very creative."

Tracy smiles and says, "This is true, and knowledgeable of the role of a woman standing behind a great man."

"A great man?" Aaron laughs.

"Yeah. She said Loretta Scott King was a supportive woman who made certain sacrifices to make sure Martin knew she was there for him no matter what."

Aaron laughs and says, "Martin, Loretta. Do you guys filter any of your conversation through reality?"

"Baby, this is blowing up. I mean, even Chapin Street is settling down. The extent is almost empty. Ford Street, Fifth, Nassau Street. All the usual drug spots are quieting down substantially."

"Well, all glory to God then, but as for all that, about Martin and Lo? I think your mom has way too much thought time on her hands."

Tracy grins and says, "Oh, speaking of on hands—so I can get you up off my momma case—guess what I did today?"

Aaron just smiles and says, "Please don't make me cringe."

"You so silly and a holy man too. I was at the laundromat, and I saw Mini Slaughter."

"Mini… Mini! Yeah, she uses to sing at this church down the street from us. I used to love to hear her sing solos."

"Everyone did, so I asked her if she be interested in singing at the next Off Glass, being that we're at The Great Cross. Was that okay?"

"Yeah, yeah. Did she say she'd do it?" Aaron takes her by the hand and pulls her to his lap.

"Don't worry, I got her. I'm was sure Martin would expect nothing less from Loretta."

As she gently kisses him on the lips, just then they both turn as they hear the sound of a key in the door.

Suddenly Lisa opens the door and rushes in, saying, "You guys are not going to believe this!"

As she paces in front of Aaron and Tracy, Lisa explains, "Ya know that music is always a big attraction, at least at the last three Off Glass. Anyway, I heard an old friend of mine was back in town from our school days, and so I went by her house, and there she was,

so I told her what was going on, and I asked her if she'd be inter-
ested. She'd already heard about it, and she said yes! *So*. We now have
Heather Thomas to sing at the next Off Glass at The Great Cross!
So! What'd ya think?"

Aaron and Tracy just stare. Lisa can see the disbelief…just not
the kinda disbelief she was looking for.

She asks, "What!"

Tracy frowns and explains with a very low-key enthusiasm, "I
just asked Mini Slaughter to sing at The Great Cross."

Aaron shakes his head and says, "And you were just saying 'don't
worry.'"

Lisa's hand covers her mouth.

"Jeez, they hate each other…like a fat boy loves beans they hate
each other. Ever since that contest awarded Heather the full scholar-
ship instead of Mini."

Aaron adds, "Yeah, and most of the black community felt Mini
was robbed because of Heather's father's influence with the school
board, to be honest, including me."

Lisa nods and says, "I didn't think there was a clear-cut winner
to me. I can't say Heather went in knowing she'd win. That was the
rap. She did look as shocked as everyone else."

Aaron shakes his head and says, "Ladies, wait. You know what?
That was years ago. God has put this thing together and gave it the
wheels it's riding. Now, maybe it's God's will that this feud should
end the way it began…with both girls singing their hearts out on the
big stage in front of the hometown crowd."

Tracy agrees, "But, baby, how we gonna get them to agree?"

"Yeah, that thing got really ugly that night between those girls,"
Lisa adds.

Aaron looks into Lisa's eyes and says, "I say we trust God."

Suddenly there's a knock at the door. Lisa and goes to opens it.
The man at the door looks right into Lisa's eyes. They both pause as
their eyes seem to lock.

The man says, "You're Lisa. I've seen so many pictures of you,
and though they captured your essence of you, right now I under-

stand that none of them could have possibly captured the fullness of the beautiful woman that stands before me."

Tracy calls out, "Who is it, Lisa?"

"Uh, oh…it's defiantly for me." She smiles.

He extends his hand, and taking hers, he kisses it.

"I'm Eddie Boyd, but friends calls me School."

Lisa exhales, "Yeah, talk about ya back-to-school specials. Hey, wait, your Aaron's friend from prison, aren't you?"

"Yeah, he here?"

"Come on in. Aaron! It's for you!" She cuts her eyes at School and whispers, "For now."

He smiles, and then he sees his friend, and his joy is made complete as they embrace.

The excitement of the conversation stems mainly on what School has read about the Christian off Glass movement that's getting state notoriety so soon after its conception and, of course, the latest word of their friend, All Day.

Chapter 57

In for a Penny

At Deerwood Estates, Mickelson is visibly upset as he looks over the records of the profit taken out of St. Augustine.

"Mr. Cole, what do you make of this? Seems the profit margin is decreasing in St. Augustine of late some 26 percent in the last three months."

Cole, who is reading *The Florida Times-Union,* turns the state and local front page to Mickelson. It reads: NEW YOUTH CHRISTIAN MOVEMENT IS TAKING OLD CITIES BY STORM.

Mickelson smiles and says, "Yes, I saw that, but 26 percent? I can't imagine that many young people coming to the realization that there is more to life than filling their beloved dope pipe. Please. I find it easier to believe that perhaps Vega's product is on the street and has taken away from our profit margin."

"There is always that." Cole nods as his eyebrows raise.

"I believe perhaps we should take a more vested interest in Blain, Rodgers, and Billips. Perhaps you should pay them a little visit. Just to make sure we have the right understanding with regard to what we expect on our investment returns."

Cole smiles a most sinister grin and says, "That sounds like my kind of duty."

Chapter 58

Just Talk

Meanwhile, back at Aaron's, the girls are gone to bed while Aaron quizzes School on the guys he left at Graceville.

"So they sent All Day to Loddy Faith-Based Camp."

"Yeah, dog. He didn't seem to expect it either. They say it's a camp for, like, sick people, ya know. He should be right at home, giving, like, last rights and all, but he's a short-timer anyway and say when he gets out, he'll be by to visit."

Aaron smiles and says, "Yeah, I hope so. We could use him here. Could be a start over for him too. I tried to find him on the internet to see what he was even in for, but he wasn't in the system, at least not under Adam Louis Lawrence Day. I mean, how many of them can there be?"

School laughs and asks, "So that's his real name, uh?" But then he changes the subject. "Hey, so what's up with Lisa, dude, she free?"

Aaron jokes, "Naw, she's about fitty bucks an hour."

"What?" School smiles with excitement.

"I'm messin' with ya, dude."

School grins and says, "Oh man, got me all up in my wallet!"

"Dude, she digs you, ya know. She could use someone real too."

"You saying that like she's ya little sister, and ya wonder what's going on inside my heads? Yo, bro, I'm feelin' her straight up, ya know. She can be a keeper, but will she wanna stay, is all I'm askin'."

"Ya know I'm the wrong one to be asking that, bro. But I think she sees you. I think you see each other really."

Aaron throws a pillow in School's chest.

"Dog, I'm going to bed. Ya got enough cover out here?"

"Oh, yeah, bro, I'm straight. I see ya in the minute."

Chapter 59

No Way Out

Some hours later that night, Jonny Blain lays in his king-size bed, fast asleep. He feels a warm sensation under his cover. He wakes to find he's pissed on himself. Quickly he jumps up from the bed; at the same time, he knocks over a bowl of water from his nightstand that wasn't there when he went to bed.

"What the…"

Suddenly he notices a man in the dark, sitting in his desk chair with his legs and arms crossed. He clears his eyes, and as they adjust, he can see the man called Cole.

Cole smiles and says, "I've always wondered if those fingers in the warm water really made a man piss in his sleep."

The expression on Jonny's face is of confusion and fear and an anxiety that suggests he may yet piss again.

Cole continues, "You seem afraid, Jonny, and that's good. You should be very afraid. Yeah, see, my employer—your employer—is losing sleep over these latest numbers. You're not stupid enough to think I won't kill you dead about the numbers, are you, Jonny?"

Jonny takes a deep breath and says, "Mr. Cole, I'm not trying to beat anyone. We had a problem, but we're working some new prospects. The numbers will be right back up in no time, I promise you."

Cole unfolds his arms, and his 9mm with silencer is now visible. Jonny eyes widen.

"Relax, Jonny. Hell, it's a good thing you already pissed, uh?" He laughs. "You got a problem with this movement thing of your cousin's. We thought these chumps would get better jobs and spend

239

more money. They probably will too. But you need to hedge your bets. We don't want to see what else this Aaron Daniels has up his sleeves. Tell ya what. kill him. He's no martyr. They will forget him. People will be so torn up they'll need a hit. It's business as usual."

"Kill him?" Jonny asks with a surprised look on his face.

Cole looks at Jonny with eyes that cut right through the dark. The look on Cole's face is very serious. He was clicking his silencer off. But then Jonny can hear the silencer click back on.

"Is there a problem, Jonny?" Cole looks with concern in his eyes.

Jonny shakes his head.

"No, Mr. Cole…not at all."

"Good, Jonny. Take a week. You truly don't have two. Understand?"

"Yes…yes, I do."

"Good…very good. Know that he's your cousin. But that'll get you close to him. He need never see it coming. I'll let myself out. Oh, tell ya mother I like what she did with the study and the kitchen. I might have went another way. 'Course it was kinda hard to truly appreciate it in the dark. Ya know… I almost mistook her room… for yours."

Cole looks into Jonny's eyes and again unsnaps the silencer from his gun.

Chapter 60

Courage of Faith

It's Thursday evening. A light rain falls upon the old city, and traffic is slowed as the sudden rain has the many tourists scrambling to get back to their rooms for shelter.

Near the church at The Great Cross on San Marco, a twenty by ten feet army tent has been put up so that the program director can choreograph the activities.

They have long since gone, and only Lisa, School, and the singer, Heather Thomas, remains. She looks over selections of music in search of one or two spirituals that her voice would do justice to as the featured artist.

The rain has settled some, and the tapping sound of the rain against the top of the tent is overshadowed by the sound of voices coming closer to the tent.

Tracy enters the tent with Mini, and suddenly there is an awkward silence as the two singers lay eyes on each other for the first time since high school.

"What is she doing here?" Heather asks.

Mini turns to Tracy and demands, "Am I the featured singer or what?"

"Featured!" Heather replies.

"Well, who else? Not you!" Mini snaps.

Now they begin to fire insults at each other. Their complaints are both simultaneous and loud.

Suddenly School shouts, "Hey! Are you kidding me right now? I've only heard about what you both bring to the table, and I hear you two have…issues, but aren't you both forgetting something? It's not your table, ladies. This thing is way bigger than the both of you. There are going to be people here that are going to feel in their own right that theirs should be the lead voices also. We are here to ask them to be humble for a greater good. And we're gonna need a lot to go right if we're gonna have a prayer of pulling this off. And it's not about fame or fortune but people who need hope for something like a clean place to lay their heads and a decent meal to eat. 'Cause before God's own eyes, it's the right thing to do!"

The four women pause, and their eyes turn to School. He stares back at them. "I could bite a midget right now!"

School continues, "Okay, like chapter 21…no…yeah, that's it—the book of James. Ya'll know about James, right? The Lord's brother? Y'all know…spiritual…stuff, right?"

School begins to walk back and forth.

"Don't it say, 'In there the wrath of man will never bring forth… the righteousness of God?' Where you two are taking this—that's not a real place. I ain't never heard you guys sing or nothing, but I've heard talk of it and from people I trust, and they say you are the… stuff. God made you to be these voices like lights that shine through the darkness of the human heart. Can y'all feel that?"

He asks, "Can you guys imagine the power you two would generate, stepping out there together? That alone would be a great message of hope."

There is a pause of silence, but then Mini nods her head.

"Together?" Mimi says softly as she looks at Heather.

Then Mini's and Heather's eyes meet.

Heather kind of whispers, "Together."

Mini is visually confused, but she smiles and says, "Together, uh, ya know, that just might be worth thinking about. I mean, considering the people who know our history…"

Heather nods and says, "Yeah, and then again…you're not all together that bad." She laughs. "Truth be told… I think you have a pretty terrific voice."

School shakes his head and says, "Yeah, now that's real."

The girls begin to smile and then laugh.

Mini walks over beside Heather and asks, "So you see anything in that song book we can cut up on?"

Heather nods and replies, "Ya know, a few songs do come to mind now that I have back… I mean a partner."

The rain has all but disappeared, and School steps outside the tent into the night. Darkness has overcome the sky, and the lights of cars combined with the glistening of the wet, grassy churchyard create a cascade that simmers the landscape along San Marco Avenue. He can hear the harmonies behind him, and his mind gets lost in the music being arranged, so lost he doesn't notice the tent opening and closing behind him, and Lisa walks out.

"Tell me you're not like in search of an unsuspecting midget out here, are you?"

School turns and says, "Yeah, it's something my grandma used to say, and she was kinda tall, so you never really knew who she was eyeing, ya know."

They laugh, but then it's like he sees her as though by candlelight.

"Why don't you have a boyfriend?" he asks.

Lisa is caught off guard.

"No, don't be direct." She laughs. "I guess I'm…well, looking for… I don't know…someone who's…strong and confident, experienced, maybe traveled. He could even have a prison record and be very direct."

They both laugh. School gently reaches over and takes her hand.

"See, now I'm feeling you so much. We vibe, but if Im'a be honest, I'm not sure of… I don't know… Where do we go from here?"

Lisa smiles while nodding her head and says, "Yeah, I mean, we live with Trace and AD. Their whole thing…got me really checking myself too. I mean, I want what they got, but they got that right from the start. I see them having fun. I have fun with them. I ask myself, if that's being a Christian, what am I so afraid of? What am I gonna be missing if it's already in my heart? I've been baptized and everything." She laughs.

He laughs as well and says, "Yeah, it, like, rubs off on ya, don't it? I been in prison for two years. I'm, like, supposed to be trying to get you in one of these hotel rooms across the street, but it's like this… What we're doing right now. just talking, I'm really feeling… an intimacy here, and I'm thinking maybe we're blessed like them to, ya know, maybe if I—that is—if we both want ta do this right… maybe we won't ever have ta do this again, ya know. Mean me… I could live with that."

Lisa's eyes swell with tears as she is visibly surprised and pleased.

"Wait, you mean you'd consider us staying together, you and I, for like…a blessed thing? You're not just saying that 'cause you've been locked up a long time?"

School shakes his head and says, "That has mostly nothing to do with it."

They both burst out laughing. Lisa puts her hand on her hips, shaking her head in confusion.

"That's game."

School is shocked and says, "No!"

"You are *so* lying." She laughs.

"I'm being real right now!"

Lisa smiles and asks, "So what was it that sold you so hard on me?"

"Oh, Lord."

"No, tell me! See I told ya, game."

"Okay. You have personality. I love your attitude. You have character. You're beautiful, funny, fine to death, and"—he mumbles under his breath—"you do…have a job."

"Wait what! No, hell no, you did not just say that!"

"What! I want nice things in life, hey!"

School breaks out as Lisa swings at him. He zigzags in the field of the wet grass as she tries desperately to connect.

Chapter 61

Showtime

In Jacksonville Bobby comes in from work and finds Cricket in the study at his desk, doing some paperwork.

"Hi, babe," he greets as he kisses her quickly, and then he falls on the couch, kicking his shoes off and putting his feet on the table.

"Uh, long day?" she asks.

"Oh, long isn't even the word."

"New case?" She asks.

"If only. Cases I can handle. They're clear, you have a story to look over, you find a point of law, you attack. Sillenia's really on the Aaron Daniels bandwagon with this Off Glass thing, trying to extend some of its good will into Jacksonville. Of course, because of our personal relationship, I'm cochairman of the Aaron Daniels's committee for a better tomorrow, which I should have seen this coming after the speech she gave me that started about stopping the rain." He yawns then continues.

"Today I felt like I was in a circus. Do you know that Aaron evidently mentioned that he may need someone to screen some calls coming at him about appearances? Seems there are people offering him money for him to speak. Today she made it part of my duties as his former attorney of record officially. I don't know anything about contract law. I was his criminal attorney of record.

"At least I have Kaddie who is thrilled to be involved in the 'Daniels Initiative,' or whatever she wants to call it. And then who does she expect to call? I mean, granted this thing did take off, but really, do you know, she's even cut my workload. She's got Kaddy screening my cases for…"

He looks over and notices that Cricket hasn't even looked around.

"Penny, what are you doing?"

She turns and smiles at him, asking, "Tightrope walker?"

"Uh?"

"Did you know that there are more than six hundred churches in Jacksonville? I've got some two hundred delegates that contacted me about the Off Glass at The Great Cross gathering!"

Bobby drops his head and says, "You're kidding…"

She shakes her head and continues, "No, about six hundred. I'm sorry, honey, but this is the one baby, the one that's supposed to spill into Duval County sponsoring monthly concerts and helping people get off the street and in schools and good jobs."

"How come that sounds a lot like the same speech Sillenia gave me?"

Again, Penny smiles and says, "Okay, maybe I called her this morning and asked for some help, but this is big, Bobby. We could be part of something really special."

"Penny…look, honey, these things have a shelf life, They happen all the time. They take off, honey, but they also land, and we go on. It's not like the nation's gonna sit up and take notice."

Just then the phone rings.

Bobby gets up and walks over around the desk to answer it as he continues, "All I'm saying is, don't get bent out of shape when it starts to slow down in a month or two."

He picks up the phone and answers, "Hello… Yes, this is Bobby Cox… Yes, I represent Mr. Aaron Daniels."

He rolls his eyes. Penny smiles at him as if to say, "I'm sorry."

He continues on the phone, "Yes… Excuse me, did you say Harpo? Yes, yes, I'm sure he'd be interested. Wait a minute, are you the same Harpo located in Chicago? Yes, we have a fax number."

Cricket covers her mouth, her eyes stretched in shock. Bobby looks over at Cricket and gives the fax number. She is elated with laughter at the look on Bobby's face.

Chapter 62

Cry Out

Back in St. Augustine, Jonny Blain sits in the study of his house and meditates on the sofa. He is stretched out, looking at the giant fish tank and the many exotic fish swimming along. Slowly he dozes off into sleep. Soon he finds himself in a dream.

He's back in high school in a basketball game against the school's biggest rival in Palatka. The score is tied up with seconds left on the clock.

The team sits on the bench as the coach screams strategy at them over the noise of the crowd. Jonny rocks back and forth and nods his head. He looks down the bench and sees Aaron listening to the coach's instructions.

Jonny begins to feel the confidence and excitement he's shared so many times when teamed up with his teammate, his best friend, his cousin. But then he begins to remember the words of Cole telling him he must kill him.

He looks again at the crowd that's screaming. Now he sees his father in the crowed slowly shaking his head no. His face looks surreal. He looks again and sees his grandfather, Pastor Mason. The pastor speaks, and his voice resonates over the sound of the crowd.

He says, "What would you give for your soul? What would you take…for Aaron's life?"

The team puts in their hands, and Jonny reacts and puts his hand in.

Aaron puts his hand on top of Jonny's and smiles, looking Jonny in the eyes.

Aaron says to him a phrase that they've shared over the many years of competition, "Think it's a game? Play it to win!"

Aaron has said this to him hundreds of times. Jonny quickly jerks his hand back.

"Oh! Aaron, I'm sorry!" he screams.

He then looks around and see his mother in the stands. Cole is sitting behind her, his grayish-blue eyes staring right at Jonny. The coach's voice is suddenly tuned out, and Jonny hears a verse from the Bible in the midst.

"Touch not my anointed, nor do my prophet any harm."

Jonny eyes open, and he is again in his study. He wipes the sweat from his forehead, but as he sits up for a second, it seems all his fish are at one side of the fish tank and staring at him. Then suddenly they all disperse, each to their own direction.

Then the bell rings. Jonny is startled and then presses the intercom.

"It's us, Chain Gang and Lil Boy."

Jonny presses the buzzer and lets them in. Soon they are in the study.

Jonnie is visibly agitated and begins to explain, "Look, we have a problem. We need to increase production, and fast!"

Chain Gang shakes his head, saying, "Eaiser said than done. JB, we're kickin' out Godfather deals to what few customers that's still buying, but a lot of jugs are still hooked into that job placement, free schooling shit with them people with AD."

Jonny snaps, "Yeah, well, do me a favor, don't keep reminding me! We gotta do something quick 'cause AD is runnin' out of time, dog. He runnin' out of time!"

Lil Boy shows concern in his face as well in his voice, "Out of time?"

The two boys look at Jonny. They are puzzled.

Lil boy asks, "Out of time, what you talking 'bout, Jonny?"

Jonny turns to them with tears in his eyes.

"Look...we gotta hit him."

Lil Boy stands up.

"What? Hit AD. Dig this, dog… What we do…it ain't all that. You know it, them jugs even know it. If anything, they want better jobs to buy bigger dope, dog, slow ya roll."

Jonny stands and yells, "We ain't got no choice, okay! The man that put us on says we got one week from last night, dog, that's it!"

Chain Gang rubs his head.

"Damn… AD…that's hood, dog. I say we stand up against the man 'fo we hit one of our own. We got his shit. We got guns."

Jonny shakes his head and says, "We can't fuck with these people, dog. We don't even know where they're at, and they know all about us, our families, they running the popo. I'm thinking if we could make some real money fast, maybe we can buy AD some time. This thing of his will slow down, I know it!"

Lil Boy looks into the fishbowl and says, "You know, maybe there's another way."

He turns to Jonny and says, "This new dude that they strapped you with…this Clay dude. Now, he don't sound like somebody they were all about pushing around. I mean, think about it. That scary cat Cole that we see every now and then. He give us that look. Why wasn't he brought in to get the brother onboard?"

Jonny thinks about it

"Yeah, know it does look like if everything goes south, it all lands on me."

Lil Boy is animated and says, "Yeah, 'cause they know he 'bout that life! I say we get that kinda protection behind us. I'd rather be working for a brother anyway if we gonna be working the hood."

Chain Gang is uncertain and says, "I don't know, dude. I mean, I know I ain't about hittin' Aaron, but how we gonna make this guy just buck?"

Li Boy smiles and says, "See, that's what you boys missin' down south. Unions! Dude, once you got the men, you got the power. This dude came here to set up, right? The other side saw him, and they didn't want a war, so they dealt with him, right? But in the end, we're the engine making the whole thing run. I say this is how we take back a little bit of the control now 'cause they already wildin'."

Jonny nods and says, "Ya know what, that could work. He locked down the Shores quick and even came in looking to buy some property to branch out, so he ain't no lightweight. We sneak him some play in like the work crew migrant worker in, like, Hastings and Elkton, Armstong with the Shores and the beaches if we can get him to pump our weight for a minute. And we purpose a buyout of our own for a small percentage, our personal take…"

Lil Boy nods in agreement, saying, "Yeah, and those jugs in the Shores and the beaches already got good jobs, and that cheese."

"Good thinking," Chain Gang adds. "Just gotta keep this away from Rodgers and Billips."

Jonny smiles and says, "That should be easy enough. He's a baller like us. He can't stand 5.0 anyway. Screwing them just sweeten the pot a little."

Chapter 63

Near the Cross

The morning has come of the gathering at The Great Cross. Thousands of people have shown up, and even the tourists in nearby hotels and motels have gathered along the sidewalks.

Reverend Mason is preparing to speak, studying his notes. Aaron is in the tent with him. He notices Reverend Mason's meditation. He is entranced for a while. Aaron is silent. Suddenly the reverend begins to smile, his head still in his hands. Aaron observes as the pastor is now in laughing. Then Pastor Mason looks up at Aaron who smiles with confusion.

"Did you get, like, a revelation from God?"

The pastor stands and looks Aaron in the eyes and says, "Yes. Indeed I did."

Aaron breathes a sigh of relief and asks, "So you're ready?"

"I am. In fact, I am more than ready to hear what it is God has put into your heart to speak."

Aaron looks stunned.

"Uh…"

"This was the revelation that the Lord had put upon my heart. That which I have prepared to say…they've heard those words, and they've never been swayed before. That which must be said…should be pure, of a pure heart, a pure motive. He chooses your heart, Aaron, a heart that he himself has prepared for this day."

Aaron's jaw drops as he looks through the crease in the door of the tent. The crowd seems enormous.

He turns back to the pastor and exclaims, "Jesus!"

"Yes, my son. Remember what he has taught you. In doing so, I will tell you this: Do not worry what you will say. He will give you what you should say."

Just then Bobby and Penny come into the tent. Bobby puts his arm around Aaron's shoulder and looks over at the pastor.

"Man, what a crowd! Pastor, I hope you're ready to bring forth the word!"

The pastor points at Aaron and smiles. Penny and Bobby both look at Aaron.

Penny starts to speak but is cut off by Bobby, "We just wanted to say they're ready...and good luck, or maybe not luck...more like whatever you'd say at something like this."

Aaron looks at Bobby and asks, "They're ready, aren't they?"

His eyes turn back to the pastor.

The pastor hands Aaron his Bible and says. "Let not your heart be troubled nor let it be afraid."

Aaron walks out on the stage, and it is assumed that he is there to introduce his grandfather Pastor Mason. But then Aaron begins to speak.

"First, I want to thank you all for coming here today. For some of you, this is a festivity, a church outing, and I get that. But some of you are here because you're really here to listen for something old and yet something new. In the book of First Corinthians, third chapter, the Apostle Paul spoke of the foundation of God being Christ Jesus, and we accept that as gospel. He also spoke of us building on that foundation as using gold and silver. Precious stones, wood, hey, and stubble. Paul spoke of our rewards and losses in such a manner as to suggest this was our life's review of what we had done. I thought it interesting that today, as I looked over the denominations of the Christian faith, that many of you think you build with gold while others...do not. You may even dare among yourselves to suggest some may build with stubble.

"Now, I didn't go to seminary school. I went to prison. I'm very much one on the outside looking in. But knowing that the devil is so crafty, as I'm sure we all do, what if the real gold standard of God was found in our inclusiveness? I mean, have you ever considered what is left on the table because we are so divided? Or even what we could become if we were somehow made whole? The shelters we could build, the food, and transportation to medical, in short, the will of God as the strong bearing the weak.

"And I'm sure many of you have thought about how vast our reach and how plentiful we have become in this America. But even as we have led the world in technology and entertainment and sports... we should be leading in our humility by evolving into a self-contained unit of outreach and growing our communities. I mean, it's not like they couldn't use our help in feeding God's sheep.

"It's time to put aside our differences, our denomination, and become a nation of Christians in action toward all mankind. The time is coming and indeed has come to occupied. The Lord said, whosoever will come. He didn't say come and be Baptist or Methodist, but come. These denominations have two things in common. They derived from the thinking and understanding of some man. And they separate and divide the awesome power of the living God through the children of God, keeping us one from another

We are under attack by our mortal enemy who has submit us under the laws of God and accuses us of being a house divided, in hopes we shall fall. We all remember the tragedy of September 11... of the great loss of life. People for as great as those Twin Towers where no one mourned the buildings that were destroyed that day. We cried for those children who would never see their mothers or fathers again.

"They were mighty and majestic and beautiful, but it was what they housed that were our national treasure. At the end of the day words like *pentacostal* is only a title, a house, a building. Who are we inside? Truly, I tell you the Sabbath was made for man, not man for the Sabbath. Let it be known this day before *God's* own eyes that at last, more than anything in the end, we were trying to be Christians as hard as we could.

"I tell you, maybe this is the mountain the Lord has said we can move by faith, even the faith the size of a mustard seed. If you can agree that our hands can fit perfectly one inside of another, we then can agree we are not alone, and together the numbers before us may not seem so...big, so big."

Aaron walks off to the sound of silence, only the sound of his shoes against the stage made of wood, and then slowly they begin to clap their hands and even cheer. They do this for a few minutes.

Aaron stands in the tent as Bobby, Penny, and the pastor stare with looks of approval.

Aaron listens, but his face is blank, and he says, "They clapped their hands, and they cheered…but did they hear me, Pastor? Do they know what was said?"

The pastor walks over, and he puts his hand on Aaron's shoulder.

"Did you hear you? You have asked them to trust in the power of God. Now I must ask you to also trust in that same God…as you would say…feel me."

Aaron laughs and says, "Yeah, I feel ya, Grandpa."

Sillenia enters the tent and walks over toward Aaron. She looks over toward Bobby.

"Did you tell him?" she asks.

But before Bobby can answer, School and Lisa comes into the tent, holding hands. They are hurried.

"Yo, AD, you got ya peace on you!"

"Yeah, right here."

As Aaron reaches in his back pocket, Pastor observes with a stunning look of concern on his face.

"A peace!"

Aaron pulls out his pocket Bible, and School grabs it, and he and Lisa start to thumb through it.

Aaron turns to the pastor and says, "Yes, my peace."

The pastor is relieved to laughter.

"Okay, I get it…peace." But then he interjects as Lisa and School seem desperately in searching of scripture, "You know I am a pastor. Maybe I can help you, what are you looking for?"

School and Lisa looks up to the pastor, and School explains, "Well, after a while, some of those groups started saying something about John 10:16. Then they started—I don't know—mingling with each other."

"I thought I saw a priest hugging a Jehovah's Witness," Lisa adds while still searching.

"Oh my god. Are you sure?" The pastor is visibly moved.

Then he replies, "The Lord had just healed a man born blind. He also conveyed to this man that he is the Son of God. The Pharisees were questioning Jesus when he said in the book of John in the tenth chapter, the sixteenth verse. 'And other sheep I have which are not of this fold; them also I must bring...and they will hear my voice; and there will be one flock and one shepherd.' Maybe the Lord is bringing about his word even now in their hearts."

Sillenia runs to the tent door and looks out into the crowd.

"Oh my god, they're still filming. Bobby, did you tell him?"

"I was about to." Bobby turns to Aaron and says, "Aaron, Harpo Productions is here. They asked permission to film the event. They said there is a chance that if this is something special, it'll air, but there is a catch."

"A catch...what's the catch?" Aaron asks.

"Well...you'll have to do a cameo."

"Okay, that's no problem."

School walks over and looks Aaron in his eyes, put his hand on Aaron's shoulder, and asks, "Aaron, did you know Harpo is Oprah spelled backwards."

"Oprah... Winfrey!"

Cricket goes to the tent door. She looks outside into the crowd.

"My god, they're like long-lost friends. Like a family reunion of sorts. The one common bond—their love of Jesus...their love of God. There is a jubilee of joy among them."

School joins her in gazing into the crowd. He turns and looks back at Aaron.

"Yo, AD...boyz from the hood."

Aaron and the rest spread the tent doors, and some of the former dope dealers and addicts are among the makeup of the crowd.

Then the music begins. Heather enters the stage from one end, Mini the other. Their voices harmonize in incredible octaves, and the crowd is silenced in amazement. They go on and on, and then they begin to sing *Amazing Grace*, this in a way unheard of, with the arrangements and octaves unprecedented.

Then they sing "His Eye Is On the Sparrow." The orchestra is entwined with rhythm in midair and a block away at Dairy Queen. People migrate to the patio and the parking lots at the nearby hotels.

Bypassers in cars pull over in restaurant parking lots to hear the songbirds sing, hanging onto every word, every note, and then they are joined by a group of men dressed as 1950s gangster-style zoot suits with round brims and pinstripes.

They act as choir and do a dance routine as the ladies sing "Something's Got a Hold on Me," and the people go crazy, and truly a good time is had by all.

Chapter 64

When It All Comes Together

That night at the federal building, Rollie is in his office, working a little late. That was the plan, but he's been on the phone with Sillenia for an hour now. Her excitement is contagious even though over the phone, and he enjoys hearing her. His buzzer rings.

"Hold on, honey." He changes lines. "Yes, Betty?"

"Rollie. Ms. Stockwell is here from NCIC."

"Thank you, Betty. Send her in, and why don't you call it a night, Betty, thank you."

He switches back to Sillenia.

"I gotta go, babe. How long before you're back?"

Ms. Stockwell comes in, and Rollie motions her to take a seat. Rollie hangs up.

"Ms. Stockwell."

"Yes, Agent Wade. I heard you were working late. I'm here because of the background check you wanted on Antrarious Cole's unit during the war. Well, as you know, in any war, there are casualties, and MIAs are sometimes labels given missing soldiers who, for whatever reasons, are considered missing, unconfirmed dead."

"And?"

"Well, I don't know if this is important or not, but we have an MIA: Sulivan Toilver, born 1956 in New Orleans who has an older sister Janet Ryder, born 1940, also in New Orleans, and the interesting thing is…she married a Franz Cole who happened to have fathered Antrarious Cole."

"Sir Cole's uncle was in his unit?"

"More than that, sir. Apparently, they are rumors they ran a list of black bag operations as a duo, smuggling things into the states. It was Cole that filed report of his uncle's capture. I thought that was kinda convenient, sir."

Rollie nods with a smile and says, "I'd say so, and out of character. He specializes in extraction of MIAs in enemy territory, yet he leaves his mother's brother. Let me see the date on that." Rollie looks over the paperwork. "This guys a sport. He's no doubt assumed another identity, and he's had almost thirty years to fortify his position, damn it. We didn't go back far enough."

"So what do you want me to do, sir?"

"Okay, from that date, we need a missing person's report on possible POWs from that unit. Cross-reference with their hometown recovery records. Somebody came out of that jungle, but they didn't go home because they'd be recognized as an imposter. See if any of them match up with the names submitted to the St. Augustine faculty, also cross-reference them with staff of the St. Augustine Police and Sheriff Department, both city and county."

"Yes, sir." She grabs her paperwork and starts toward the door.

Rollie then calls her, "Ms. Stockwell, what made you check, I mean the MIAs?"

She pauses and turns and smiles.

"Danny, I mean Agent King, we've been dating, and he was keeping me abreast as to how important this case is to both of you. He stopped by my house the night that nice Mr. Ling was killed. He really felt bad for his wife. It was his idea really."

"Nice Mr. Ling? You knew him?"

"Yes, sir. I live about a block down. Danny stopped by that night. He was so torn up he didn't even realize his clothes were wet."

"Wet?" Rollie's thoughts of that day's weather plays back in his mind of a complaint of the heat. He doesn't remember any rain, just the opposite.

"Yes, sir. Some kids unplugged a hydrogen. He drove right through it. I'm really worry about him sometimes. He's not as brick and mortar as he'd like to think he is."

Rollie smiles and says, "We'll take good care of him, Ms. Stockwell, I promise."

"Thank you."

Ms. Stockwell leaves, and Rollie turns and opens his blinds. His mind wanders as he stares into the city. Then his buzzer rings.

"Yeah, Betty, I thought you had gone."

"You've got a call from someone on a secured line. I held it until you had finished. He sounds important."

"Okay, put him through"

"Agent Wade, I'm under here in Old Town and can't talk long, but be advised of a possible hit ordered on one Aaron Daniels. Take precautions. He's a good kid."

Chapter 65

Rock Beach

Jonny Blain's SUV pulls up on the curb in front of a sign along the Highway A1A just down from St. Augustine Beach.

Jonny, Chain Gang, and Lil Boy exit the vehicle.

The sign reads Rock Beach.

Chain Gang laughs and says, "How da hell a beach called Rock Beach. Think it's a gang of bassers hiding out here, getting they stupid on!"

Lil Boy looks around and says, "Damn, sho ain't nothing out here but weeds and brush I see. We gotta walk down through these woods to get to the beach?"

Jonny looks around and says, "Yeah, guess so. This is where he said he'd be. I don't see no ride though. Let's check it out. Maybe we early."

The three make their way through the given path through the shrubberies. They come up on a line of large rocks. Beyond them, they see Danny sitting in a beach chair facing the ocean. They're three other chairs and a table with a bottle of Hennessey cognac and three other glasses and a cooler of ice.

The men make their way from beyond the rocks through the beach sand dunes.

Danny smiles at their approach.

"Welcome, gentlemen. I hope you didn't have trouble finding the place?"

"How the hell did you find it?" Jonny asks.

"I do my homework. I suspected at our first meeting that per- haps we should get together somewhere that Officer Friendly won't be popping up. I don't see him even knowing about this place."

"You suspected, uh?" Lil Boy asks. "Tell me something, man. Who are anyway, man? I'm trying to figure how you just come in outta nowhere, and in the OT area, my turf, is where I spotted you. Now you serving in the Shores. For all we know, you could be 5.0."

Danny gestures to the three men to take a seat and have a drink.

"First, it's good practice to walk the field you plan to play on. You want to know your product is appreciated. You blaze your own trail. Get to know the demographics. You know how to distribute and who would be your best worker to put in that area."

Jonny and Chain sit and pour a drink. Lil Boy is still standing and still visibly heated.

"You forget the part where you ask permission to work the turf!"

Danny rolls his eyes and looks at Jonny, asking, "Is he kidding?"

Lil Boy steps closer, exclaiming, "What, am I kidding!"

Danny holds up his hand as to halt Lil Boy, then he points his finger at Jonny. Lil Boy looks at Jonny to find a red laser beam aimed at his chest. Danny points again, this time at Chain Gang. There is also a laser on his chest. Jonnie and Chain Gang's eyes spread, and their mouths drop open. Lil Boy looks back to Danny. Danny stands up and walks nose to nose with Lil Boy.

"And then there were two… Now, we play a little different where I come from, yeah. This was to become a hostel takeover, but I thought I might have found some promise here for myself along with some young brothers wanting to make a come up. If you boys want a lesson in how to hustle turf from a master, then I can use you. I can't use stupidity. This America, little boy. You have only the rights you can defend. That's why you're here. So I show hope you boys got something to tell me, or you are about to have ya self a very bad day after I inform Mickelson you tried to go behind his back."

The three boys' eyes meet.

Danny smiles and continues, "Now, I'm guessing you boys maybe want ta get from under a white boy's fist. Why's he running a black man's world anyway?"

Jonny gives an exhale then says, "This is business. And yeah, he disrespecting the tone."

"I can't tell," Danny explains. As he stands toe to toe, looking into Lil Boy's eyes, Danny continues, "See, now the way this works is if I sit down before you, then we'll finish this in another life. Now if you thinking anybody could be out in the bush with laser lights, then try ya luck, but I really would suggest ya sit ya ass down, little boy."

"Man, sit yo ass down!" Chain Gang replies with a shout.

Lil Boy slowly sits.

Danny looks back at Jonny and asks, "You want to do business?"

"Yeah, but it's a little tricky. See, this is just between us."

Danny nods and says, "I suspected as much. In our last meet, I sensed that there was something…more to discuss, but being that you're so giving to the double cross. Why should I trust you, and please don't tell me we're all brothers here. Tell me, what did you have in mind?"

Jonny runs down a game plan in which Danny would buy drugs from him at a bargain price from his people, extending them access to new territory, then his boys would distribute the surplus at market value when they pull a hostile takeover of their own.

Danny pretends to be not interested, and Jonny sweetens the pot. This is what Danny's been looking for, but he really didn't see this coming so soon. Still, he can't make it too easy, but finally, he agrees.

"Okay… I'll have five of my guys pick up from you, through the real estate office as you wish, this prepay thing, as you wish. But come Friday night, if you don't deliver as you promise, you all dead." Danny smiles and adds, "Oh! and I will be at the game."

That Wednesday Danny sends five undercover agents to Jonny's real estate agency.

They each leave ten thousand dollars. They each leave with tickets to the St. Augustine Yellow Jackets football game. Each ticket stub has a stamp on the back.

"Keep the stubs. There'll be two sets of officers at the game with dogs at the gate there. Rodgers and Billips' men."

Danny gets back to Rollie and fills him in, "So what do you want to do, Rollie?"

"Hard call. My first thought is to go ahead and pick up Rodgers and Billips at their end of shift Friday. That'll take two firearms out of play and also keep them where we can put our hands on them once this all goes down. I know they'll already have their men schedule for the game by then, and by now, with Mickelson thinking he's got you, he may let Cole make a play for them. But I can't risk not letting the other's buyers show their faces."

Danny nods and adds, "Yeah, plus what if it's a rip-off? Jonny is in control of the funds until he's not. The boy looks like he's got some rabbit in him, and he's damn scared of Cole. We'd have no dope, no real evidence to connect to Mickelson to Cole, to Fells, or Billips."

Rollie shakes his head and says, "That could be a real place, Danny. From what Sillenia was telling me on the phone last night, there's a lot of people fighting for their lives back down there. Rodgers and Billips are already in no-man's-land, counting the days they wake up ended."

Danny smiles and asks, "So you think they're feeling the pressure?"

"Yeah, Danny, I do, and if we want this to go down, Billips and Rodgers are key. Mickelson knows this. Yeah, we'll have them called away on assignment, and we'll take 'em later their after shift."

Chapter 66

All Is God's

Thursday evening Aaron, Tracy, School, and Lisa are in their apartment when the doorbell rings. Aaron opens the door, and to his surprise, there is Darryl, the street hustler. Darryl is fidgety and visibly uncomfortable.

"Hope ya don't mind me stopping by? I, uh... I... Okay, I went and got the job at the restaurant, and I was doing really good, yeah know. I was working hard and learning things, and...and then I messed up."

Aaron smiles and shakes his head, asking, "What did you do?"

"I...uh... I got, like, an advance from the lady manager, Mrs. Martha, and I was on schedule to go to work, but that night... I got high...so I didn't call, didn't show, nothing."

Aaron nods and asks, "You want your job back?"

"Yeah...but I don't know what to say. I'm ashamed. Some of them people know me. They knew this would happen."

School walks from around the corner to the door.

"Yo, I couldn't help but overhear, partly 'cause I was eavesdropping, so what da you think, AD, is this the man I was looking for or what?"

Aaron's eyes light up, and he nods, still looking at Darryl.

"I was just thinking the same thing."

The two men take Darryl by the arms and sit him in the living room among the girls.

School announces the news, "Ladies, the newest member of our staff!" The girls clap their hands.

Darryl smiles.

Lisa asks, "So what's his position?"

AD answers, "Counselor. He's who we're sending people that have fallen down so he can instruct them on what it takes to get back up."

Darryl's mouth drops, exclaiming, "Me! Hey, I'm a dishwasher!"

Lisa is quick to say, "And there're some dishes in the sink if this is like your motivation."

Darryl stands and says, "No! You don't understand. I was getting high last night! So who am I to council anybody?"

Aaron explains, "Anybody and everybody who's ever felt like you when you knocked on my door will relate to those emotions and connect with you in ways we couldn't possibly. People sick and tired of being sick and tired may want help right now, but not many of them would have knocked on that door. It's not supposed to be easy. It's supposed to be fought though. People who have been where you just came from, and wanting what you have, they need someone to tell them that first fight that urgency to take the money out of your pocket.

"They need to review the last few times they went down that street and how hopeless they felt. They need to remember how good they felt when they are doing for someone they love some good. No one can do a little crack without going all in. They need to believe they got better days, man."

Darryl stands and says, "I mean, you guys need help, I'm sure, but you don't promote a man after he messes up!"

"Yeah, ya do," Tracy replies as she tosses another pistachio in her mouth. She continues, "Honey, we were just reading that the other night. Remember you said you'd make a mental note?"

Aaron reaches over on the living-room table and grabs the Bible. "Yeah, and I did make a mental note."

Aaron thumbs through and comes to it. "It's Second Corinthians 5:18, 'Now all things are of God's, who has reconciled us to himself through Jesus Christ, and has given us the Ministry of reconciliation,' that is, that God was in Christ reconciling the world unto himself, not counting their sins to them. And has committed to us the word of reconciliation. Now, I think we are ambassadors for Christ. So that's the job, Mr. Ambassador, and you've got the qualification and the ball. People need you. Your friends need you. They're counting on someone who can relate to them. We don't need another dishwasher in the world, but we can always use a man bearing light."

Darryl slowly shakes his head and says, "So, yeah, it makes sense, man! You sure you want to take that kind of chance on me?"

School nods and says, "'Cause you knocked on that door in our hour of need! It is written, no one can—can!—come unless it has been granted him by God!"

Darryl looks at Aaron. Aaron thumbs back to John 6:65 and points it out to Darryl.

He tells Darryl, "You cared enough to come. Now stay. Learn about the armor that keeps you safe from temptation: the love in your heart for those that may need you. You didn't fall to stay down. You can't. As God gives you strength to stand, so you shall."

Lisa leans over to Tracy and says, "You don't think he looks like he'd be more motivated if he could just wrap his hands around a few dishes just ta bask in the rinsing of the plates?" Tracy rolls her eyes at Lisa. "What? It's like a muse, is all I'm saying."

Chapter 67

Hush Little Baby

Thursday morning, about 3:00 a.m. There's a dirt road just south west of King Street off Whitney Street in St. Augustine. The dirt road is called Grant Street.

There is an old abandoned house most frequented by those given to the night because of its setting, so far away from the road, as well as the large overlapping tree limbs that drape over half of the side of the house, its limbs brushing against the ground.

A car sits behind these limbs, perfectly concealed in the darkness.

The two young men in the front seat pass a joint between them as another guy in the back seat rolls down his window and tossed a freshly used condom into the night. Beside him, a very pretty and shapely young lady feels along the floor of the back seat in search of her hot-red thong. Finding it, she then holds them against the car window to see which side is inside out. As she begins to slide back into her underwear, she spots the guy in the driver seat holding up a bag of crack as though to check the quantity of the sack.

Her eyes stretch, and she becomes complimentary.

"Damn, you boys know how ta put it on a girl. I mean damn! I ain't gonna be doing much of nothing for a week!"

The men look at each other and laugh.

She continues with a seductive smile on her face, "Maybe I'll just wait for y'all to come back in town, and we make this a regular thing, ya know, y'all look out."

As the man in the front seat hands her the baggie, she begins to search through her purse, looking for her stem.

The man in the back seat turns to her and says, "Hell naw, you ain't finda hit that shit up in here. You got yours. You gonna need ta dip."

She nods and says, "Oh, okay, I'm straight, my bad."

As she exits the car, the car starts and slowly begins to make its way onto the dirt road.

The young lady finds a seat on a step beside the deserted house. She takes one of the pieces from the baggie and breaks it. The sound of the snap is pleasant as it signifies the potency of the drug. She places the smallest of the broken pieces on her pipe, but instead of the sizzle, the rock-type substance isn't liquefying; it turns into the intoxicating gas, and there is only the smell of smoke. She quickly thumps the substance from her pipe and places the other piece into her mouth and then spits. The taste is of Orajel and peanuts.

Quickly she jumps up and runs to the edge of the road. She can see the taillights of the car in the distance as it is slowing down to stop at the corner Stop sign.

She begins to run toward the car, screaming, "You sons of bitches! You come back here, motherfuckers!"

The guy in the back seat looks out of the window and yells back, "Hey, we got our nuts! You got yours!"

She can hear their laughter as the car turns the corner and is gone.

Her stride breaks, and she falls to her knees, her hands and knees now submerged in the dirt; her pipe in one hand, a bag of nuts in the other; her face a mass of tears that begins to beat the ground beneath her face.

She raises her head and screams, "*No!*" as she tosses the baggie into the direction of the Stop sign.

Now the ground begins to bead all the more as a soft drizzle begins to deflect the dirt against her skin like tiny little dots. As she rises to her feet, the sky seems to open, and the rain begins to drop heavily, and she races to find shelter behind a large oak tree near her.

There is a chill in the air, and her fragile sweater is unable to stretch enough to cover her legs.

She slumps behind the tree, trying to pull the sweater around her legs and knees without success, and wonders if she should dash for the house; but then just as suddenly as the rain had begun, it stops, and she notes the favor of the rain as it's washed the dirt from her legs and feet.

She starts toward Whitney Street and then toward King Street. She stops at a puddle just before King Street and birdbaths a little more before she begins to walk King Street.

Her thoughts are of shelter. She thinks of Archie's house, a dope trap about a mile down the road. There hasn't been lights or water in about five months, so she duck into the tree line to take a piss. She can deal with the candles, but the stench of that bathroom is not an option.

She reaches King Street as a PT Cruiser passes and seems to slow down and take notice. She makes her way to the top of the hill and across the tracks. She starts toward Archie's when the PT Cruiser comes up from behind her just as a drizzle begins.

This time it stops just twenty feet up the street from her. She begins to run quickly toward the car. The window comes down.

"Need a ride?" the driver asks.

He's an older man, about mid-forties, dressed nice, and he smells really good.

She climbs in quickly as she can't believe her good fortune. She notices eight-by-ten glossies in the back seat of his car, but only through shadows of passing street lights.

"You a cop?" she asks.

The man smiles and says, "No. I'm not. Are you? What's your name?"

"Tammie." As she begins to survey the vehicle for clues, she asks, "And no, I'm not a cop. So what are you doing tonight?"

He smiles and says, "Well, I was hopping on doing something... nice." He takes a look at the young lady and smiles. "I mean, you're sure you ain't no cop?"

She smiles and places her left knee upon the edge of the car seat as she looks away out of the passenger-door window. The shift raises her skirt, and her red thong is now hard at work.

"No, I'm not a cop. So what are ya taking about getting into?" she asks.

"Well, I'd like to start with breakfast at Denny's first. Now, I'ma give you forty bucks anyway before we even leave there, and I'ma pay the check on whatever we eat. Is that acceptable?"

Tammie glances over at the driver and nods her approval with a smile.

Once at Denny's, just as the food arrives, the man stands and takes the bill in hand. He then reaches into his wallet and places the money on the table for the food.

He then hands Tammie $40 and says, "Tammie, I'm afraid I have deceived you, but I'm paying you for your time as promised." He continues, "But I came out here tonight looking for another kinda date."

Tammie is visibly confused as the man turns, and just behind him at the door, another man stands there.

Tammie looks at the door and softly speaks the words, "Daddy."

Her father walks over to the man and shakes his hand and thanks him.

The man leaves, and her father asks, "May I join you?"

She is stunned, surprised, and embarrassed all at the same time.

"What are you doing here?" she asks.

Her father stares out into the parking lot.

"What am I doing here? You know I heard a man ask another man about two weeks ago, 'How can you rest peaceably at night, knowing that ya little girl was out there among a world of people who just don't look at her the way you look at her? People that are unable to see your little girl the way you see your little girl. Would any one of them protect her the way you would without thought of life or death? Which one of them would give her the shirt off their back if she was cold or give her their last if she were hungry?'"

Tammie eyes begin to bulge with tears as she can see the sincerity in her father's eyes.

"All of a sudden. I couldn't sleep, baby. I couldn't help wondering. I lay in bed, and I got all of these snapshots of how I couldn't get you to stop crying, and I'd sing to you and rock you, and I used to get so jealous that your mother would take you, and you would just shut up."

They both laugh.

"I remember every day. Sometimes even at work I'd stop suddenly in thought of how I was going to win your heart that day, and even though it took what felt like years…the day finally came when you knew me. When you gave me your okay to hold you and to feed you. I never even knew I could feel such a thing. So I joined this program called Dads for Daughters for dads that want to help their kids maybe come home, and they put us with the police department. They give you a list of all the known hangouts, and we take turns picking up girls and bringing them to breakfast."

Tammie takes a deep breath and shakes her head. There is a proud smile she tries to suppress.

"Uh-uh, you did not just tell me you set this whole thing up… to see me."

He smiles and nods. But now holding back their tears becomes harder.

She asks, "So how's Mom? I mean…she's okay, right?"

Her father looks her in her eyes and says, "She misses her baby too."

Tammie takes a deep breath and says, "Daddy, all we do is fight. Look, if all you want is some sleep, I don't know what to tell ya—"

But he cuts her off.

"Yeah, you're right. We fight, but not hard enough, not nearly enough, not for each other. Not to lessen the distance that divided us one from the other. I have held you in one hand, baby, and I have gotten up early in the morning to get you back to sleep and then went right out to work, glad to make the day 'cause I knew what I was working for. You're my heart, you and ya mother both. You are my heart.

"I've always loved you like that, and maybe I'm not very good at showing you what you need to see…but it's there, baby, I promise you. Tammie, if I thought you'd let me I'd hold you in my arms right now in front of all these people just like when you were my little baby and sing ya 'Hush Little Baby' ta ya fell sound ta sleep, and I know ya grown. I don't need nobody to tell me you grown. Now I've done some things wrong in this world, some things ya can't get back. I wasn't great at being your age. None of us are. We just don't want our kids to know.

"When I think about it now, maybe that's what the Lord meant when he said confess your sins. Maybe he was saying 'to your children' so they won't get screwed up, wondering what's wrong with them. But not making sure you was ready for this world—inexcusable. A man should never let himself get that busy, and I and your mother, we're asking for a do-over. And we don't know what we don't know, but we're asking you to work with us, and let's see if we can't get through this as family."

There is a warm smile on Tammie's face, and the anger, the frustrations, the events of only hours ago feel like distant memories.

She asks, "So…are we gonna take something home for Momma?"

Her father smiles and says, "I know just what she'd want." He moves around the table to her side and hugs her.

There are now tears of joy in the eyes of both father and daughter as she reminds him, "Oh, and don't forget…when we get home, you owe me a song."

Chapter 68

Fear

It is the day of the game, and there is a great anticipation and excitement throughout all St. Augustine. But in the living room at a duplex in Ocean Palms, just down the street from Jonny Blains, there is a much more solemn mood.

A man and a woman are sitting on their living-room sofa. Their son makes his way from the dining room with a chair, and placing the chair facing them, his words are staggered and sad.

"Mom, Dad... I'm in a lot of trouble, and I can't see my way out."

His father reaches out to him and asks, "Son, is this about the thing at U of F? Did you take the money?"

Jonny shakes his head and says, "I wish it was that simple, Pop."

As he stands up and begins to pace, he says, "It all started a long time ago. I meet this guy when I went to Miami that summer just before my tenth-grade year. The dude was getting dope for like a fourth of the cost, and he started selling me the dope at half his price, and to make a long story short, before long, I had people working for me."

"Jonny, are you in some kinda trouble with the law?" his mother asks.

"No, Mom. It's worse. I got with these people who...insisted I work for them."

"The mob!" his father asks.

Jonny just nods and says, "Now I'm having trouble moving the stuff, and to make it right, they want me to take somebody out."

Tears begin to stream down his face as his mother rushes to him.

"Oh no, baby, you can't. You'll be throwing your life away like that. They'll always hold that over you, no!"

He embraces his mother as his father sits and stares into Jonny's eyes. Suddenly there is a look of realization on his face.

"My god…they want you to kill Aaron, don't they?"

Jonny's eyes begin to pour as his head drops into his mother's shoulder. He then nods, still holding his mother.

"If you don't do it, they'll kill you," He replies, still looking in Jonny's eyes. But then suddenly he can see what Jonny is afraid to say.

"You've put all of us are at risk, son? Otherwise, you wouldn't be telling us, would you?"

Jonny can only drop his head again.

His father raises from his chair and says, "Boy, what the hell you done got us into! You ain't never wanted for nothing, and you done put all our lives at risk! You going straight to the police, and ya gonna take ya chances!"

"I can't. They own the cops. They got two cops working for me!" he screams.

"Oh my god!" his mother cries out as she covers her mouth in the shock of the unthinkable.

Now there isn't a dry eye among them.

She turns to her husband and asks, "My god, what are we going to do?"

Jonny's father holds her in his arms and says, "It's gonna be okay, baby," as he looks up into Jonny's eyes again.

"Jonny, you do nothing, ya hear! I'll handle this."

"But, Dad, I'm running out of time."

"*I said I'll handle it!*" he shouts, and then he says calmly, "Ya friends, they out there waiting for you. Just go, and I'll handle this."

Chapter 69

The Chase to the Place

The day is cooling as the sun begins to set. The perfect night for a football game, and tonight none is bigger than this football game as the undefeated St. Augustine High football team takes on the also-undefeated and county rival, Nease High School.

Both teams feature the collegiate sought-after seniors such as Nease record setting Q B , and S. Augustine's high-powered offence primed by a running back core by committee, and a defense headed by a young group of sophomores and juniors.

Dillard is en route to the stadium hours before the game when his cell phone rings.

"Yeah."

"It's Rollie. What's your location?"

"I'm heading to the school. They'll have metal detectors at the gate. I'll stash a piece so I'll have Danny's back. It's still on for tonight, right?"

"Yeah, look, I got Pam meeting you at the Gyro Restaurant in the St. Augustine Square downtown. I need an ETA."

"I can be there within the hour."

"I'll relay that, ponytail. Keep your eyes open."

"Will do, Chief!"

Dillard reaches the stadium and makes the plant of a weapon. He starts out, and as he is locking the gate, he is surprised.

"Mr. Dillard?"

He turns to find Principal Strickland.

"Mr. Dillard, what are you doing?"

Great, Dillard thinks to himself.

"Sir, I painted some of the lines over this morning for the big game. I was just checking to see if they had dried."

Strickland looks suspicious but says, "Okay…good. I'll check over the field myself later. I trust you'll be on call tonight for maintenance?"

"Oh, yes, sir. Only way to get in. There's no tickets left." He laughs, but Strickland doesn't.

"Just remember, Mr. Dillard, you are here tonight to act in a professional capacity. You are not a spectator, got it?"

"Oh, yes, sir." He thinks, *I won't even look toward the field while they're playing, sir.*

"Good. You may go."

Dillard walks off, thinking, *Man, what a putz.* Unknown to Dillard, he is being observed from a distance by two of Mickelson's men who just made the drop-off to Fells.

From the car, one of them spots Dillard.

"Hey, I know that guy."

His partner says, "That's the maintenance man. I watched him one night with Ricks. He's all right."

The other man continues to stare.

"Naw, man, I know him from the war. Dessert Storm. That guy's a war hero. You'd think he could do better than a janitor. I heard that guy took out two all-terrain vehicles and pull three GIs from a burning vehicle before it exploded."

"Yeah?"

"Yeah."

The other man watches as Dillard gets into his car and begins to think, *Why is he sweeping out johns?*

"Follow him, don't get to close. I'll call Cole."

Soon Cole is on the phone.

"Dillard, the janitor? I ran him. There was no mention of any military record."

"So what do you want us to do?" the other man asks.

"Are you on him now?"

"Yes, sir."

"Take him and ask him what he's really doing at the school. But I know I'm not gonna like the answer, so if it's cute, take him out!"

Cole hangs up the phone and then dials another number.

The sleeper answers, "That janitor, he's not right. I'm taking him out. Keep your eyes open tonight at the game. Watch for anyone who showed up in those photos I sent you. I got a feeling we're close to shutting this down."

"I'm on it. What if they get too close?"

"No, they don't get too close. They get to Fells too late, if anything. You understand!"

"I do." Then the sleeper hangs up.

Dillard makes his way down US 1 South. He notices the tail. Soon he is downtown at the Gyro Restaurant.

As he walks to the door, he notices Pam (his contact) sitting at a table through the window. Dillard goes inside and takes a seat just up a few rows from her. She knows what he is doing. She sits, and reaching into her purse, she pulls out a pin and pad (part of their tactical training).

Dillard reads her move and picks up a menu. With his right hand hidden from the window behind him, he begins to sign. "Voyeurs" is the message. She then notices the men through the window behind him across the street in the crowd, doodling. They are suspicious in that they are not moving but appear to be waiting for someone. Knowing Dillard's keen eye, she trusts him. Soon Dillard orders a sandwich. Pam notices, as Dillard eats, he looks over a newspaper and taps his car keys on the table.

He's going for his car just north of their position, she thinks.

Then she calls the waiter and pays for her coffee. She leaves, never making any contact with Dillard. She goes to her car and calls for backup. Most of their units confirm their positions miles away at the game.

Dillard comes out, and she watches him go to his car. Suddenly a man comes up on Dillard. She can't see, but she's sure he has a gun. They both get into Dillard's car and drive off. Pam begins to follow.

Dillard drives down San Marco with the gun trained on him from the man in the passenger's seat.

"So what's this a carjack?" Dillard asks.

"Just drive, get on US 1, and go north.

Dillard reaches over.

"Hey!" the gunman responds.

"I'm just putting on my seat belt, sport. It's the law."

"You better understand something, sport. You don't do nothing you don't ask me first."

Now Dillard is on the open road and says, "Okay, so I'm gonna ask you again, what's this all about?"

"Just drive," the gunman insists.

"*Okay.*"

Dillard begins to mash the accelerator. The car is quickly up to seventy and climbing.

"Slow down!" the gunman shouts.

"Or what? Or you'll shoot me. This wasn't a well thought out plan, was it? I mean, you shoot me, we crash, the whole thing gets public quickly. Hey, want to see what she really can do?" Dillard applies more speed.

"I'm warning you!" the gunman shouts.

As he points the gun at Dillard's head, Dillard looks in his rearview mirror.

He sees a sedan coming up fast and says to the gunman, "Friends of Yours?"

The gunman grabs the rearview mirror and turns it quickly to look.

In an instant, Dillard grabs the gunman's hand and slams on the breaks. The gunfires just pass Dillard's head, shattering the driver's-side window as the gunman is thrown back and then forward into the windshield. Dillard pulls the gun man back and chops him under the throat with the gun as he hits the gas.

The sedan, which also hit breaks, tries to regain control as Dillard cuts across the medium and races back south with gun in hand. The sedan follows and does not notice Pam who is still traveling North in observation.

Dillard pushes about eighty when he comes to notice the miniature piano factory on the other side of the highway.

Timing his break, he darts back across the turn lane into its entrance. Making a sharp right, he hook slides in his car, jumps out, and takes aim.

The sedan comes into the entrance to suddenly see Dillard's car. With nowhere to go, he attempts to avoid the car and runs into the concrete stairs at the base of the building.

Dillard makes his way to the sedan to find the driver is unconscious.

Seconds later, Pam pulls in. Dillard has disarmed the sedan driver and has him on the ground away from the sedan.

"Dillard! You all right!" Pam screams.

"Yeah, why wouldn't I be? You didn't call for a whole lot of back up, did ya?"

"I did, and yeah, they're not coming. Someone seems to have felt trying to take you while letting you drive would wind up a bad career move."

Pam looks around at the subdued perpetrators lying disarmed on the ground and says, "I guess they were right."

Dillard is hurried and says, "Okay, don't call the locals! If you have to wait, get some of our people on this. SAPD can't know I'm alive."

As he hurries to his car, she asks, "Where are you going?"

Dillard pulls the other gunman out to the ground.

"It's the biggest game since Tebow verse James? I'm going to a football game."

Rollie, being driven by Agent Hutch, speeds down I-95 South en route to St. Augustine High School. His chin rests against his hand as he stares into the highway terrain. Hutch notices after a while that Rollie is unusually quiet.

"You okay, Boss?" he asks.

"Uh? Oh...yeah, I just—"

Just then the phone rings. Quickly Rollie reaches inside his jacket and grabs his cell phone.

"Rollie."

"Hi, Boss, it's Betty. You wanted me to check on those work orders."

"Yeah, Betty, what cha got?"

"Boss, on those dates you gave me, I found no reports of fire in the area or vandalism. There isn't even any record with the city of an issued work order or anyone signing off on the repair of any fire hydrant near the Ling house."

"Thanks, Bet." Rollie hangs up.

"Hutch, what's our ETA?"

"About twenty minutes."

"Make it ten!"

"You want the noise?"

"And the lights, hit it!"

Rollie then phones Danny.

"Yeah."

"Danny, look, there's a chance you've been made!"

"What? how?"

"That visit you made out to the Ling widow. It was a designed play to draw us out."

"So the man died for nothing. I'm in the parking lot, Rollie. There are six officers under with me, and Dillard's on the way. I got sharpshooters. I'm going in. We gotta do this, if just for the widow Ling."

"I'll be there in ten. I don't know why they would have let it get this far knowing what they've known for so long, Danny, but we can't rule out war against the establishment, so be on your toes and tell those sharpshooters to stay alert."

Danny gets out of his car and looks around. He sees the surveillance van assigned to serve as command post. The other agents undercover posing as patrons make their way to the gate. They give the tickets and keep the stubs as they go in. Danny goes in last.

He makes his way through the crowd and finds Jonny Blain sitting exactly where he said he would be.

Showtime, he thinks to himself as he makes his way up the stands.

"What's up, Jonny?"

Jonny smiles and says, "Glad you could make it. It should be a good game."

"It should at that, but being this is our first time out, why don't we get this thing on, and afterward we could all enjoy the game a little bit better. I mean, hey, Jonny. I paid up front, I ain't used to that shit."

"Relax, bro, we can't do nothing till after kickoff. That's when they settle, and my man can handle his business, ya dig. It'll all be over by halftime."

"Halftime."

Danny's surprised. The longer this takes, the more time that someone has to notice and leak the arrest of Rodgers and Billips. He remains calm.

Dillard makes his way from his car and races to the gate. He almost pulls his badge out but then quickly switches it to his employee gate pass.

As he enters the gate past the officer, he is immediately met by Principal Strickland.

"Mr. Dillard! I've been waiting for you. Please follow me!"

Dillard is still undercover, and they've captured the attention of the officers. Since he doesn't know who's dirty, he complies. Strickland walks ahead of him, leading him toward the paint shed beyond the stands.

"Mr. Dillard, the referees are complaining. They won't start the game because one of your lines was not drawn clear enough."

Strickland unlocks the master lock and opens the door. Dillard walks in and toward the shelves of paint.

Just then he hears the drumroll indicating the kickoff.

Wait a minute, that's the kickoff, He thinks to himself. He starts to turn when Strickland, already with gun in hand, fires twice, hitting Dillard in the back.

Dillard grabs the shelves and pulls them on top of him. Strickland fires two more times into the cluster.

Just then there is a girl's voice.

"Mr. Strickland, they're looking for you in the coach's box, something about eligibility."

Strickland's gun is hidden by the open door, and so he eases it into his waist and buttons his coat. He then quickly observes the cluster and, seeing no motion, locks the shed and starts back toward the stands.

Chapter 70

The End Game

Cole rides in the back of one of Mickelson's limo toward St. Augustine. The fact that no one has called in on Dillard has caused Mickelson concerned. Cole has been sent out on damage control and to look out for feds personally.

Danny, sitting with Jonny Blain, observes the concession stand rolling a close cart that fit nicely behind the stand. Jonny taps his shoulder.

"Concession stands open. Why don't ya get yourself some goodies, and ah...don't forget the stub."

Danny nods. He has people in position at the base of the stands watching. He gives a signal, and they (one by one) make their way over to Mr. Fells's stand. Each one passes him a ticket; each one is handed a large bag. They start going toward the gate in three-minute intervals.

After a phone call, Danny stands and shakes Jonny's hand, saying, "Save my seat. I'll be back."

"That's the whole point, brother, keep you coming back."

The first man reaches the control van where Rollie is waiting.

Now Cole's limo is turned onto Highway 16 just as his phone rings.

"Yeah."

"I just saw your friend in the photo you sent me shaking hands with Jonny Blain. They seem quite friendly."

"You shittin' me? They're at the game together?"

"What are your instructions?"

282

"That's too close. Shut down shop, now!"

"It's done."

The sleeper hangs up his phone and starts toward Mr. Fells's stand.

Meanwhile, another phone is ringing over and over.

"Sir, still no response from Agent Dillard."

Rollie turns to his man and orders, "Keep trying."

Finally, Dillard's eyes open. He hears the phone. Pushing the paint shelves off his body, he grabs his phone and answers.

"Got him, sir."

Rollie grabs the phone and demands, "Where you at, ponytail?"

"Chasing down your sleeper. It's Strickland, the principal."

"What? You sure?"

Dillard pulls the two slugs out of his bulletproof vest.

"Let's just say I'm not extremely unsure. He put two bullets in my back."

"You okay?"

"Yeah, I'm wearing my vest." He kicks the shed door open.

"We got Fells on sells. Get yourself to the north side concession stands. He's there. Take him quietly."

"Gotcha."

Rollie calls his sniper on the north-side tree line and orders, "Unit two can you see Dillard, he should be making his way to the north-side concession stand."

The spotter nods and says, "Yes, sir, I got him."

"Okay. Fells—that's our man. Keep him in your sights. If you see a weapon, take him out. There're kids everywhere to use as a shield."

"Yes, sir, uh...wait, sir... He's doing something, looks like he's dumping something."

Fells begins dumping bags of dope into a canister filled with hydrochloric acid as Strickland acts as lookout. Soon as he finishes, Strickland grabs him by the arm.

"Quick. We must leave. They're waiting to get us out of here come on!"

Strickland and Fells start behind the north side of the stands.

Dillard's phone rings.

"They're on the run, moving toward the north side of the stadium. Where are you?"

"North-side back."

"Find them!"

Dillard pulls out his badge and lets it fall around his neck. Retrieving his weapon, he weaves through the few people but still too many to get a visual.

"Unit two!" Rollie calls. "You still got 'em?"

"Yes, sir, but I won't much longer, not if they make it around the stadium."

"Do you see a weapon?"

"Negative!"

Fells and Strickland reaches the edge of the stadium when Strickland sees Dillard weaving through the crowd. He reaches for the restroom door, and snatching it open, he grabs Fells by the arm and swings him into the restroom. He then pulls his gun. Dillard sees Strickland raising his gun toward him once again; he has Dillard at a disadvantage.

Dillard reacts, dropping to one knee. He reaches for his weapon when suddenly there are two loud thumps. Strickland's arm drops back to his side. His glasses are cracked, and one lens is stained with blood. He stumbles forward.

Quickly Dillard raises and rushes over to catch Strickland's body, and he throws him inside the restroom, observing the two bullet holes in the open restroom door.

He then rushes into the restroom where Fells is making his way to his feet.

"You! Stay down and keep your hands where I can see them!" Dillard commands Fells as he aims his gun at him. He then gets on his cell phone. "Rollie, I got one down, Fells is in custody, and uh, tell the boys damn good shootin'."

The football game has barely reached halftime when Cole's limo eases down Lewis Speedway Drive to watch units of police car lights flashing. The coroner is also there.

Cole notes all these things, and then he tells the driver, "Get us out of here."

Another man stands quietly outside the game, also observing. He is watching his only son being escorted off to jail. He stands in the shadow near Aaron's car when there's a voice from behind him.

"It's all over now, Mr. Blain."

The man begins to pull a revolver from his coat pocket when the man behind him gently places his hand over Mr. Blain's hand.

"No...no, don't do this. Sir, your son has ruined enough lives tonight. It's all over now. You don't have to be another victim." The man reaches into Mr. Blain's pocket and removes the gun into his own pocket.

Just then Danny spots the two of them by Aaron's car and makes his way through the crowed.

He calls out, "Talvin, everything all right?"

"Yeah, we straight. Hey, you guys gonna need me to make a statement?"

Danny shakes his head and says, "Naw, Lil Boy. We wouldn't want you to blow your cover. What's up with that anyway, Lil Boy? Why you still using that name, dude? You know you look like three old men on food stamps?"

"Oh, whatever, man, and why justice just be coming on the case without giving anybody a heads up?"

Danny smirks and says, "Yeah, 'cause like we felt we should check to see if DEA might be involved with some street-level dealers in St. Augustine."

"Actually, Danny, there's more to Mickelson than even we know. We thought it was just dope, but he's got some interesting buffers when it comes to get info on the man. I was trying to come up the back door like soldier boy. Best I can do now is give ya the lay of Jonny's land and dealings."

As the two cousins walk away, Lil Boy turns back to Mr. Blain, driving back to his wife.

It's about eleven o'clock now at Deerwood Estates in Jacksonville. Cole sits in Mickelson's office.

"I can see the morning copy of *The Florida Times-Union* newspaper," Cole says as he glances over at Mickelson at his desk.

"We'll be the paper's front page. Well...not us, but they got Fells and Blain, they got Rodgers and Billips. Hell, it won't be long before one of them starts to talk, and they'll be banging on the door soon enough. I tried to tell ya. We could have took out the cops, we work with city boy, but no, you had a bigger picture, a grander scheme. Why ya always gotta be so magnanimous all the time, uh? Well, shit's hit the fan, old boy, and I'm afraid I'll be bailing out. And all this... Nothing personal... I just..."

Just then there's a knock on the office door, and Ricks enters.

"Mr. Mickelson! I..."

Ricks stops in his tracks as he is stunned to see Mickelson sitting in his chair, his head leaning backward as blood flows out of his mouth down both sides of his chin.

Then Ricks look over to see Cole sitting at his desk in the corner.

Ricks is speechless as he stares into Cole's bitter grayish-blue eyes.

Cole looks at Ricks and says, "Believe me... It was something he ate."

Ricks gulps as he looks to Mickelson's corpse, but then he looks back to Cole.

"Actually, I was coming to tell him, uh, you, that there's some suspicious activity going on outside. I mean, we got mail trucks, telephone repair men, satellite dish vans. I'm thinking they're not all who they seem to be."

Cole replies with sarcasm, "Ya know what, Ricks, I'm thinking yer right. Get all the men in position, call the lawyers. If they knock, answer. If they don't, well, mailman or not, he's kicking on my window. I'm filling his ass with lead, ya got me! Then you meet me at the vault."

Ricks and Cole both exit the office. Minutes later, Ricks joins Cole in the vault at the center of the mansion. Cole is gathering bonds, jewelry, and cash into two satchels as Ricks stands at the door of the vault, watching the hall.

Cole cuts his eyes over to notice Ricks is watching the hall and slides back a secret panel in the vault's wall. He then quickly presses a code on the keypad, and the wall adjusts into an escape hatch. He then eases his weapon from his waist. Just as he takes aim at Ricks, Rick's attention is called to the steely reflection, and he sees Cole's intentions.

Ricks jumps outside the vault, and the bullet misses. Then Ricks quickly slams the vault door close, unaware of the escape hatch. Cole makes his way through the hatch, sealing it. Then he makes his way into the in pass where he finds another such panel. Now he's into the drain tunnels. Cole walks the tunnel for about a quarter of a mile till he can see an opening just ahead.

Placing the satchel down, he takes his weapon in his hand. He then slowly and methodically makes his way out, surveying the bush around the tunnel's mouth.

Then he goes back, holsters his weapon, and proceeds. After about three quarters of a mile, he comes upon a well-camouflaged Range Rover. Placing the satchel down, he begins taking the camouflage from the vehicle. Taking a key from his pocket, he mashes the button to unlock the door. The sound indicates the vehicle's unlocked. Cole picks up the satchel and walks to the driver's-side door.

As he is about to open the door, the vehicle sounds off again to indicate that it has just locked.

A voice comes from Cole's rear, "Antraious Cole."

Cole drops the satchel and begins to turn. His natural instinct says, reach for your weapon, but the sound of what must be twenty or so bolt-action weapons locking and loading overrides that instinct, and he stops all movement.

"Not quite the payoff you had in mind, I'm guessing? I'm betting what's in that bag could retire the average-size village on a tropical island… But you weren't looking for the big score, were you? It's the only way this makes sense. You didn't tell anyone that you made my man. You had to let everyone take the fall while you make off with the goods in the confusion.

"I'm going out on a limb and guess Mickelson is already dead, isn't he? The only man who can link you directly to the cop's murder, his bargaining chip…except this vehicle puts you in the area of at least two dead men, just circumstantial, but enough to get a search warrant to search for the murder weapon.

"Thank you for that, Mr. Cole, for taking procession of this vehicle. Now, if you would please, sir…lock your fingers behind your head, drop to your knees, and we'll get you someplace safe before some of these cops start feeling an insanity defense coming on."

Rollie places Cole hands behind his back and cuffs them.

*****

The following weekend at the home of Bobby and Cricket, Aaron is being honored before his big send-off to Chicago.

School, Lisa, Rollie, Danny, Sillenia, Mr. Philmore, Tracy, and others are in attendance.

Danny receives a call and finds Rollie pulling him aside.

"That was Duke. We tried to move in on that house off Blanding Boulevard, central to Mickelson's communication just now. It exploded."

Rollie is troubled, asking, "Dear god, how big? was anyone injured?"

Danny nods and says, "No, which brings me to the bizarre. The house imploded, Rollie. The fire marshal found cross-the-counter accelerants centrally located in that house. If we hadn't already been on the scene, all would be lost in a matter of minutes."

"So are you saying we found something in the debris?"

Danny shakes his head and answers, "So far, we found what we believe to be a number cipher of some kind of code. Our analysts are on it even as we speak."

Rollie nods and says, "Good work, Danny. There is more than meets the eye about that whole setup. So many layers to peel. Can't help wondering what is at the heart of this onion."

Across the room, Bobby and Aaron slip away from the crowd and into Bobby's bedroom.

Then Bobby opens the glass door and says, "So what do ya think, AD?"

Aaron looks out and is quite taken at simmers of light that glisten the waters of Bobby's swimming pool.

"Ah, man, yeah, let's move the party out here!"

He slips off his clothing, and his bathing suit is underneath.

"I have another surprise for you as well." Bobby then leads Aaron to the poolside where sitting in a lounge chair is a man whose hat covers his face.

"All Day!" Aaron screams as the two embrace. "So they let you go?"

"Your friend Bobby here is a better lawyer than even he knows."

Bobby shrugs his shoulders and says, "Don't ask! Anyone wants something to drink?"

Aaron and All Day agree on apple juice, and Bobby is off to the kitchen.

"So what, are you on paper or what? Ya got to do this show with me, I mean, hey, you're a—"

All Day shakes his head and says, "Young priest, please, slow down. I'm simply here to wish you luck. You are the instrument chosen for this task. I have that which I must do also. You have found a great lesson through our Lord. You trust God, and now he shall glorify you even as you glorify his name."

"But you..." Aaron starts to speak

"No, Aaron. You now go and take your swim that we may join the others."

Aaron looks upon the water and says, "Oh man, yeah. Will you excuse me for a few laps. It's the one thing I've wanted to do since I got out that I hadn't had time for."

"Certainly, young priest."

Aaron dives off the far end of the pool swimming. Underneath the water there is a great echo within the its stillness. Aaron can hear All Day's voice as he strides underneath the water.

"Young priest, you are a solider to the kingdom of God. Therefore, since we are receiving a kingdom which cannot be shaken, serve God acceptably with reverence and godly fear. Let brotherly love continue. Do not forget to entertain strangers..."

Aaron's head rises out of the water, and he wipes the chlorinated water from his eyes.

"How'd you do that? I could hear..."

Aaron looks around to find he is alone.

Suddenly Bobby comes back out with two glasses of apple juice as Aaron exits the pool and surveys the area for All Day.

"Hey, Bobby, where did All Day go?"

Bobby laughs and says, "Oh man, I know what you mean. Sometimes when you hit a grove and it's all coming together, and you realize it's hours later, and hey, that's probably going to be like the norm for you these first few months. It gets easier as you find your baring."

"What?" Aaron laughs, but then he notices there are only two glasses.

Bobby hands Aaron an apple juice and begins to drink the other. Aaron is confused. He looks over where All Day sat, and there is a piece of paper in the chair. As Bobby is talking, Aaron walks over to pick up the paper. It reads simply: "Do not forget to entertain strangers, for by so doing, some have unwittingly entertained angels."

The paper then slips from his hand by a sudden wind and over the privacy fence.

Bobby calls out, "Aaron... Aaron, are you okay?"

Aaron begins to laugh and says, "Yeah, Bobby. I'm fine. Actually, I'm better than fine... I'm blessed."

Elsewhere at a maximum security federal facility, a cold, hard doors slam in a hallway where the only sounds are shoe leather, officers commands, and deafening silence.

Antavious Cole is led away to his new home for now in cellblock C. The doors open, and his leg irons are removed. Once inside, he turns backward. Sticking his hands through a slot, his cuffs are removed.

More doors slam as the officers make their way off the maximum-security custody block.

Cole does a survey of this his new home. A toilet and a bed. The cold hard walls. There is a look of contempt on his face, anger in his heart.

"I should have taken the bullets," he mumbles.

He turns to the bars and sighs as the futility of escape starts to sink in. Then he notices a ray of smoke coming from the cell just next door. He realizes he's not as alone as he once thought. This person must be sitting on the floor his back against the wall. Cole walks over to the wall and wipes his lips.

"Hey…over there…spare a smoke?"

A pack of Tops roll-ups slide in front of his cell. He takes the pack and finds the cigarettes already rolled, and there is a lighter as well. Glancing at the wall, he takes five.

Then the voice from behind the wall says, "Get cha self four or five."

Cole smiles and slides the pack back. After a while, he begins to rant.

"Can you believe this place? A cage of obscurity. No one should be made to live like this. To be among the whole wide world and yet not be allowed to coexist. Why don't they just put a bullet in ya head and be done with it? By the way, I'm Cole."

As the man behind the wall retrieves the lighter from the floor. The voice from behind the wall begins to speak most solemnly.

"Perhaps this is the place we've painted for ourselves, at least some, for what may be misconstrued as an inability to coexist. Perhaps we are rendered mercy from the blunt trauma of a bullet to the brain, for indeed, it takes away that which is hope. A man should have hope that he may discover that which is hidden deep within himself, even from himself. As for me, I am called All Day, and I believe as long as a man takes breath, he still has hope."

The End

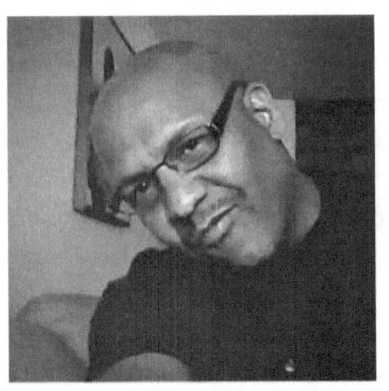